IT IS NOT ENOUGH TO THINK ABOUT OUR DESTINY: IT MUST BE FELT.

MIGUEL DE UNAMUNO, *The Tragic Sense of Life*

———————

GOD BE IN MY HEAD, AND IN MY UNDERSTANDING;

GOD BE IN MY EYES, AND IN MY LOOKING;

GOD BE IN MY MOUTH, AND IN MY SPEAKING;

GOD BE IN MY HEART, AND IN MY THINKING;

GOD BE AT MY END, AND AT MY DEPARTING.

SARUM PRIMER

———————

SOME OF THOSE HABITS OF THE MIND

WHICH ARE THROUGHOUT THE BIBLE REPRESENTED AS ALONE PLEASING

IN THE SIGHT OF GOD,

ARE THE VERY HABITS WHICH ARE NECESSARY

FOR SUCCESS IN SCIENTIFIC INVESTIGATION,

AND WITHOUT WHICH IT IS QUITE IMPOSSIBLE TO EXTEND

THE SPHERE OF OUR KNOWLEDGE.

JOHN HENRY NEWMAN, sermon preached July 7, 1826

HABITS
OF THE
MIND

Intellectual Life

as a Christian

Calling

JAMES
W. SIRE

InterVarsity Press
Downers Grove, Illinois

InterVarsity Press
P.O. Box 1400, Downers Grove, IL 60515
World Wide Web: www.ivpress.com
E-mail: mail@ivpress.com

InterVarsity Press® is the book-publishing division of InterVarsity Christian Fellowship/USA®, a student movement active on campus at hundreds of universities, colleges and schools of nursing in the United States of America, and a member movement of the International Fellowship of Evangelical Students. For information about local and regional activities, write Public Relations Dept., InterVarsity Christian Fellowship/USA, 6400 Schroeder Rd., P.O. Box 7895, Madison, WI 53707-7895.

All Scripture quotations, unless otherwise indicated, are taken from the Holy Bible, New International Version®. NIV®. Copyright ©1973, 1978, 1984 by International Bible Society. Used by permission of Zondervan Publishing House. All rights reserved.

Excerpts from John Henry Cardinal Newman, The Idea of a University, ed. Frank M. Turner, ©1996, used by permission of Yale University Press.

Selections from A. G. Sertillanger, The Intellectual Life, ©1987, used by permission of the Catholic University of America Press.

The poem by Wendell Berry featured in chapter seven is from A Timbered Choir by Wendell Berry. Copyright © 1998 by Wendell Berry. Reprinted by permission of Counterpoint Press, a member of Perseus Books, L.L.C.

Cover photograph: Alinari/Art Resource, N.Y.

ISBN 0-8308-2273-9

Printed in the United States of America ∞

Library of Congress Cataloging-in-Publication Data

Sire, James W.
  Habits of the mind: intellectual life as a Christian calling/James W. Sire.
    p. cm.
  Includes bibliographical references and indexes.
  ISBN 0-8308-2273-9 (paper: alk. paper)
  1. Thought and thinking—Religious aspects—Christianity. 2. Intellect—Religious
aspects—Christianity.   I. Title.
  BV4598.4 .S57 2000
  230—dc21

                                                00-040911

19	18	17	16	15	14	13	12	11	10	9	8
15	14	13	12	11	10	09	08	07	06		

To Marjorie,

whose intellectual realism

keeps in check

my romantic flights of fancy

Contents

Preface

*Calling is the truth that God calls us to himself so decisively that every-
thing we are, everything we do, and everything we have is invested with a
special devotion, dynamism, and direction lived out as a response to his
summons and service.*
OS GUINNESS, *The Call*

The topic of *Habits of the Mind* is the intellectual life, especially its
integral nature. First, thinking is integral to our call to be what God
wants us to be. God calls every one of us to think and to do so as
well as we can. We are to love God with our mind as well as with
our heart and soul and strength (Lk 10:27). How we ever thought
otherwise is not the topic of this book. That fact, which should but
does not astonish us, has been covered very well by others such as
Mark Noll. Here I am much more interested in getting on with our
call to love God with our minds by thinking as well as we can with
the intelligence with which we are endowed.

Some of us, however, are called specially to a life of the mind. It is
not a call that makes us either better or worse. But it is a call that
must be heeded. For as Os Guinness says, "A life lived listening to
the decisive call of God is a life lived before one audience that
trumps all others—the Audience of One. The caller is God."[1] The
central goal of this book is to identify, describe and encourage those
habits of the mind that are central to fulfilling our call to glorify God
by thinking well.

Second, thinking is rarely a matter of cold, heartless, calculating logic. Thinking feels. Sometimes when I am reading—and thinking while reading—my mind becomes so hot, so affected by the implications of the ideas, that I stop to cool off. John Henry Newman talks about the mind enraptured by the "music of the spheres." A. G. Sertillanges speaks of being lifted on the downy wings of truth. There is indeed a unity between thinking and feeling. Unity, in fact, stands behind all aspects of our human *being*. I have, therefore, let my emotions be displayed as I agonize and play, think and feel, through a major theme of this book: how thinking feels.

So this is a very personal book, the most personal I have written. I have not hesitated to convey my feelings, my emotions, about the subjects I am dealing with. Moreover, I think I am learning to trust my emotions and even my gut feelings, willing to put them on display. Some might say that I am learning to be vulnerable—a term reflecting, in part and sadly, the move toward a therapeutic understanding of Christian faith. But should anyone conclude that this is really happening, be it known: I shall battle them long and hard with all the abstract intellect at my personal disposal! So there!

As I was writing this book, I had the privilege of lecturing in the Miguel de Unamuno Room in the University of Salamanca. Oddly, the topic was "responsible technology," an analysis of the implications of technology on our social destiny. I picture Unamuno listening from the walls. What did he think? Whatever it was, one thing would have been clear. His thought would have been flavored by passion. "It is not enough to think about our destiny: it must be felt," he wrote.[2] So I too would long for those who read this present book: let your thoughts be felt; let your feelings be thought. Our goal will be Unamuno's goal: to speak as and to address "the man of flesh and bone; the man who is born, suffers, and dies—above all, who dies; the man who eats and drinks and plays and sleeps and thinks and wills; the man who is seen and heard; the brother, the real brother."[3]

Third, thinking well is integral to acting righteously. Truth and spirituality are of a piece: to know the truth is to do it. There is no dichotomy between the two. To *be* spiritual is to know/do the truth.

So my primary goal in this book is to encourage you to think more and better than you did before reading it, to strive toward "the perfection of the intellect," to enjoy the proper habits of the mind. Though I discuss some specific biblical, theological and philosophic notions, I am far more interested in stimulating good Christian thinking and prompting it to be put into action than I am in propagating a set of ideas.

My best thinking is, however, woefully lacking in finality—even for myself. I have worked off and on for several years thinking about and writing this book. The subject is important, too important for me to publish what is still in flux in my own mind. I have wanted to wait for the last word, the final formulation, to take shape. A book on the intellectual life should be the product of settled conviction. Or so I thought. Now I have abandoned this goal. Even when I sound certain, that certainty is not absolute. Rather, may all I say reflect the wisdom of the ancient intellectual who said:

> When someone is honestly 55% right, that's very good and there's no use wrangling. And if someone is 60% right, it's wonderful, its great luck, and let him thank God. But what's to be said about 75% right? Wise people say this is suspicious. Well, and what 100% right? Whoever says he's 100% right is a fanatic, a thug, and the worst kind of rascal.[4]

* * *

A caveat for author and reader: Always when one presumes to instruct or advise others about complex matters, there is a great danger. Dom Camillo points this out. We run the risk, he says, "of reincarnating Jesus' message in a new culture or ideology which is destined, like all others, to perish, incapable of expressing God's thought and fit only to be a vehicle of suffering for Christians yet to come." Lord save us—reader and author alike—from the evil consequences of our best but erring thoughts!

One guard against erring thoughts is the witness of the intellectual communities, both specifically Christian and generally intelligent. I have tried to submit my thoughts to these communities by consulting and quoting frequently from others across a wide spectrum of intellectual commitments. It was a delight to find ample justification for this in, of all places, a Renaissance Italian author:

> Yes, I use a great many quotations; but they are illustrious and true, and, if I am not mistaken, they convey authority pleasurably. People say that I could use fewer. Of course I could; I might even omit them entirely. I shan't deny that I might even be totally silent; and perhaps that would be the wisest thing. But in view of the world's ills and shames it is hard to keep silent. . . . If anyone asks why I do so abound with quotations and seem to dwell on them so lovingly, I can merely reply that I think my reader's taste is like mine. Nothing moves me so much as the quoted maxims of great men. I like to rise above myself, to test my mind to see if it contains anything solid or lofty, or stout and firm against ill-fortune, or to find if my mind has been lying to me about itself. And there is no better way of doing this—except by direct experience, the surest mistress—than by comparing one's mind with those it would most like to resemble. Thus, as I am grateful to my authors who give me the chance of testing my mind against maxims frequently quoted, so I hope my readers will thank me.[5]

Six and a half centuries later I say, "Thank you, Petrarch." Your maxim on maxims has come in rather handy—not least in its ardent admission of authorial self-deception. May your insight help us twenty-first-century readers to detect when our minds have been lying to us about ourselves!

*   *   *

I am delighted to acknowledge my debt to several scholars who have recently published books on the topic of Christian thinking. Mark Noll, Os Guinness, David Gill, Brian Walsh, Richard Middleton and George Marsden have each contributed to the development of my own views. I will only occasionally refer to their work, not because it hasn't helped shape my own perspective but because their work is an established given. There is no need to document or give detailed explanation of American and evangelical anti-intellectualism. Noll in *The Scandal of the Evangelical Mind* and Guinness in *Fit Bodies, Fat Minds* have done that. There is also no need to outline the history of the decline of a Christian presence in the academic world. Marsden has done that in *The Soul of the American University*. Nor is there need to outline a Christian worldview. Walsh and Middleton have done so in *The Transforming Vision* and *Truth Is Stranger Than It Used to Be*. Moreover, I have addressed this in *The Universe Next Door* and *Discipleship of the Mind*. David Gill has fleshed out the dimensions of the Christian mind in *The Opening of the Christian Mind*, as has Gene Edward Veith Jr. in *Loving God with All Your Mind*. The book that most parallels the themes and approach of my own is J. P. Moreland's *Love Your God with All Your Mind*, published as I had the present book well under way on paper and in my mind. I will let others judge between them.

I see in the present book a unique focus on "intellectual life" itself—not what a Christian should think but how a Christian can think better—with more accuracy, more attention to implications for life, more experience and acknowledgment of the presence of God in whatever is thought. For this I have not so much quoted my evangelical contemporaries as plumbed the riches of Christian thought of earlier centuries and other traditions.

*   *   *

It has taken me several years to write this book. Though I had outlined it roughly before starting, the topic soon got away from me and the book, like Topsy, just "growed." Even in its first conception it was never like a pine tree with a straight trunk pointing in a single upward direction. The more it growed, the more it became like an elm or, better, a live oak. Branches went off in a dozen directions and then grew like the twigs. Only from a far distance—perhaps only *sub species aeternitatus*—could a unified form be seen. Then as it matured, a few themes appeared in different forms in a number of different chapters. I found that what I had written about reading had the same overall structure as what I was writing about knowing and doing. I saw as well that the intellectual disciplines were almost identical to the spiritual disciplines. Then I noticed the profound similarity between the engagement-abstinence disciplines and the active-passive character not just of thinking but of reading as well. Finally, another two chapters conceived at different times for different overall goals suddenly emerged as mirror images of each other but, in the final trim, were completely cut.

Chapter one introduces the intellectual life by looking at several definitions of the word *intellectual* and concluding with my own. A major source for this definition is John Henry Newman, whose own character as a Christian intellectual (the subject of chapter two) has long intrigued me, as has his concept of the "perfection of the intellect" (chapter three). Two succeeding chapters examine my own concept of *intellectual life*, first in relation to its distinctly mental dimension (chapter four) then in its moral dimension (chapter five).

Then follow three chapters detailing intellectual practice: intellectual virtues (chapter six), intellecual disciplines (chapter seven) and thinking by reading (chapter eight). A chapter on Jesus as a reasoner, even a "logician," provides one reason (of several that could be examined) that we both can and should reason (chapter nine). The final chapter (chapter ten) challenges us as Christians to accept the responsibility to think well and in so doing to seek first the kingdom of God and to glorify God. With this structure undergirding the argument of the book, I trust it has become a tree and not a pile of dead branches.

My intent in all this could be summed up in a comment made by George Santayana about William James as a professor at Harvard University: "A philosopher who is a teacher of youth is more concerned to give people a right start than a right conclusion."[6] May the habits of our minds lead us to more than notebook knowledge.

Finally, I wish to thank those who have reviewed this work in manuscript form and offered excellent advice; for all its faults this book is better for the contributions of Harold K. Bush Jr., Steve Garber, Douglas Groothuis, Don Meeks, Terry Morrison and James Strauss. A special thanks goes to James Hoover, my stalwart and longtime editor, who has saved me from several significant gaffes. And thanks go also to Ruth Goring, the final editorial eye on these meanderings. The remaining faults are my own.

So I offer now my conception of some of the proper habits of the mind. *Tolle, lege; tolle, lege.*[7]

I

CONFESSIONS OF AN INTELLECTUAL WANNABE

I *remember it very clearly. It was a sunny day in the fall of 1954. We* were standing in front of the Museum of the Nebraska State Historical Society. I said to the young woman who would one day be my wife, "I'd really like to be an intellectual."

When I reminded her of this forty-three years later, she said. "It's funny that I married you. You were such a snob."

The word *intellectual* has certainly had its detractors, so many that one might wonder why anyone would want to be one. Perhaps I was a snob, seeking a place in the university sun. Certainly my origins were humble enough. Born on one ranch—literally, my mother gave birth to me in the ranch house—raised on another ranch, educated for the first six years in a one-room schoolhouse where one teacher, a high-school graduate, taught from four to eight children individually because all of them were in different grades: to be sure, I did not have the benefits of a great Montessori elementary education.

My parents did, however, instill in me a love for reading. *The Saturday Evening Post* and *Collier's*, staple reading in my rural community, arrived regularly. So before the end of the sixth grade, I had learned to read well and had developed a taste for good literature. By the seventh grade we had moved to Butte, a county seat of six hundred (now five hundred) people with a high school of ninety. There were twenty-three in my graduating class.

I loved the beauty of the ranch land, and in my childhood days I roamed the hills above our tiny house in the wooded valley of Eagle Creek. But as I grew older I came to dislike, then detest, the work of ranching. Milking cows was one thing. I didn't like it, but it came easy. Lifting bales of fresh-cut hay, shocking wheat and riding a horse through the tall marijuana that grew wild and unharvested— that was another matter. Great clouds of pollen would rise from the marijuana, my eyes would water and close, my nose would drip, and I would sneeze my way back to the ranch house, letting the horse find the way.

When we moved to Butte, I escaped much of the agony. But the University of Nebraska was the great escape. My uncle, only sixteen years older than I, had escaped before me. He had become a pharmacist and an amateur photographer with a Rollicord, a Leica and a wife who was also a pharmacist and photographer. I loved them and I loved their cameras. My aunt was city always, my uncle was country-turned-city with a love, like mine, for the beauty of the country and a loathing, like mine, for the mindless work.

The conversation with my future wife in front of the State Historical Society could almost have been predicted, but only given the knowledge that I had rejected not only the work of ranching and farming but the anti-intellectual tone set by my father.

Intellectual: A Populist Version

I learned very early from my father that intellectuals were not to be trusted. Dad was a rancher, a farmer, a county assessor, for seven years a county agricultural agent, then again a farmer and rancher, cream-station manager and cattle-feed salesman. He was appointed to the job as county agent in 1945 just as World War II was ending. A college degree was normally required, but no one was qualified. Most men who otherwise would have been were in the military. Dad had had to leave college, Nebraska Wesleyan University, before the end of his first semester because of illness and a financial disaster at home. Over the years he had become known for his work as a 4-H leader, a county assessor and an active breeder of purebred Herefords. So he was appointed county agent.

Egghead: A person of spurious intellectual pretensions, often a professor or the protégé of a professor. Fundamentally superficial. Over-emotional and feminine in reactions to any problem. Supercilious and surfeited with conceit and contempt for the experience of more sound and stable men. Essentially confused in thought and immersed in mixture of sentimentality and violent evangelism. Subject to the old-fashioned philosophical morality of Nietzsche which frequently leads him into jail or disgrace. A self-conscious prig, so given to examining all sides of a question that he becomes thoroughly addled while remaining always in the same spot. An anemic bleeding heart.

LOUIS BROMFIELD
"The Triumph of the Egghead"

Then the soldiers came home, went to college and became more qualified than my father. So he lost his job to a younger man, much more educated, much less wise. I think that all his life Dad had railed against pointy-headed intellectuals. After he lost his job, these comments surfaced with greater regularity.

The last time I remember hearing my father complaining about the intellectuals was not long before his death. I had asked him why the new bridge across the Niobrara River had been placed a half-mile downstream from the old one. "To save a tiny tract of wetlands," Dad said. "The road should have just gone straight across the river, but those pointy-headed environmentalists (nuts and radicals, they are) put up a fuss, and it cost a lot more to reroute the road."

I can only imagine how my father might have exploded had he picked up *The Saturday Evening Post* and begun to read there the opening lines of *Rameau's Nephew*:

> Come rain or shine, my custom is to go for a stroll in the Palais-Royal every afternoon at about five. I am always to be seen there alone, sitting on a seat in the Allée d'Argenson, meditating. I hold discussions with myself on politics, love, taste or philosophy, and let my thoughts wander in complete abandon, leaving them free to follow the first wise or foolish idea that comes along, like those young rakes we see in the Allée de Foy who run after a giddy-looking piece with a laughing face, sparkling eye and tip-tilted nose, only to leave her for another, accosting them all, sticking to none. In my case my thoughts are my wenches.[1]

"A man with too much time on his hands," we might say today. My father's words would be unprintable. What I imagine would have been his definition of an *intellectual* is not unprintable.

The average American would rather be driving a car along a highway than reading a book and thinking. The average Frenchman would rather be drinking an extra bottle of wine than watching a play by Racine. The average Britisher would rather fill up a football-pool form than listen to Elgar's *Enigma*.

GILBERT HIGHET
Man's Unconquerable Mind

Dad would have simply defined an *intellectual* as someone educated beyond his intelligence.[2] At times it seemed to me that he thought anyone who had a college degree, let alone a doctorate, was indeed so educated.[3] But perhaps my father was unwittingly echoing Bertrand Russell, who would surely fit most people's definition of an intellectual:

> I have never called myself an intellectual, and nobody has ever dared to call me one in my presence. I think an intellectual may be defined as a person who pretends to have more intellect than he has, and I hope this definition does not fit me.[4]

Intellectual: An Ideological Version

One needn't be limited to negative definitions coming from populists. There are also negative academic definitions of an *intellectual*. Paul Johnson—who, like Russell, is himself an intellectual—attacks the breed of secular thinkers who he says have set themselves up as kings and high priests of a modern, not just secular but religionless world.[5] Speaking of the first intellectuals who began to emerge as the credibility of the church began to be shattered in the Enlightenment, Johnson writes:

> The secular intellectual might be deist, sceptic or atheist. But he was just as ready as any pontiff or presbyter to tell mankind how to conduct its affairs. He proclaimed, from the start, a special devotion to the interests of humanity and an evangelical duty to advance them by his teaching.[6]

Like a modern Prometheus, the intellectual felt confident that he (and it was always a he) could select or reject any or all wisdom from the past, diagnose, prescribe and cure all social ills, and expect that even "the fundamental habits of human beings could be transformed for the better."[7]

If we look back to the sixteenth century, the era in which the class of independent word-workers emerged, we may notice several types who reappear in subsequent history: withdrawn scholars, militant freethinkers, militant defenders of the establishment, skeptics, failed politicians, curious seekers of novelties and polyhistorians.

LESZEK KOLAKOWSKI
Modernity on Endless Trial

In writing such a description Johnson says he is trying to be "factual and dispassionate," but the book itself belies him. He may often be factual—in fact, he may always be factual—but he is seldom dispassionate. Johnson has a much blunter instrument than a stiletto to grind, and grind it he does, then relentlessly swings it. Down come some of the tallest of intellectual trees in the forest of modern society—from Jean-Jacques Rousseau to Karl Marx, from Bertrand Russell to Jean-Paul Sartre. It may be well to fell these trees, but to use the term *intellectual* to describe only those Johnson finds perhaps justifiably reprehensible is to play into the hands of those who are anti-intellectual for less than worthy reasons.

Power, power everywhere,
And how the signs do shrink.
Power, power everywhere,
And nothing else to think.

MARSHALL SAHLINS
Waiting for Foucault

If I had had in mind either the populist definition of my father or the academic and ideological definition of Johnson, I would never have yearned to spread my branches in their woods.

Intellectual: A Fundamentalist Version

But there was one intellectual who was worse than the populist and the academic versions. This was the intellectual according to biblical fundamentalism. I was fortunate. I did not encounter this version in a fever-pitched form. I knew something was awry with what I saw symbolized by Bob Jones University.

Still, the form it came in was strong enough. "If you go to the godless University of Nebraska, you are likely to lose your faith," I heard my Baptist pastor say. He probably said no such thing, but I heard him say it anyway. I knew he wanted me to go where his children went—Bethel College in St. Paul, Minnesota. I wanted to go there too, because I wanted a Christian education. My father, despite his anti-intellectualism, wanted me to have an education, but not at an expensive private school like Bethel. It had to be the University of Nebraska, the major public university in our state. So that's where I went.[8]

But I went with some trepidation—not much—and a great deal of Nebraska rancher bull-headedness. I encountered skepticism, atheism and agnosticism, but none of them ever fazed my faith. "You read lots of books," my atheist anthropology professor told me, "but you read all the wrong ones." He was actually more correct than I then gave him credit for, for I was reading what I now think of as the mad ravings of a man who claimed to have worked with the great Egyptologist Sir Flinders Petrie. I remember him telling a packed fundamentalist church in Lincoln that the buzzing hornets referred

---

Fundamentalism created major problems in several ways for the life of the mind. First, it gave new impetus to general anti-intellectualism; second, it hardened conservative evangelical commitments to certain features of the nineteenth-century evangelical-American synthesis that were problematic to begin with; and third, its major theological emphases had a chilling effect on the exercise of Christian thinking about the world.

MARK NOLL
The Scandal of the Evangelical Mind

---

to in Joshua were really the engines of Egyptian aircraft. Archaeologists had found the buttons worn on the uniforms of the pilots. Well, here was a pseudointellectual masking as intellectual and putting himself at the service of the church.

When I asked my anthropology professor if he had ever met this archaeologist, he said, "Yes, he came by to visit me. He's a nice old man." After that, what intelligent person would want to be a Christian and intellectual? Well, I for one.

I soon met other Christians who were brighter than I. We supported each other, had our faith deepened by daily devotions, group Bible studies, prayer meetings and intelligent Christian speakers. There was never any question in the InterVarsity Christian Fellowship I joined that Christianity was somehow intellectually second-rate. It obviously was not.

Still, there was considerable reason for my pastor and other fundamentalists to be concerned about *intellectuals*. And this warning sticks with me and, if anything, is stronger in me today than ever before. Both Jesus and the apostle Paul had some hard words for those who thought they had the truth tacked down tight. Paul especially is known for his warning: "Knowledge puffs up, but love builds up. The man who thinks he knows something does not yet know as he ought to know. But the man who loves God is known by God" (1 Cor 8:1-2). The warning here is against intellectual pride.

But Paul's strongest warning comes in his first letter to the Corinthians:

> Where is the wise man? Where is the scholar? Where is the philosopher of this age? Has not God made foolish the wisdom of this world? For since in the wisdom of God the world through its wisdom did not know him, God was pleased through the foolishness of what was preached to save those who believe. . . . For the foolishness of God is wiser than man's wisdom, and the weakness of God is stronger than man's strength. (1 Cor 1:20-25)

Again he writes to the Colossians: "See to it that no one takes you captive through hollow and deceptive philosophy, which depends on human tradition and the basic principles of this world rather than on Christ" (Col 2:8).

Anti-intellectualism is a disposition to discount the importance of truth and the life of the mind. Living in a sensuous culture and an increasingly emotional democracy, American evangelicals in the last generation have simultaneously toned up their bodies and dumbed down their minds. The result? Many suffer from a modern form of what the ancient stoics called "metal hedonism"—having fit bodies but fat minds.

OS GUINNESS
Fit Bodies, Fat Minds

Many Christians have interpreted these passages to mean that Christians should avoid the world of scholarship and philosophy. This is surely not a proper understanding of Paul's word. He is not objecting to good thinking but to inaccurate thinking, especially of the sort that insists on its accuracy. Paul is rather pitting God's genuine knowledge against claims to human knowledge.[9]

It has always puzzled me that some Christians have thoroughly rejected the life of the mind, for Jesus commanded us to use our mind: "Love the Lord your God with all your heart and with all your soul and with all your mind and with all your strength" (Mk 12:30). But anti-intellectualism is a major strain in American Christianity, and it's not likely to fade away anytime soon.[10] As Mark Noll says, "The scandal of the evangelical mind is that there is not much of an evangelical mind."[11]

Is the only good intellectual a dead intellectual? That's what the first three definitions would suggest.[12] But those three just can't be the only choices.

The Intellectual Cast of Mind

One way out of the morass of anti-intellectualism spawned by populism, ideological conservatism and misguided fundamentalism is to look at what constitutes the basic nature of an intellectual cast of mind.[13] Surely we can reach less tendentious conclusions than that to be an intellectual is to be some sort of cultural or religious pariah. In his study of anti-intellectualism in America historian Richard Hofstadter gives us a helpful list of the qualities characteristic of intellectual life: "disinterested intelligence, generalizing power, free speculation, fresh observation, creative novelty, radical criticism."[14]

To be sure, each one of these qualities carries with it an implied ability. It assumes, for example, that one actually could have an intelligence that pursues truth regardless of its implications for one's life or the life of one's community or country. It assumes that one can speculate without the restraints of prejudice, self-interest or prior commitment to a way of life or set of values. It assumes the ability to see with eyes no longer clouded by past vision. It assumes that newness of vision and novelty of notion are, at least for the most part, virtues. And finally, it undermines all of the above by recognizing radical criticism as an essential element, not at the moment noting that if radical criticism is turned back on the other qualities, it is possible that none of them will remain. Radical criticism is indeed the sharpest ax in the intellectual forest, and it has been wielded so well by those masters of the hermeneutic of suspicion—Marx, Freud, Nietzsche—that the whole notion of intellectual is suspect.[15] But this is to get ahead of my story. We will look at some of the work of these critics later.

Hofstadter distinguishes between *intelligence* and *intellect*.[16] Intelligence is simply mental ability, being able to use the mind well in a wide range of circumstances. In this sense, most professionals—lawyers, doctors, editors, accountants, engineers—use their intelligence much of the time. But, says Hofstadter, deferring to Max Weber, professionals live *"off* ideas, not *for* them."[17] Living off ideas is employing *instrumental* knowledge: knowledge for the sake of something

---

To me an intellectual is a person who has devoted his or her life to thinking in general terms about the affairs of this world and the broader context of things. . . . That is, their principal occupation is studying, reading, teaching, writing, publishing, addressing the public. . . . Often . . . it leads them to embrace a broader sense of responsibility for the state of the world and its future.

VÁCLAV HAVEL
The Art of the Impossible

---

other than knowledge itself. The intellectual, on the other hand, has an almost religious dedication to ideas as such, which, when it is not balanced by playfulness, can quickly turn to ideological fanaticism.[18] True intellectuals, however, have fun with ideas; they move them around, back and forth, turn them on their heads, submit them to ironic reflection, test them with their imagination and don't get so enamored of their own brilliance that they become nothing more than sophisticated, arrogant prigs.[19]

There is a spontaneity about the intellectual life. It is not fueled by a passion directed solely toward one objective. And because of this the true intellectual occasionally sees some things, makes true observations and has insights that few if any before him have seen or had. If there is any danger in this, it is not in having a one-track mind but in having a mind with so many tracks that it either arrives at many places at the same time or never gets out of the station.

My experience resonates with Hofstadter's description of the intellectual life. Though Hofstadter was yet to write his book when I said to Marj, "I would really like to be an intellectual," it was Hofstadter's notion that seems now to have been implicitly mine.

One ought to make good use of one's intellect in order to live a morally good life. Stated another way, one ought to lead an intellectual life. But many of us do not lead intellectual lives. Many of us are anti-intellectual. Many do not use their intellects beyond those uses they cannot avoid—its cooperation with the sensory powers in acts of perception, memory, and imagination.

MORTIMER ADLER
Intellect: Mind over Matter

So what shall we say about the desire to be an intellectual? Should we wannabe one? If being an intellectual is dangerous, if it is hazardous to the health of both the intellectual and society, if it is biblically problematic, is it worth it? I am not yet ready to answer that question.

What I mean [by an intellectual] is a person playing a particular role. It is the role of the thinker or writer who engages in public discussion of issues of public policy, in politics in the broadest sense, while deliberately not engaging in the pursuit of political power.

TIMOTHY GARTON ASH
"Prague: Intellectuals and Politics"

But I am ready to offer an initial definition of what an intellectual is and how that relates to being a Christian intellectual. These will stand at this point as proposals. In the chapters that follow I will examine other positive contributions to these definitions and suggest how any person who still "wants to be a Christian intellectual" might take positive steps in that direction. But first the definition:

An *intellectual* is one who loves ideas, is dedicated to clarifying them, developing them, criticizing them, turning them over and over, seeing their implications, stacking them atop one another, arranging them, sitting silent while new ideas pop up and old ones seem to rearrange themselves, playing with them, punning with their terminology, laughing at them, watching them clash, picking up the pieces, starting over, judging them, withholding judgment about them, changing them, bringing them into contact with their counterparts in other systems of thought, inviting them to dine and have a ball but also suiting them for service in workaday life.

A *Christian intellectual* is all of the above to the glory of God.

We will get a further perspective on these definitions when we consider the perspective of John Henry Newman, surely one of the great intellectuals of the nineteenth century. Of course Newman is one of those good intellectuals who is also a dead intellectual. But his death for us is rather an illusion. For Newman is not only now very much alive in God, he is a living intellectual presence in many twentieth-century minds, mine included. I hope to show why in the next two chapters.

II

JOHN HENRY NEWMAN AS AN INTELLECTUAL

I *have long had a love affair with John Henry Newman. I was introduced* to him in Professor Howard Fulweiler's course in nineteenth-century prose, taken in graduate school one fall over thirty years ago. From the moment I first read portions of his *Apologia Pro Vita Sua* and *The Idea of a University* I was hooked. In that course he was a good figure to admire, for Fulweiler was an easily self-confessed high-church Episcopalian, and it was obvious that Newman was one of his favorite authors.

There was perhaps another reason as well. I had become known in the department as a vocal but not obnoxious Christian and a member of a Southern Baptist church. This gave Dr. Fulweiler—who himself had recently received his Ph.D.—a foil in the class. I was his source of contemporary opinion for what "evangelicals" were currently believing or, perhaps in my case, actually thinking. Now normally this issue would not come up in a graduate course in

English literature, but with nineteenth-century writers like John Stuart Mill, Thomas Huxley and of course Newman, the question of religious belief was clearly relevant. Newman's whole life was wrapped up in issues that distinguished the major religious orientations of the day: Dissenters, evangelical Anglicans, "broad church" Anglicans, high-church Anglicans, Catholics and a growing number of defectors from any religious belief at all. So more than once, with a wry smile Fulweiler would ask me, "So, what do the evangelicals think about that issue?"

What I remember from those days, however, were Newman's lectures on the founding of the first Catholic university in Ireland. From those lectures I remember most Newman's eloquent, even passionate, description of the Christian mind, what he variously called "the perfection of the intellect" or "the imperial intellect" or the "philosophical habit of mind." This passage especially almost struck me dumb:

> That perfection of the intellect which is the result of education, and its beau ideal, to be imparted to individuals in their respective measures, is the clear, calm, accurate vision and comprehension of all things, as far as the finite mind can embrace them, each in its place, and with its own characteristics upon it. It is almost prophetic from its knowledge of history; it is almost heart-searching from its knowledge of human nature; it has almost supernatural charity from its freedom from littleness and prejudice; it has almost the repose of faith, because nothing can startle it; it has almost the beauty and harmony of heavenly contemplation, so intimate is it with the eternal order of things and the music of the spheres.[1]

This is by no means the only passage of appropriately purple prose to leap from the pages of *The Idea of a University*. The entire set of published lectures is itself one of the highlights of nineteenth-century prose. Deliberately Ciceronian in prose style, Newman can still stir the blood while he fires the imagination and sets the mind spinning.

The following chapter will focus on Newman's notion of "the perfection of the intellect." This chapter, however, will focus on Newman himself—the cast of his mind, the practice of those habits he called "philosophical." Newman was, of course, a Roman Catholic for about half of his life. Moreover, his radical development from Protestant to Catholic took up much of his intellectual energy. Protestants such as myself have much to learn from Catholics, especially from one like Newman who represents in such a magnificent fashion what a Christian intellectual can be. Primarily, however, I have selected Newman because I know of no Christian thinker—scholar, cleric or both, as Newman was—who has given us such a vivid picture of the "perfection" toward which all Christians should aspire to the limit of their ability.

So here we will look at the individual cast of Newman's mind. For that we need to know more about Newman the man and his age.

Newman the Man

Born in 1801, Newman grew up in a modestly Christian family and attended a private school. At age fifteen, after an illness, Newman had a profound religious conversion. Though this conversion was not marked by "those special Evangelical experiences," nor were Newman's parents evangelical, Newman's early religious training was evangelical. He was, for example, "firmly convinced that the Pope was the Antichrist."[2] Newman was studious, and because of excellent test scores he gained access to Trinity College, Oxford.[3] Then, despite a very poor—but misleading—showing as an undergraduate, he wrote a stellar essay and was elected a fellow of Oriel College.

Newman was early attracted to the religious life and knew he "wanted to go into the Church."[4] In 1824 he took Holy Orders, becoming a curate at St. Clement's, Oxford, and in 1828 the vicar of St. Mary the Virgin, Oxford. From this post he preached sophisticated sermons (many more like lectures) to a growing number of

Oxford students and faculty. The basic orientation of his religious devotion never altered, and though his ecclesiology and theology were to take some dramatic twists and turns, and though he experienced doubts and occasional serious depression, he remained a convinced Christian, engaged in controversy and writing many essays and open letters, throughout his long and productive life.[5]

A few key turning points will serve to finish the backdrop to the more detailed picture I want to draw of Newman's cast of mind. From his early training as an evangelical, Newman first became attracted by Enlightenment rationalism, subjecting "all questions to intellectual scrutiny" and eventually losing confidence in the "emo-

---

Lead, Kindly Light, amid the encircling gloom
Lead Thou me on!
The night is dark, and I am far from home—
Lead Thou me on!
Keep Thou my feet; I do not ask to see
The distant scene—one step enough for me.

JOHN HENRY NEWMAN
"The Pillar of the Cloud"

---

tional and intuitive approach to religious certitude" that characterized the evangelical faith of his day.[6] It was in fact a modest skeptic, Richard Whately, whom Newman credits with teaching him "to think for himself."[7] This was only a temporary preface, however, to a growing interest in a new movement toward a more traditionally Catholic approach to Christian piety and ecclesiology. Newman, in fact, became a major figure in this so-called Oxford Movement that began with a sermon by John Keble in 1833 and was spurred on by a series of *Tracts for the Times*, many of which Newman wrote.

In 1841 Newman wrote the famous, or infamous, *Tract 90*, suggesting that the Thirty-nine Articles defining the doctrines of the Anglican Church were really more Catholic than Protestant. This caused a furor among many Anglican clergy and intellectuals, as rumors spread that Newman, despite his constant and eloquent denials, was about to convert to Catholicism. And the rumormongers in all strains of Christian commitment—Dissenters, Anglicans and Catholics—eventually had their fears or hopes confirmed. In 1845 Newman was received into the Catholic Church.

Newman was soon ordained priest in Rome by the pope and joined the Oratorians, "a community of secular priests living under a rule but not under vows." In this semimonastic order Newman could keep his property, the most important of which to him was his library.[8] In 1852 Bishop Paul Cullen of Armagh asked him to deliver a few lectures on education toward the founding of the Catholic University of Ireland. This sparked the lectures that became *The Idea of a University* and were followed by his appointment as the university's first rector, a post he held till 1856.

His next major move came when Charles Kingsley, a popular novelist, wrote, "Truth for its own sake had never been a virtue with the Roman clergy. Father Newman informs us it need not be, and on the whole ought not to be."[9] Newman responded with his *Apologia Pro Vita Sua* which not only answered Kingsley but finally brought Newman commendation from across the religious spectrum. Always admired by a few, he finally secured the respect of many.

Newman continued to serve the Catholic Church in a variety of ways, writing, teaching, administering and gradually winning the admiration of most who knew him or about him. Late in life his alma mater, Trinity College, Oxford, fêted him and made him its first honorary fellow (1878), and for his contribution to Catholic faith Pope Leo XIII made him cardinal (1879). He continued to write and edit during the last ten years of his life, dying of pneumonia on August 11, 1890. "The pall over the coffin bore his cardinal's motto 'cor ad cor loquitur' [heart speaks to heart]. On his memorial-tablet were inscribed the words he had chosen—'Ex umbris et imaginibus in veritatem.' Out of unreality into Reality."[10]

The Cast of Newman's Mind

No brief list of appointments and accomplishments can begin to do

justice to the quality and significance of the life of a man like Newman. Even Ian Ker's masterful and massive biography (745 pages)
cannot do the job. This book's topic is smaller, of course, but it also
has fewer pages. Still, if we can get a sense of the cast of Newman's
mind, it will advance a major aim of this book: to encourage the
development of a Christian mind in every one of its readers.

Very oddly, some would suggest that Newman could never be a
hero of a book on the Christian mind. Thomas Carlyle, for example,
said that "Newman had not the brains of a moderate-sized rabbit."[11]
And Henri Bremond remarked that "among his intellectual equals
he had the least inquiring mind of the last century." History and the
facts have belied both Carlyle and Bremond. Newman had a su-

**A religious mind is ever marvelling, and irreligious men laugh and scoff at it
because it marvels. A religious mind is ever looking out of itself, is ever
pondering God's words, is ever "looking into" them with the Angels,
is ever realizing to itself Him on whom it depends, and who is the centre of
all truth and good. Carnal and proud minds are contented with self;
they like to remain at home; when they hear of mysteries, they have no
devout curiosity to go and see the great sight, though it be ever so little out
of their way; and when it actually falls in their path, they stumble at it.**

JOHN HENRY NEWMAN
Parochial and Plain Sermons

---

perb and original intellect. Rather than coursing down the well-
worn paths of theological and philosophical discourse, he took his
own route, bringing such insights as could not have been the work
of anyone else. His contribution to the understanding of the development of Christian doctrine, his analysis of the theology of justification, his innovative treatment of the justification of belief: all bear
the unique stamp of his powers of imagination and ratiocination.[12]
"He had a lively mind," writes Owen Chadwick, and it was always
working.[13]

In *The Idea of a University* Newman wrote, "Thought and speech
are inseparable from each other. . . . Style is a thinking out in language."[14] Near the end of his life Newman noted that "he had never

been able to think well without a pen in his hand, 'and now that I cannot use it freely, I cannot use my mind.' "[15] Because of this we can see something of Newman's mind at work just before he began to doubt the legitimacy of the English Church:

> I write—I write again—I write a third time, in the course of six months—then I take the third—I literally fill the paper with corrections so that another person could not read it—I then write it out fair for the printer—I put it by—I take it up—I begin to correct again—it will not do—alterations multiply—pages are re-written—little lines sneak in and crawl about—the whole page is disfigured—I write again. I cannot count how many times this process goes on.—I can but compare the whole business to a very homely undertaking . . . washing a sponge of the sea gravel and sea smell. Well—as many fresh *waters* have I taken to my book [*Lectures on Justification*].[16]

One wonders how he would have gotten on with a word-processing computer.

A Passion for Truth
In his thought and consequently in his writing Newman was always driven by a passion for truth. Not long after his conversion Newman read Thomas Scott's *The Force of Truth*. It struck him pro-

---

**By the time he passed the age of thirty-five he had become the solitary thinker. His ideas developed under his own meditation.
He read many books, and thought about them much, and on occasion discussed them. But his mind was his own.**

OWEN CHADWICK
Newman

---

foundly. Scott, Newman said, "followed the truth wherever it led him, beginning with Unitarianism, and ending in a zealous faith in the Holy Trinity."[17] In this comment two themes which were to characterize Newman's whole life combine in perfect union: truth and obedience to the truth. This is a thread we will pick up below.

The passion for truth is the underlying assumption of everything Newman thought and did.[18] Railing against the retreat from reason

---

[Newman] seemed to one listener to be like an eagle swooping unerringly upon its prey. He might lead the hearers into mystery; he never lost his consciousness that the universe is a very mysterious place and that mortal mind can only touch its fringes; but he never left his audience muddled by mystery, or confused about what they heard.

OWEN CHADWICK
Newman

---

that had begun to characterize Christian thought in his day, he writes: "That there is a truth then; that there is one truth; that religious error is in itself of an immortal nature; . . . that the search for truth is not the gratification of curiosity; . . . that truth and falsehood are set before us for the trial of our hearts . . . this is the dogmatical principle."[19]

Newman contrasts this principle with the principle of liberalism, which he rejects:

> That truth and falsehood in religion are but matter of opinion; that one doctrine is as good as another; that the Governor of the world does not intend that we should gain the truth; that there is no truth; . . . that belief belongs to the mere intellect, not to the heart also; that we may safely trust to ourselves in matters of Faith, and need no other guide.[20]

John Henry, we cry out, where are you when we need you! Perhaps not as much has changed in the past hundred years as we might think. But back to the point.

Newman is passionate about truth itself, not just an endless search for it, but the real, embodied, blood-and-gut reality itself. And he is fascinated both by how it can be acquired and how its acquirement can be made certain.

First, how can it be acquired? That question immediately brings us to the second half of the theme: the willingness to follow what one begins to perceive might be true. "Great men alone can prove great ideas or grasp them," he wrote. "Moral truths are 'gained by patient study, by calm reflection, silently as the dew falls' and do not

---

Truth is too sacred and religious a thing to be sacrificed to the mere gratification of the fancy, or amusement of the mind, or party spirit, or the prejudices of education, or attachment (however amiable) to the opinions of human teachers, or any of those other feelings which the ancient philosophers suffered to influence them in their professedly grave and serious discussions.

JOHN HENRY NEWMAN
Fifteen Sermons Preached Before the University of Oxford Between A.D. 1836 and 1843

---

show well 'in the argument of an hour.' "[21] The close relationship between knowing and doing, believing and obeying, theory and practice, emerge in a host of ways in his writings throughout his life. Consider these:

[1833, during his trip in the Mediterranean] Good thoughts are only good so far as they are taken as means to an exact *obedience,* or at least this is the chief part of their goodness.[22]

[1841?] If virtue be a mastery over the mind, if its end be action, if its perfection be inward order, harmony, and peace, we must seek it in graver and holier places than in Libraries and Reading-rooms.[23]

[April 20, 1845] It is so difficult to know whether it [the inclination to leave the Anglican for the Roman Catholic Church] is a call of *reason* or of *conscience.* I cannot make out if I am impelled by what seems to me to be *clear* or by a sense of *duty.*[24]

[1856, on the character of a Catholic university] I want the same roof to contain both the intellectual and the moral discipline.[25]

A Passion for Holiness

To say only that Newman had a passion for truth and that this meant obedience had to follow is not strong enough. Newman had

in fact an "unremitting quest for holiness" regardless of its connection to anything else—truth, sentiment, pleasure—anything.[26] Early
in his pastoral work at St. Clement's he wrote: "Those who make
comfort the great subject of their preaching seem to mistake the end
of ministry. *Holiness* is the great end. There must be a struggle and
trial here. Comfort is a cordial, but no one drinks cordials from
morning to night."[27]

How did Newman conceive of holiness? One of his clearest
explanations is in two sermons preached while still the Anglican
rector of St. Mary the Virgin in Oxford.

> To love our brethren with a resolution which no obstacles can over-
> come, so as almost to consent to an anathema on ourselves, if so by
> we may save those who hate us,—to labour in God's cause against
> hope, and in the midst of sufferings,—to read the events of life, as
> they occur, by the interpretation which Scripture gives them, and
> that, not as if the language were strange to us, but to do it
> promptly,—to perform all our relative daily duties most watch-
> fully,—to check every evil thought, and bring the whole mind into
> captivity to the law of Christ,—to be patient, cheerful, forgiving,
> meek, honest, and true,—to persevere in this good work till death,
> making fresh and fresh advances towards perfection—and after all,
> even to the end, to confess ourselves unprofitable servants, nay, to
> feel ourselves corrupt and sinful creatures, who (with all our profi-
> ciency) would still be lost unless God bestowed on us His mercy in
> Christ;—these are some of the difficult realities of religious obedi-
> ence, which we must pursue, and which the Apostles in high mea-
> sure attained, and which we may well bless God's holy name, if He
> enables us to make our own.[28]

The second sermon again addresses the path to holiness:

> Let us strive and pray that the love of holiness may be created within
> our hearts; and then acts will follow, such as befit us and our circum-
> stances, in due time, without our distressing ourselves to find what
> they should be. You need not attempt to draw any precise line
> between what is sinful and what is only allowable: look up to Christ,

and deny yourselves every thing, whatever its character, which you think He would have you relinquish. You need not calculate and measure, if you love much: you need not perplex yourselves with points of curiosity, if you have a heart to venture after Him. True, difficulties will sometimes arise, but they will be seldom. He bids you take up your cross; therefore accept the daily opportunities which occur of yielding to others, when you need not yield, and of doing unpleasant services, which you might avoid. He bids those who would be highest, live as the lowest: therefore, turn from ambitious thoughts, and (as far as you religiously may) make resolves against taking on you authority and rule. He bids you sell and give alms; therefore, hate to spend money on yourself. Shut your ears to praise, when it grows loud: set your face like a flint, when the world ridicules, and smile at its threats. Learn to master your heart, when it would burst forth into vehemence, or prolong a barren sorrow, or dissolve into unseasonable tenderness. Curb your tongue, and turn away your eye, lest you fall into temptation. Avoid the dangerous air which relaxes you, and brace yourself upon the heights. Be up at prayer "a great while before day," and seek the true, your only Bridegroom, "by night on your bed." So shall self-denial become natural to you, and a change come over you, gently and imperceptibly; and, like Jacob, you will lie down in the waste, and soon see Angels, and a way opened for you into heaven.[29]

Newman knew that such holiness was not easy to come by. One must want to change, and that desire itself has to be developed: "Is not holiness the result of many patient, repeated efforts after obedience, gradually working on us, and first modifying and changing our hearts?"[30]

A few years prior to his conversion to Catholicism, Newman discovered that holiness is not to be acquired by a severe asceticism but by ordinary discipline.[31] The life of a saint, he wrote, "is a narrative which impresses the reader with the idea of moral unity, identity, growth, continuity, personality . . . the presence of one active principle of thought, one individual character . . . an inward life."[32] And while Newman never aspired to be recognized as a saint, he clearly aspired to have a life identified by moral unity, "one active principle of thought." Indeed, his passion for holiness along with his pas-

---

Those who saw Newman at the sacrament were conscious that he was much with God. But he prayed in his own way. He had a lively mind and could not rest in long silences. He needed a lot of material for his prayers, a lot of thinking about Biblical texts or devotional authors. The mode was unusual. He thought best with pen and paper, and prayer was no exception.

OWEN CHADWICK
Newman

---

sion for truth is the hidden bedrock undergirding his whole life—personal, intellectual, pastoral, professorial, clerical.[33]

Acquiring Truth

Assuming, then, that one has a passion for the truth and is willing to live by that truth when it becomes known, how is the truth acquired?

Newman is no innovator here. The human mind is made for truth, and the arts and sciences as practiced in Newman's day were taken by him as the main ways to acquire knowledge about the world around us. The main way one arrives at religious truth, however, is through reason and revelation (Scripture, Christian tradition and the individual human conscience).[34] *Tract 73* deals with this topic at some length and subtlety. First, reason has a role to play with regard to revealed truth:

> As regards Revealed Truth, it is not Rationalism to set about to ascertain, by the use of reason, what things are ascertainable by reason, and what are not; nor, in the absence of an express Revelation, to inquire into the truths of Religion, as they come to us by nature; nor to determine what proofs are necessary for the acceptance of a Revelation, if it be given; nor to reject a Revelation on the plea of insufficient proof; nor, after recognizing it as divine, to investigate the meaning of its declarations, and to interpret its language. . . . This is not Rationalism.[35]

But there are limits to reason too:

> But it is Rationalism to accept the Revelation, and then to explain it away; to speak of it as the Word of God, and to treat it as the word of man; to refuse to let it speak for itself; to claim to be told the *why* and the *how* of God's dealings with us . . . and to assign to Him a motive and a scope of our own; to stumble at the partial knowledge of what he may give us of them; to put aside what is obscure, as if it had not been said at all; to accept one half of what has been told us, and not the other half; to assume that the contents of Revelation are also its proof; to frame some gratuitous hypothesis about them, and then to garble, gloss, and colour them, to trim, to clip, pare away, and twist them in order to bring them into conformity with the idea to which we have subjected them.[36]

Like all traditional Christians, Newman saw the Bible as the prime revelation, though part of the reason he became more and more attracted to Catholicism is that he saw a growing role for the teaching office of the church, first the councils and later, and more important, the pope. Moreover, as Newman studied the history of the church he came to reject what he called the " 'ultra-Protestant principle,' according to which 'every one may gain the true doctrines of the gospel for himself from the Bible.'"[37] Rather, the early church formed the doctrines, using the Bible only "in vindication of its teaching."[38] In short, Newman believed (and Protestants do not) that the church teaches and then the Bible justifies the church's teaching.

Surely Newman was not sanguine about the ability of any human mind to easily achieve a knowledge of truth—whether secular or sacred. The mind is an instrument of great complexity; it is subject to all sorts of extraneous desires that lead it astray; it proceeds by fits and starts and often flags in the process of gaining clarity. One of the most eloquent passages Newman ever wrote describes the mind at work:

> The mind ranges to and fro, and spreads out, and advances forward

with a quickness which has become a proverb, and a subtlety and versatility which baffle investigation. It passes on from point to point, gaining one by some indication; another on a probability; then availing itself of an association; then falling back on some received law; next seizing on testimony; then committing itself to some popular impression, or some inward instinct, or some obscure memory; and thus it makes progress not unlike a clamberer on a steep cliff, who, by quick eye, prompt hand, and firm foot, ascends how he knows not himself, by personal endowments and by practice, rather than by rule, leaving no track behind him, and unable to teach another. It is not too much to say that the stepping by which great geniuses scale the mountains of truth is as unsafe and precarious to men in general, as the ascent of a skilful mountaineer up a literal crag. It is a way which they alone can take; and its justification lies in their success. And such mainly is the way in which all men, gifted or not gifted, commonly reason,—not by rule, but by an inward faculty.[39]

This is, of course, Newman describing the workings of any vitally active mind, but we can be certain that much of this description came from deep introspection of the workings of his own mind. Newman was to think long and hard about the "inward faculty," and in *The Grammar of Assent* he eventually lights upon the term "Illative Sense" to give it a concrete label.[40] His discussion there is too complex to summarize in this chapter. Suffice it to say that Newman has in mind a distinct mental faculty, to be equated with neither logical inference nor intuition. A sense of this we can see from a comment he made in a letter: "You must be patient, you must wait for the *eye* of the soul to be formed in you. Religious truth is reached, not by reasoning, but by an inward perception. Any one can reason; only disciplined, educated formed minds can perceive."[41] Or again: "We judge for ourselves, by our own lights, and on our own principles; and our criterion of truth is not so much the manipulation of propositions, as the intellectual and moral character of the person maintaining them, and the ultimate silent effect of his argument or conclusions upon our minds."[42]

First principles especially—what I usually call presuppositions—are not to be grasped by reason but by the conscience:[43]

> Conscience . . . teaches us, not only that God is, but what He is; it provides for the mind a real image of Him, as a medium of worship; it gives us a rule of right and wrong, as being His rule, and a code of moral duties. Moreover, it is so constructed that, if obeyed, it becomes clearer in its injunctions, and wider in their range, and corrects and completes the accidental feebleness of its initial teachings.[44]

Or again:

> The conscience is the connecting principle between the creature and his Creator; and the firmest hold of theological truths is gained by habits of personal religion. When men begin all their works with the thought of God, acting for His sake, and to fulfill His will, when they ask His blessing on themselves and their life, pray to Him for the objects they desire, and see Him in the event, whether it be according to their prayers or not, they will find everything that happens tends to confirm them in the truths about Him which live in their imagination, varied and unearthly as those truths may be.[45]

Truth, however, is not solely the province of the individual intellect, *eye* of the soul or conscience to determine. This would lead to the exaltation of a principle Newman rejected throughout his life: the principle of "private judgment," the principle deriving from the Protestant Reformation and one that has had, as far as Newman is concerned, disastrous consequences. It is the principle that led to the "Rationalism" we have already seen him reject.[46] Rather, truth is often the result of a conflict between claims to truth.[47] Moreover, "Truth is wrought out by many minds, working together freely."[48]

There is no doubt that there is a tension in Newman's treatment of "private judgment," which often seems to characterize his own original thinking, and the judgment of his colleagues and especially of the tradition of the church.[49] As Ker puts it, "Indeed, it is in these exploratory letters that we see a vigorously independent and original mind, yet imbued with a profound sense of authority and tradition, in the actual process of forming a balanced theory of the teaching office of the Church."[50] As he agonizingly worked through the issue of the infallibility of the pope, a dogma enunciated in 1870 which he personally opposed, Newman carefully presented a balanced case. Ker comments, "What is so impressive ultimately about this last chapter [of *Apologia Pro Vita Sua*] is its refusal to adopt any one particular point of view to the exclusion of other considerations and factors."[51]

What I find most striking, however, are the famous final words on the subject of conscience, which he calls "the law of God as apprehended in the minds of individual men."[52]

> Conscience is the aboriginal Vicar of Christ, a prophet in its informations, a monarch in its peremptoriness, a priest in its blessings and anathemas, and even though the eternal priesthood throughout the Church could cease to be, in it the sacerdotal principle would remain and be given a sway.[53]

Only under the most extreme of circumstances would it be appropriate for the "dictate" of conscience to override that of the pope: "Unless a man is able to say to himself, as in the Presence of God, that he must not, and dare not, act upon the Papal injunction, he is bound to obey it, and would commit a great sin in disobeying it."[54] Then Newman concludes: "I add one remark. Certainly, if I am obliged to bring religion into after-dinner toasts, (which indeed does not seem quite the thing) I shall drink—to the Pope, if you please—still, to Conscience first, and to the Pope afterwards."[55]

We must note well that Newman did not view conscience as the judgment of any private individual on his or her own. Conscience, he said, is "the connecting principle between the creature and his Creator."[56] Nonetheless, it seems to me that Newman as an individual thinker practices the principle of "private judgment" in spite of himself. But is it not the only way any person can act? When one submits to the judgment of another, one is making a private judgment that submitting is right. When one refuses to accede to another—be it parent, friend, spouse, teacher or pope—one exercises "private judgment."

What we get in Newman and in the teaching of traditional Christianity in general is the teaching that our private judgments, especially when they seem to belie the common understandings of the church (no matter how defined—Catholic, Protestant, Mennonite, Orthodox), are especially prone to error and therefore should be made with the greatest of care and humility. "The fear of the LORD is the beginning of wisdom" (Ps 111:10): if we honor that truth with obedience, we will at least have our heart in the right place.

A Passion for Certitude

Before examining a specific instance of Newman's mind at work, let us look at one more passion: his passion for certitude.[57] This passion was accompanied by a passion for exactness (for expressing precisely what he really thought) and a passion for being real and not just *notional* about his beliefs.

We look first at his desire for accuracy. Because he thought with his pen, he wanted to get down everything he said exactly as he wished it said. He was always willing to take the consequences for what he wrote, as his vast number of published rejoinders and private letters to critics show. But he tried hard to write in such a way that all could be defended and little would have to be retracted.[58] Concerning the work of two of his colleagues who presumed to accept Newman's notions and then go further, Newman wrote to E. B. Pusey,

> I think my sympathies *are* with them; but really I cannot determine whether my opinions are. I do not know the limits of my own opinions. If Ward [one of the two colleagues] says this or that is a development from what I have said, I cannot say yes or no—It is plausible; it may be true—I cannot assert it is not true; but I cannot with that keen perception, which some people have, appropriate it. It is a nuisance to me to be *forced* beyond what I can fairly go.[59]

Just so far and no further, Newman insisted. What one believes should not just be theory, not just notional, but real. The distinction has roots in the evangelical distinction between a nominal and a real Christian, but is developed by Newman in a far richer form. In his first book, *The Arians of the Fourth Century* (1833), the very notions of *true* and *false* were defined for him in terms of *real* and *unreal*. In *Parochial Sermons* (1834) Newman "insists that all religion 'must be *real*.' To profess a religious belief as true, and yet not be able to 'feel, think, speak, act as if it were true,' is to believe 'in an unreal way.' "[60] This, of course, is another way of saying that Newman's passion for truth is linked with his passion for a holiness characterized by obedience.

It is in *The Grammar of Assent* (1870), however, that Newman gives the fullest expression of the distinction between the real and unreal.[61] There the distinction undergirds his highly original and complex study of the justification of belief. Newman had long wanted to pursue the issue of why as Christians we are believing what is true. The time came to him in his intellectual maturity, and

---

The love and pursuit of truth in the subject-matter of religion, if it be genuine, must always be accompanied by the fear of error, of error which may be sin. An inquirer in the province of religion is under a responsibility for his reasons and their issue.

JOHN HENRY NEWMAN
The Via Media

---

the results are, if not convincing, an original step toward the justification of our faith. In this his most philosophical work Newman sets himself the task of understanding how we are justified in believing doctrines of the Christian faith that we cannot strictly prove by rational inquiry.

I cannot presume to summarize the often torturous progress of this argument.[62] It will suffice to give its flavor in a few quotations.

> Certitude . . . is the perception of a truth with the perception that it is a truth, or the consciousness of knowing, as expressed in the phrase, "I know that I know," or "I know that I know that I know,"—or simply "I know."[63]

It is the characteristic of certitude that its object is a truth, a truth as such, a proposition as true. There are right and wrong convictions, and certitude is a right conviction; if it is not right with a conscious-ness of being right, it is not certitude. Now truth cannot change; what is once truth is always truth; and the human mind is made for truth, and so rests in truth, as it cannot rest in falsehood. When then it once becomes possessed of a truth, what is to dispossess it? but this is to be certain; therefore once certitude, always certitude.[64]

What brings this certitude is the "illative sense," a term not origi-nal with Newman but one rarely used. "It is the mind that reasons, and that controls its own reasonings, not any technical apparatus of words and propositions. The power of judging and concluding, when in its perfection, I call the Illative Sense."[65]

Among the three passions—for truth, holiness and certitude—it is the latter alone, it seems to me, that is problematic. The search—nay, the *passion*—for certitude fueled the Enlightenment project. Descartes, the first genuinely modern philosopher, thought he had

---

Men are satisfied with themselves, not when they attempt, but when they neglect the details of duty. Disobedience blinds the conscience; obedience makes it keen-sighted and sensitive. The more we *do*, the more we trust in Christ.

JOHN HENRY NEWMAN
Parochial and Plain Sermons

---

found, through self-reflection, a way of securing philosophic certi-tude. And while subsequent philosophers such as David Hume (before Newman) and Friedrich Nietzsche (after Newman) have profoundly challenged this optimism, the subsequent intellectual culture accepted the notion that philosophic certitude was possible, largely adopting the methods of science as the way to such certi-tude.[66] While Newman rejected both Descartes's method of doubt and the scientific methods of finding certitude, he still accepted philosophic certitude as a proper and reachable goal. Newman tried to show just how it is that human reason in the form of the illative sense performs, under God, this function. Despite the intensity of Newman's quest and the sophistication of his reasoning, few today think he achieved his goal.

Still we need to see just how for Newman this illative sense works out in his practice. We can get a glimpse of this by looking at Newman's mind at work on the issue that gave him the most difficulty of his whole life: which is the true church—the Anglican Church or the Roman Catholic Church?

Newman's Mind at Work

Perhaps the best way to see Newman's mind at work is to follow him as he began to doubt his view of the Church of England as a *via media*, a proper halfway house between evangelicalism and Roman Catholicism. More accurately, in the words of Avery Dulles, "Newman and his colleagues maintained that the Catholic Church had three branches: Orthodox, Roman, and Anglican."[67] For about six years the Tractarians, as Newman and his friends were called, engaged in controversy from the first tract till the final *Tract 90*, the last straw for the bishop of Oxford, who asked that no further tracts be published.

We pick up the story in 1839. Since the first of the *Tracts for the Times* was published in 1833, Newman had been the major force in the Oxford Movement. He had written many of the tracts themselves, tracts whose main purpose was to promote a mid-position between the evangelicals (Protestant in their reading of the Thirty-nine Articles) and Roman Catholics. "In the spring of 1839 my position in the Anglican Church was at its height. I had supreme confidence in my controversial *status*, and I had a great and still growing success, in recommending it to others."[68] Such a position was, of course, a more Catholic version of Anglicanism than was currently prevalent in the English Church.

The beginnings of Newman's doubt came both suddenly and unexpectedly as he engaged in the seemingly innocent pursuit of scholarship. He had turned his attention to a controversy in the early church. The exact nature of that controversy need not be delineated here. It concerned the ancient heresies of the Donatists and the Monophysites. An article by Nicholas Wiseman, a Catholic scholar, had pointed out that the expounders of these heresies had appealed to antiquity as justification for their position but had been "silenced by a living authority (the Church)."[69] The key words were those enunciated by St. Augustine: "Securus judicat orbis terrarum."[70] (The full sentence reads, "The world judges with assurance that they

---

If there is one comprehensive thing that can be said for Newman's writing, it is that he has a "voice"; it is his own and no one else's. To me, at least, it is a voice that never fails to start up, radioactive from the page, however musty the physical book.

M U R I E L   S P A R K , foreword to
Realizations: Newman's Own Selection of His Sermons

---

are not good men who, in whatever part of the world, separate themselves from the rest of the world.")[71] Only the Roman Catholic position is consistent with the notion that "the deliberate judgment, in which the whole Church at length rests and acquiesces, is an infallible prescription and a final sentence against such portions of it as secede."[72] This meant that any version of the church—not just Dissenters and Anglican evangelicals but Tractarian Anglican *via media* promoters as well—was a church in apostasy. The shock to Newman was intense: "By those great words of the ancient Father, interpreting and summing up the long and varied course of ecclesiastical history, the theory of the *Via Media* was absolutely pulverized."[73]

But Newman was not to convert quickly to the Roman Church. A week later he thought that Wiseman's article should be studied and answered. Then a few days later he suggested to a friend that St. Augustine might well agree "that grace could be 'given even in a schismatical Church.' "[74] Later still the challenge to Newman's Tractarian view died away: "After a while I got calm, and at length the vivid impression upon my imagination faded away. . . . My old conviction remained as before."[75] He had, he said on reflection, "determined to be guided, not by my imagination, but by my reason."[76]

Six more years passed before Newman resolved the issue and the "shadow of a hand upon of the wall" of 1839 became a reality. As the confidence in a middle position became for him more and more untenable, he came to feel that "it was 'irrational to believe so much' as Anglo-Catholics did without believing 'more.' "[77] The change, however, was gradual, as he explained to Henry Wilberforce in October 1844:

> They [my reasonings] are not present—the impression remains, but the process of argument is like a scaffolding taken down when the building is completed. I could not recollect all the items which went to make up my convictions, nor can I represent it to another with that force which it came to my mind. Corroborations too are generally coincidences resulting from distinct courses of thought or from the bodies of fact which require a certain frame of mind to appreciate.[78]

In July 1844 he wrote to John Keble, reflecting on his dilemma: "I feel myself very unreal."[79] Part of his problem was fear that he was somehow unholy: did he have a secret fault that kept his illative sense from working? He wrote his sister that he could convert "tomorrow—it is the fear that there is some secret fault which is the cause of my belief, which keeps me where I am waiting."[80]

Eventually he made the move. Ker concludes, "He had only one real reason for joining the Roman Church, and that was his belief that the Church of England was in schism."[81] But for him it was enough. On October 9, 1845, he was received into the Roman Church. From this finally settled judgment he never wavered.

We could now ask, Was Newman right? Are all churches but the Catholic Church apostate? On this Protestants and Catholics will disagree. My point is not to follow Newman in the specifics of his reasoning about this one—granted important—issue. It is rather to show how Newman's mind worked and to encourage us to follow him in following what we perceive to be the truth and its consequences in action.

We could also be far more detailed in our analysis of the general workings of Newman's mind. He, as much as—perhaps more than—any other intellectual, has given us a running account in *Apologia Pro Vita Sua* and his letters. Fueled by fear of hypocrisy, by constant vitriolic and personal attacks on him and his ideas, and by self-reflection to ascertain that what he thinks is certain is indeed true, Newman vividly reveals the machinations of his mind. Who among us, even if we had his powers of expression, would be willing to be so candid?

I close this chapter with a studied summary of Newman's mind written by historian Owen Chadwick. I would hope that what I have said above will help justify his conclusion:

> Let us take him as a mind of unity; growing, articulating, arranging, acquiring new truth from meditating on old truth or even, though more rarely, from new information found in books; but a man with the same mind all his life; the same despite one conversion at the age of forty-four; a mind with principles formed early, and then expanded, adapted, recast, and yet recognisably the same principles—so that some of his best writing on subjects which he treated in books as Roman Catholic is found in books which he wrote as a Protestant. This is not to say that the mind stood still; never was a mind so unceasingly in motion. But the motion was always growth, and never revolution. Occasionally he entered some cul-de-sac of the mind and then retreated. But he needed to retreat far less than most men who think a lot. If he got into what looked like a dead end he would pause, and consider, and peer about, and wait, and finally discover that after all he could see a way forward.[82]

Does Newman, then, illustrate the definition of an intellectual given at the end of chapter one? How does Newman understand the life of the mind? The next chapter will throw further light on these questions.

III

THE PERFECTION OF THE INTELLECT

What does it mean to be an intellectual? To have a developed or developing mind? What is its demeanor? What is its scope? What are its tasks? What does it do? What does it mean to think well and to think responsibly?

This is a huge subject. I will have to treat only a small slice of it. But a philosophy of a thousand thoughts begins with one proposition. And not a few will follow here, the most important ones being from John Henry Newman.

A Source for Our Reflection

About 150 years ago, 1852 to be more precise, John Henry Newman was asked to provide the intellectual foundation for the formation of the new Catholic university in Dublin, Ireland. He delivered five lectures on this topic, to which others were later added. These have been published in various forms but finally have become known most widely as *The Idea of a University*. Newman's task was specific, and some of what he said is limited in scope to the historical situation of which it was a part—the founding of a specifically Catholic university for the education of Irish students otherwise forced to get their education from an Anglican university. Nonetheless, much of what he said then has had a profound impact on the theory and practice of higher education for almost a century and a half.

As Frank M. Turner says,

> No work in the English language has had more influence on the public ideals of higher education. No other book on the character and purposes of universities has received so frequent citation and praise by other academic commentators. . . . Newman provided the vocabulary, ideas, and ideals with which to discuss the concerns, character, and purpose of the university and of higher education generally.[1]

This work is so important, so pregnant with ideas, so insightful in detail, so encompassing, that an entire book could be dedicated solely to its implications for the scope of Christian education today.[2] This chapter focuses on only one of its central ideas: "the perfection of the intellect," which Newman sometimes called the "imperial intellect."

The Perfection of the Intellect: Texts from Newman

I have struggled long and hard over how to present Newman's notion of the perfection of the intellect. The texts in which the notion is expounded are so rich, the subideas so intertwined, not to say entangled, that the central features of the notion do not lie on the surface, quotable phrase by phrase, but are woven in a tapestry as complex and beautiful as the Unicorn Tapestries in The Cloisters. I have decided to let Newman speak at length for himself. So here are five sections from *The Idea of a University* and one from an earlier sermon, "Implicit and Explicit Reason," to set the stage for our analysis.

If you are not used to reading nineteenth-century prose, I encourage you to take a deep breath and slowly read these passages aloud. You will hear the phrases move ashore in your mind like the waves—large and inevitable—on Waikiki Beach on a good day for surfing. Try it.

THE DISCIPLINED INTELLECT

But the intellect which has been disciplined to the perfection of its powers, which knows and thinks while it knows, which has learned to leaven the dense mass of facts and events with the elastic force of reason, such an intellect cannot be partial, cannot be exclusive, cannot be impetuous, cannot be at a loss, cannot but be patient, collected and majestically calm, because it discerns the end in every beginning, the origin in every end, and the law in every interruption, the limit in each delay; because it ever knows where it stands, and how its path lies from one point to another.[3]

THE ENLARGEMENT OF THE MIND

The enlargement [of the mind] consists, not merely in the passive reception into the mind of a number of ideas hitherto unknown to it, but in the mind's energetic and simultaneous action upon and towards and among those ideas which are rushing in upon it. It is the action of a formative power, reducing to order and meaning the matter of acquirements; it is making the objects of our knowledge subjectively our own, or, to use a familiar word, it is a digestion of what we receive into the substance of our previous state of thought; and without this no enlargement is said to follow. There is no enlargement unless there be a comparison of ideas one with another, as they come before the mind, and a systematizing of them. We feel our minds to be growing and expanding *then*, when we not only learn, but refer what we learn to what we know already. It is not a mere addition to our knowledge which is the illumination; but the locomotion, the movement onwards, of that mental centre to which both what we know and what we are learning, the accumulating mass of our requirements, gravitates. And therefore a truly great intellect, and recognized to be such by the common opinion of mankind, such as the intellect of Aristotle, or of St. Thomas, or of Newton, or of Goethe (I purposely take instances within and without the Catholic pale, when I would speak of the intellect as such), is one which takes a connected view of old and new, past and present, far and near, and which has an insight into the influence of all these, one on another; without which there is no whole, and no centre. It possesses the knowledge, not only of things, but also of their mutual and true relations; knowledge not merely considered as acquirement, but as philosophy.[4]

THE PERFECTION OF THE INTELLECT

That perfection of the Intellect which is the result of Education, and its beau ideal, to be imparted to individuals in their respective measures, is the clear, calm, accurate vision and comprehension of all things, as far as the finite mind can embrace them, each in its place, and with its own characteristics upon it. It is almost prophetic from its knowledge of history; it is almost heart-searching from its knowledge of human nature; it has almost supernatural charity from its freedom from littleness and prejudice; it has almost the repose of faith, because nothing can startle it; it has almost the beauty and harmony of heavenly contemplation, so intimate is it with the eternal order of things and the music of the spheres.[5]

THE PHILOSOPHY OF THE IMPERIAL INTELLECT

The philosophy of the imperial intellect, for such I am considering a University to be, is based, not so much on simplification as on discrimination. Its true representative defines, rather than analyzes. He aims at no complete catalogue, or interpretation of the subjects of knowledge, but a following out, as far as the man can, what in its fulness is mysterious and unfathomable. Taking into his charge all sciences, methods, collections of facts, principles, doctrines, truths, which are the reflexions of the universe upon the human intellect, he admits them all, he disregards none, and, as disregarding none, he allows none to exceed or encroach. His watchword is Live and let live. He takes things as they are; he submits to them all, as far as they go; he recognizes the insuperable lines of demarcation which run between subject and subject; he observes how separate truths lie relative to each other, where they concur, where they part company, and where being carried too far, they cease to be truths at all. It is his office to determine how much can be known in each province of thought; when we must be contented not to know; in what direction inquiry is hopeless, or on the other hand full of promise; where it runs into the abyss. It will be his care to be familiar with the signs of real and apparent difficulties, with the methods proper to particular subject-matters, what in each particular case are the limits of a rational scepticism, and what the claims of a peremptory faith. If he has one cardinal maxim in his philosophy, it is that truth cannot be contrary to truth; if he has a second, it is that truth often seems contrary to truth; and, if a third, it is the practical conclusion, that we must be patient with such appearances, and not be hasty to pronounce them to be really of a more formidable character.[6]

THE MIND AT WORK

The mind ranges to and fro, and spreads out, and advances forward with a quickness which has become a proverb, and a subtlety and versatility which baffle investigation. It passes on from point to point, gaining one by some indication; another on a probability; then availing itself of an association; then falling back on some received law; next seizing on testimony; then committing itself to some popular impression, or some inward instinct, or some obscure memory; and thus it makes progress not unlike a clamberer on a steep cliff, who, by quick eye, prompt hand, and firm foot, ascends how he knows not himself, by personal endowments and by practice, rather than by rule, leaving no track behind him, and unable to teach another. It is not too much to say that the stepping by which great geniuses scale the mountains of truth is as unsafe and precarious to men in general, as the ascent of a skilful mountaineer up a literal crag. It is a way which they alone can take; and its justification lies in their success. And such mainly is the way in which all men, gifted or not gifted, commonly reason,—not by rule, but by an inward faculty.[7]

THE INTELLECT ENERGIZING

The intellect of man . . . energizes as well as his eye or ear, and perceives in sights and sounds something beyond them. It seizes and unites what the senses present to it; it grasps and forms what need not have been seen or heard except in its constituent parts. It discerns in lines and colours, or in tones, what is beautiful and what is not. It gives them a meaning, and invests them with an idea. It gathers up a succession of notes into the expression of a whole, and calls it melody; it has a keen sensibility towards angles and curves, lights and shadows, tints and contours. It distinguishes between rule and exception, between accident and design. It assigns phenomena to a general law, qualities to a subject, acts to a principle, and effects to a cause. In a word, it philosophizes; for I suppose Science and Philosophy, in their elementary idea, are nothing else but this habit of viewing, as it may be called, the objects which sense conveys to the mind, of throwing them into system, and uniting and stamping them with one form.[8]

THE NATURE OF RATIOCINATION

[Ratiocination] is the great principle of order in our thinking; it reduces a chaos into harmony; it catalogues the accumulations of knowledge; it maps out for us the relations of its separate departments; it puts us in the way to correct its own mistakes. It enables the independent intellects of many, acting and re-acting on each other, to bring their collective force to bear upon one and the same subject-matter, or same question. If language is an inestimable gift to man, the logical faculty prepares it for our use. Though it does not go so far as to ascertain truth, still it teaches us the direction in which truth lies, and how propositions lie towards each other. Nor is it a slight benefit to know what is probable, and what is not so, what is needed for the proof of a point, what is wanting in theory, how a theory hangs together, and what will follow, if it be admitted. Though it does not itself discover the unknown, it is one principal way by which discoveries are made.[9]

Newman's Perspective in Outline

If you read all seven sections at one sitting, if you surfed the waves of Newman's Ciceronian prose and were not swamped, did you not still find yourself gasping first for breath and then in awe? Every time I reread even one of them, I do. Listen now to some of the phrases clipped and tamed:

> *the intellect which thinks while it knows*
> *and knows while it thinks*

> *the intellect: patient, collected, majestically calm*
> *discerning the end in every beginning*
> *the origin in every end*
> *the law in every interruption*
> *the limit in each delay*

> *the intellect: ever knows where it stands*
> *and how its path lies from one point to another*
> *the intellect: takes a connected view of old and new*
> *past and present*
> *far and near*

> *knowledge: not merely as acquirement*
> *knowledge as philosophy*

> *ratiocination: reduces chaos to harmony*
> *puts us in the way to correct our mistakes*

> *the beauty and harmony of heavenly contemplation*
> *intimate with the eternal order of things*
> *the music of the spheres*

"Wow!" we may respond, even to this brief, truncated set of phrases. Many more like them could be cited. They awaken our sleeping minds. They thrill us with the élan vital of their audacity.

Then we descend from our ecstatic state, and an opposite reaction sets in. Good grief! How can Newman say this even in his own century—a hundred years closer to the Middle Ages than ours, but distant enough and already plagued by a history and presence of profound doubt in the intellectual ability of us creatures of mere mud. Come off it, John Henry! You are dreaming dreams.

Both of these responses are valid. Newman has been eloquent in his description of the perfection of the intellect. But he also seems romantic, out of touch with reality. Can he be serious?

Ian Ker has an explanation:

> One obvious difficulty that faces the modern reader of the *Idea* is its strong element of hyperbole. The kind of rhetorical exaggeration that came naturally to the Victorians is unpalatable in a culture which tends to laud realism and deprecate idealism. The hyperbolism, therefore, which characterizes the *Idea of a University* is calculated to confuse and mislead the contemporary reader who takes literally what Newman and readers of his time would have seen as a kind of exaggerated "approximation" to the truth.[10]

Well, yes, hyperbole, I suppose. But I think Ker gives away too much. Even in the idealism, even in the hyperbole, there sounds a note of truth deeper than utter realism can reach. Newman was con-

---

After all, when a thought takes one's breath away, a lesson on grammar seems an impertinence.

THOMAS WENTWORTH HIGGINSON
introduction to Emily Dickinson's *Poems*

---

vinced of the complete truth of a muscular Christianity, one that emphasized the wisdom, power and righteousness of God, a God who in creating us as human beings intended us to know—not just to think, opine, guess or, worse, construct knowledge from language manufactured, slowly but whole cloth, by ungoverned, unintended, naturalistic evolution.

So before we examine in some detail the rich tapestry of the seven texts quoted above, it would be valuable to see just why such an exalted notion as the perfection of the intellect has a large measure of *reality* about it. To be *real* was for Newman to be true.[11]

The Nature of God the Creator

Newman's notion of the perfection of the intellect is set firmly in the context of a wholistic theology, a theology beginning with, obviously, the nature of God:

God is an Individual, Self-dependent, All-perfect, Unchangeable Being; intelligent, living, personal, and present; almighty, all-seeing, all-remembering; . . . who created and upholds the universe. . . . He is One who is sovereign over, operative amidst, independent of, the appointments which He has made; One . . . who has a purpose in every event, and a standard for every deed, and thus has relations of His own towards the subject-matter of each particular science which the book of knowledge unfolds.[12]

In this definition is most, if not all, of what is needed to undergird the possibility of human knowledge. Let us take the elements one by one. First is the utter primacy of God's existence. Second is the nature of the God who exists: he is intelligent, living, personal, almighty. That means that he not only is but knows and purposes and reigns as sovereign. Third, God is the intentional creator of a rational, orderly universe that is not himself. As Newman says later, "He [God] has stamped upon all things in the hour of their creation, their respective natures, and has given them their work and mission and their length of days, greater or less in their appointed place."[13]

For this reason knowledge is not made up of bits and pieces gleaned severally from the various academic disciplines:

All knowledge forms one whole, because its subject-matter is one; for the universe in its length and breadth is so intimately knit together, that we cannot separate off abstraction; and then again, as to its Creator, though He of course in His own Being is infinitely separate from it, and Theology has its departments towards which human knowledge has no relations, yet He has so implicated Himself with it, and taken it into His very bosom, by His presence in it, His providence over it, His impressions upon it, and His influences through it, that we cannot truly or fully contemplate it without contemplating Him.[14]

The universe is, then, a knowable entity, known first of all by God but also by human beings. Our knowledge of God, our theology, is itself a boon to our knowledge of the universe. As Newman put it,

"Religious truth is not only a portion, but a condition of general knowledge."[15]

This more than implies that God has made us able to know:

[God] has on rational beings imprinted the moral law, and given them the power to obey it, imposing on them the duty of worship and service, searching and scanning them through and through with His omniscient eye, and putting before them a present trial and a judgment to come.[16]

Or again:

As the structure of the universe speaks to us of Him who made it, so the laws of the mind are the expression, not of merely constituted order, but of His will.[17]

In other words, because God is the all-knowing knower of all things, we—being made in his image—can be the sometimes knowing knowers of some things.

In short, Newman's notion of the perfection of the intellect is based on a prior set of presuppositions standard among all traditional Christians—Protestant, Catholic, Orthodox.[18]

The Demeanor of the Intellect

One way to identify the specific concepts or subideas in Newman's notion of the perfection of the intellect is to consider them within the framework of demeanor, scope and tasks. We will take each in turn.

We start with characteristics that seem more moral and aesthetic than intellectual. This is appropriate because for Newman the human intellect itself rests on preconditions.

As we saw in chapter two, only the mind that is also moral will be granted access to the fullest truth. "Great men alone can prove great ideas or grasp them," he wrote. "Moral truths are 'gained by patient study, by calm reflection, silently as the dew falls' and do not show well 'in the argument of an hour.' "[19] Foundational principles, the ones most vital for the proper operation of the intellect, are determined not by human reason but through revelation (biblical or natural) grasped by the conscience.[20]

So the mind that exhibits the perfection of the intellect will be impartial, patient and majestically calm; it will be characterized, in fact, by "almost supernatural charity from its freedom from littleness" and "almost the repose of faith."

Intellect is the capitalized and communal form of life intelligence stored up and made into habits of discipline, signs and symbols of meaning, chains of reasoning and spurs to emotion—a shorthand and a wireless by which the mind can skip connectives, recognize ability, and communicate truth.

JACQUES BARZUN
The House of Intellect

A little self-reflection on our own part confirms these characteristics. When we think impatiently, with bias and in anxiety, we know we cannot trust the results. Insights gained in ecstasy—and sometimes they are—need to be subjected to the contemplation of temperate, not necessarily cold, reason. When we have arrived at a settled conviction of the truth of what we seek to know, there is indeed both a "freedom from littleness" and bigotry and a sense that what we know is as certain as the convictions of our faith.

No weight nor mass nor beauty of execution can outweigh one grain or fragment of thought.

JOHN RUSKIN
quoted in the introduction to Emily Dickinson's *Poems*

But the mind, Newman says, will also be characterized by "almost the beauty and harmony of heavenly contemplation." That seems a bit over the top. Is this the hyperbole that Ker points to? Yes, but it is appropriate. Newman does say *almost*, and that redeems him from complete idealism. Still, when the mind hums with activity, when it is working really well, how else shall we give a sense of how our thinking feels? It does seem "intimate with the music of the spheres." Should we come to think that we are doing all this for ourselves, should we come to feel that God is nowhere around—nor needs to be—then we must quickly and desperately be brought up short. All this is a gift of God, a "supernatural charity." Whatever else "the *almost perfect* workings of our mind" implies, it is not the "autonomy of the human intellect," our own or that of anyone else.

The Scope of the Intellect

Newman depicts a wide panorama for the scope of the human mind. With its knowledge of history, the intellect at its best is "almost prophetic." It takes "a connected view of old and new, past and present, far and near," and it does so grasping their influence on each other and seeing the center that holds them all together as one world, one universe of being and knowing, of thing and language.

With its knowledge of human nature it is "almost heart-searching." Newman does not elaborate on this, but it implies that the perfected intellect has a profound grasp of who we are as human beings. Is it not the case that the best of our writers—say Fyodor Dostoevsky, Geoffrey Chaucer, Emily Dickinson, William Faulkner—do indeed plumb the heart of humankind?

With its intimacy "with the eternal order of things and the music of the spheres," as we have seen, the perfected intellect has "almost

---

He who endeavors to reflect on the totality of the world and existence, that is, to philosophize, sets foot on a path that in this life will never come to an end.

JOSEF PIEPER
In Defense of Philosophy

---

the beauty and harmony of heavenly contemplation." Newman, waxing poetic to be sure, may be thinking of the vast storehouse of knowledge that has been given us by God through revelation—Scripture first of all but also those who have gone before. It is no secret that most of us acquire our knowledge by revelation. Somebody tells us. The bulk of those who know that water is composed of hydrogen and oxygen, two parts to one, do so because of revelation—from their high-school chemistry text or teacher. Of course, "the eternal order of things" suggests personal knowledge of God and, perhaps, academic knowledge of theology and philosophy.

Newman opens for Christians the entire scope of academic disciplines offered by Oxford University. In fact, in *The Idea of a University* Newman refers to a wide panorama: not just theology (for which he argues strenuously because in his day it was largely ignored) but astronomy, zoology, physics and chemistry, history, literature and even travel.[21] The professions of law and medicine are appropriate for study as well. It is hard to say what Newman would not include. His major argument is simply that any one of them taken on its own without the boundaries set by a theological understanding will inevitably come to rule beyond its own limited scope. Newman puts this in explicitly Catholic terms:

> Put out of sight the severe teaching of Catholicism in the schools of Painting, as now men would put it aside in their philosophical studies, and in no long time you would have the hierarchy of the Church, the Anchorite and Virgin-martyr, the Confessor and the Doctor, the Angelic Hosts, the Mother of God, the Crucifix, the Eternal Trinity supplanted by a sort of pagan mythology in the guise of sacred names, by a creation indeed of high genius, of intense, and dazzling, and soul-absorbing beauty, in which, however, there was nothing which subserved the cause of Religion, nothing on the other hand which did not directly or indirectly minister to corrupt nature and the powers of darkness.[22]

Surely if one wanted to illustrate Newman as a prophet, this would be one passage to quote. As George Marsden and James Tunstead Burtchaell have shown regarding Protestant and Catholic universities in America, schools founded on explicitly Christian theological principles have, in abandoning their specificity, lost even the taint of Christian character. In Marsden's terms, as Christianity has been systematically disestablished in college after college, unbelief has become established.[23]

The scope of knowledge to which the perfected intellect aspires is limitless, but never just the accumulation of facts without an interpretive scheme to center them. It is to be "the knowledge, not only of things, but also of their mutual and true relations; knowledge not

---

It is characteristic for our minds to be ever engaged in passing judgement on the things which come before us. No sooner do we apprehend than we judge; we allow nothing to stand by itself: we compare, contrast, abstract, generalize, connect, adjust, classify.

JOHN HENRY NEWMAN
An Essay on the Development of Christian Doctrine

---

merely considered as acquirement, but as philosophy." And that brings us to the characteristic tasks of the mind.

The Tasks of the Intellect

The primary task of the perfected intellect is to bring order to knowledge. The perfected mind stretches itself around facts and discerns their relationships. Newman expresses this central theme in a variety of striking ways. Here, without his permission of course, I break down his Ciceronian prose into a half-baked Senecan paraphrase which I further technologize with numbers! St. Newman, patron saint of passionate, purple prose, forgive me!

1. [The perfected intellect] knows and thinks while it knows.

2. [The perfected intellect learns] to leaven the dense mass of facts and events with the elastic force of reason.

3. [The perfected intellect consists] in, but not merely in, the passive reception into the mind of a number of ideas not previously known to it.

4. [The perfected intellect] consists in the mind's energetic and simultaneous action on those ideas that rush in upon it. It has a formative power that brings order to the flux of facts.

5. [The perfected intellect] accepts the classic laws of thought: the law

of identity (*A* is *A*), the law of non-contradiction (*A* is not not-*A*) and the law of the excluded middle (*X* is either *A* or not-*A*).

6. [The perfected intellect] makes the objects of our knowledge subjectively our own. That is, it digests what we receive into the substance of our previous state of thought.

7. [The perfected intellect] compares ideas to one another and systematizes them.

8. [The perfected intellect] not only learns but refers what it learns to what it already knows.

9. [The perfected intellect] illuminates by its locomotion, its movement onwards, toward a unifying mental center.

10. [The perfected intellect] knows where it stands and how to get where it wants to go.

Newman does not pause in his description to explain further what he means by the "formative power" of the intellect. He shuns developing his vision into a full-fledged epistemology. The closest he comes to doing that is in his *Grammar of Assent*. But even that strikingly original work, whose full title expresses the humility of its author—*An Essay in Aid of a Grammar of Assent*—is, in fact, as Ian Ker says, not an epistemology so much "a philosophical analysis of that state of mind which we ordinarily call certitude or certainty and of the cognitive acts associated with it."[24] I will leave to scholars of a more philosophical bent the task of relating Newman's views to Aquinas, Descartes, Locke, Kant, Edwards, Kierkegaard or Wittgenstein.[25]

One idea among the ten listed above deserves commentary: the perfected intellect "knows and thinks while it knows." This characteristic of the perfected intellect forever puts simple fideism out of bounds for the Christian thinker. It is not that everyone must think while they know. Most of humanity does not do that. Most intellectuals do not do that. All of us act as if we know most of what we claim to know, and we do not usually think about it. What that means, of course, is not that we do not know but that we are not exhibiting "the perfection of intellect" when we do so. Newman does not want us to try constantly to think about everything we think we know or subject every action to the process of thinking it through. We can't live that way. But we can and should use our mind much more often and much more fully than we do.

When we are in the process of discovering some truth or other or evaluating some important claim to be a fact or a true theory, our mind should be employed to its fullest. That will mean the thought-

---

In so far as a person is thinking clearly he is intelligent. A distinguishing characteristic of intelligence is the ability to discern relevant connexions— to put together what ought to be conjoined and to keep distinct what ought to be separated.

L. SUSAN STEBBING
Thinking to Some Purpose

---

ful selection of a few subjects from a mass of possible subjects about which to think. Each of us is fascinated by our own range of matters; each of us is set in a different ideological context; each has a different past and a different potential future. But when we claim to know something of serious issue, we should not only know but think while we know. That will help keep us from becoming ideologues— one of the prime temptations of all who think themselves to be thoughtful.

Several ideas in this list do, of course, seem romantic. Can we ever really know where we are? Can we ever really know how to get where we want to go? In fact, can we be confident that our goals are right and worthy? It will take more than this list of characteristics to lead us to the perfection of our own intellect. Still, the vision is luminous. Let us move toward its light.

The Intellect at Work
Newman's description of the mind at work is a marvel of metaphor both revealing and concealing what the mind is actually doing. "The

mind moves to and fro," Newman says, with such speed and agility as to "baffle investigation." In short, Newman doesn't know how the mind works. This is no great embarrassment. It just makes him one

---

The mind is certainly a very mysterious organ, I reflected, drawing my head in from the window, about which nothing whatever is known, though we depend upon it so completely.

VIRGINIA WOOLF
A Room of One's Own

---

of the gang. No one knows how the mind actually accomplishes what it does.[26]

There are checks and balances on what it does, of course. Logical inference checked by logical consistency was for Newman, as it is for all good thinkers, one of these checks. Fit with experience is another check for Newman. A sense of *reality* was perhaps Newman's own way of double-checking the truth of a claim to truth. The illative sense, which he describes at length in the *Grammar of Assent*, was for him the most important mental faculty, the use of which confirmed that sense of *reality*. But even after reading many pages of

---

**What does one mean by "the unity of the mind," I pondered, for clearly the mind has so great a power of concentrating at any one point at any moment that it seems to have no single state of being. . . .
Clearly the mind is always altering its focus, and bringing the world into different perspectives.**

VIRGINIA WOOLF
A Room of One's Own

---

preparation for its description and many pages of description, I still find that faculty as mysterious in its operation as the mind that moves "to and fro" in the passage quoted above. Perhaps I am not alone, for few philosophers have either accepted or built on this notion. In any case, for those who wish to pursue Newman at his most original—if not most convincing—the some four hundred pages of often turgid prose lies waiting. For me the mind that "moves to and fro" with great speed and mystery is sufficient. That's how my thinking feels.

The Dangers of the Intellect

The intellect is glorious. No doubt. The perfected intellect more so. But we must not think that we are home free once we have achieved something of a Christian mind—even a mind fashioned along the lines of Newman's *imperial intellect*. We are still in danger. My pastor was right. The University of Nebraska—and every other university I attended as a student—is a "godless" place both in reality and as conceived by most of its faculty and administration.

It is corrupting to hear or read the words of men who do not believe in truth. It is yet more corrupting to receive, in place of truth, more learning and scholarship which, if they are presented as ends in themselves, are no more than parodies of the truth they were meant to serve, no more than a facade behind which there is no substance.

EUGENE (FR. SERAPHIM) ROSE
Nihilism

Newman himself was not without his warnings. First, he knew that a *liberal education*, one such as would encourage the perfection of the intellect, would address only part of our need for human growth and development.

> Knowledge is one thing, virtue is another; good sense is not conscience, refinement is not humility, nor largeness and justness of view faith. Philosophy, however enlightened, however profound, gives no command over the passions, no influential motives, no vivifying principles. Liberal education makes not the Christian, not the Catholic, but the gentleman.[27]

For him the church—the Christian faith—was absolutely necessary: "Knowledge, viewed as knowledge, exerts a subtle influence in throwing us back on ourselves, and making us our own centre, and our minds the measure of all things."[28] He was aware of the problems brought on by the Enlightenment notion of the autonomy and sufficiency of human reason.

> A sense of propriety, order, consistency, and completeness gives birth to a rebellious stirring against miracle and mystery, against the severe and the terrible.
>
> This Intellectualism first and chiefly comes into collision with precept, then with doctrine, then with the very principles of dogmatism;—a perception of the Beautiful becomes the substitute for faith.[29]

To put this in biblical terms, "Knowledge puffs up" (1 Cor 1:18). As Christians we must not substitute the mind for the whole person. All is to be under the lordship of Christ. The intellect itself must be reborn. Newman put it this way, reflecting on John 3:7:

> Your whole nature must be re-born; your passions, and your affections, and your aims, and your conscience, and your will, must all be bathed in a new element, and reconsecrated to your Maker,—and the last not the least, your intellect.[30]

We could do well to take Newman's vision, revision it where necessary and begin to live in its light. But there is yet more to be said about the Christian mind, not the least of which will have to do with how to go about perfecting the mind. Newman talked about the role and goal of university education, which surely will play a part. But he gave very little—almost no—indication of how to learn to think, how to perfect the intellect. To practical-minded Americans this may seem astonishing. But at least it is an excuse for my not giving any suggestions in this chapter. That will wait for chapters six and seven.

IV

HOW
THINKING
FEELS

WHAT IS AN
INTELLECTUAL?

O*ne of the major charges against intellectuals or intellectualism is* that intellectuals are so unemotional as to be not quite human. It's not cool to be so cold.

I scratch my head and ask, "Where did that come from?" Ideas turn me on. They excite me so much that sometimes I have to rise up and lay aside what I'm reading—a brilliant novel or work of philosophy, for example—because my emotional temperature is reaching boil. Is this odd? Not, I think, to most people who spend a lot of time thinking.

Scaling the Mountains of Truth

I have already quoted Newman on how the mind works. He is worth quoting again:

> The mind ranges to and fro, and spreads out, and advances forward with a quickness which has become a proverb, and a subtlety and versatility which baffle investigation. It passes on from point to point,

gaining one by some indication; another on a probability; then availing itself of an association; then falling back on some received law;
next seizing on testimony; then committing itself to some popular
impression, or some inward instinct, or some obscure memory; and
thus it makes progress not unlike a clamberer on a steep cliff, who, by
quick eye, prompt hand, and firm foot, ascends how he knows not
himself, by personal endowments and by practice, rather than by
rule, leaving no track behind him, and unable to teach another. It is
not too much to say that the stepping by which great geniuses scale
the mountains of truth is as unsafe and precarious to men in general,
as the ascent of a skilful mountaineer up a literal crag. It is a way
which they alone can take; and its justification lies in their success.
And such mainly is the way in which all men, gifted or not gifted,
commonly reason,—not by rule, but by an inward faculty.[1]

Newman catches the excitement that often comes with thinking:
thinking hard is like mountain climbing—dangerous to the climber
and his friends, but exhilarating. No seasoned mountain climbers let
the fear of danger—the imminent possibility of reaching an uncross-

---

**We can catch a glimpse of the working of our mind, vague
and not much more satisfactory than was the X-ray screen twenty years
ago, but its nature must remain a mystery among many other mysteries.**

ERNEST DIMNET
The Art of Thinking

---

able ravine or looking up at the unscalable crag that blocks the
way—keep them from the thrill of the ascent. Nor do any intellectuals—any regular thinkers—let the fear of error stop the pursuit of
truth. Cold, are they? Yes, if you mean that they put aside the terror
some feel in facing a tough problem. Unemotional? Not at all, at
least not usually.

Joy is more often the emotion that characterizes serious intellectual endeavor. Listen to A. G. Sertillanges describe the intellectual at
work:

The intellectual is not self-begotten; he is the son of the Idea, of the
Truth of the creative Word, the Life-giver immanent in His creation.

When the thinker thinks rightly, he follows God step by step; he does not follow his own vain fancy. When he gropes and struggles in the effort of research, he is Jacob wrestling with the angel and "strong against God."[2]

And listen as well to systematic theologian Ellen Charry of Princeton Seminary describe her student days at Temple University. She was studying the Augsburg Confession, puzzling over a concept that as a nonbeliever she found intriguing but hard to understand:

Justification by grace through faith . . . justification by grace through faith— what are they talking about? So I decided to try it on. I lifted my arms up and I put over me like a dress, the doctrine. I tried it on myself. It wasn't just words. I tried it out. And I fell off the chair. It was in July, it was very hot; I was on the third floor in my study. . . . I tried it on like a dress, and I just fell over.[3]

In this chapter I want to address directly *how thinking feels*. What characterizes the life of the mind? The method I here choose to answer this question is fraught with danger and the possibility of misunderstanding, for I will examine only one aspect of the life of the mind. I am going to cordon off the humming intellect from the re-

---

Vibrating strings . . . [make] others vibrate, and it is in this way that one idea calls up a second, and the two together a third, and all three a fourth, and so on; you can't set a limit to the ideas called up and linked together by a philosopher meditating or communing with himself in silence and darkness. This instrument can make astonishing leaps, and one idea called up will sometimes start an harmonic at an incomprehensible interval.

DENIS DIDEROT
D'Alembert's Dream

---

mainder of the human person, the thinker from the actor—even, to some extent, the activity of the mind from the quest for truth, the intellectual in general from the Christian intellectual.

Impossible, you say? In the final analysis, yes. The more I think about the connection between seeking truth and seeking the kingdom of God, the more radically different—the more distinct from other intellectuals—the Christian intellectual becomes. Knowing and doing are so intimately related that if you do not act in the light

---

Ideas are not the sum and substance of thought; rather, thought is as much about the motion across the water as it is about the stepping stones that allow it. It is an intricate choreography of movement, transition, and repose, a revelation of the musculature of mind.

SVEN BIRKERTS
The Gutenberg Elegies

---

of what you claim to know, you do not really know it. Moreover, as Christians we know that what we believe to be true should be integrated into our lives. The Bible is replete with condemnations of hypocrisy.

Still, one can distinguish without dividing, and that is what I hope to accomplish in this chapter. In the following chapter I will try to show how the life of the mind discussed here becomes a vital part of a full-orbed life in Christ.

The Life of the Mind

What, then, characterizes the life of the mind? What is it like to be an active thinker? Let us return to the definition of an *intellectual* I gave in chapter one.

An *intellectual* is one who loves ideas, is dedicated to clarifying them, developing them, criticizing them, turning them over and over, seeing their implications, stacking them atop one another, arranging them, sitting silent while new ideas pop up and old ones seem to rearrange themselves, playing with them, punning with their terminology, laughing at them, watching them clash, picking up the pieces, starting over, judging them, withholding judgment about them, changing them, bringing them into contact with their counterparts in other systems of thought, inviting them to dine and have a ball but also suiting them for service in workaday life.

Where in this definition, one might again ask, is "the pursuit of truth"? Should it not be singled out as the first characteristic of an intellectual? Yes, if we were not to include in the class of intellectuals those "thinkers" who have abandoned this pursuit because they have lost hope either in finding truth or in the notion that such a thing as truth exists. We would have to exclude from the class of intellectuals figures from the past like Nietzsche and from the present such postmodern pundits as Richard Rorty. It is no use to point out that rejection of the notion of truth is self-contradictory or self-refuting: the attitude characterizes an important segment of thinking people. So to incorporate "the pursuit of truth," I prefer to let an adjective such as *Christian* or *Enlightenment* or *traditional* modify the word. The next chapter will pursue one such adjectival intellectual—the Christian intellectual.

Moreover, many who are not intellectuals also pursue the truth but do so from a stance of faith or an attitude of acceptance of an authority they trust to convey the truth. Many who devote themselves to a life of nonreflective faith do so because they are confident that their faith is justified by reality. They do not need to "think" or "reflect" profoundly to have truth high on their list of priorities. The

---

Can there exist pure knowledge without feeling, without that species of materiality which feeling lends to it? Do we not perhaps feel thought, and do we not feel ourselves in the act of knowing and willing?

MIGUEL DE UNAMUNO
The Tragic Sense of Life

---

intellectual life, however, is one of whirring intellectual activity, a fusillade of firing neurons. "The brain is always working; the turbines that I desiderate exist, they turn, they set in motion a wheel-and-pinion system whence ideas fly like sparks from a dynamo at full pressure."[4]

That is what the above definition attempts to capture. It is a mind that, as Newman says, never stops ranging to and fro, never stops clambering up mountains. So let's look more closely at the mind in motion.

The Intellect in Love

An intellectual is in love, in love with ideas. Everyone loves something. My wife loves trees and mushrooms.[5] A forest for me is the panoramic vista, the play of color, light and shadow; a forest for her is the trees, even more, tree after tree, specific trees with technical names. The forest floor is a hotbed for mushrooms—fly aminitas, death caps, puff balls. My son loves the fine craftsmanship of woodworking and building construction. When we toured together a few museums in Europe, I perused the paintings; he feasted on the antique furniture. I saw the medieval architecture and thought about its history; he examined the machinery that hung the doors and thought about his own craft of cabinetmaking. Scientist and philosopher Michael Polanyi insists that "personal, intuitive 'intellectual love'" is at the heart of science. Drusilla Scott summarizes his view, noting that intellectual love "belongs in the house of science in all its splendour, and if the rules don't allow for it they will have to change."[6]

Intellectuals qua intellectuals love ideas—all ideas, true ideas, false ideas, common ideas, odd ideas, simple ideas, profound ideas, exciting ideas, dull ideas, constructive ideas, devastating ideas. Show me an idea, the intellectual says, and I will salute it, deconstruct it, rebuild it, find its origin and predict its destiny. All the time there will be an excitement that in its quiet way—for the intellectual may all the while be sitting calmly—is like a sports lover's emotions watching Michael Jordan slam-dunk the final winning basket. Outward calm masks internal turbulence. And all for love, love of ideas.

Take this description of Octavio Paz written by a friend in his memory not long after his death:

> Conversation with him was a constant exploration. Although he did have the "irritable nature" that Horace ascribes to poets and was invariably serious about all issues, he could also show an almost childlike enthusiasm in the breadth and degree of his intellectual curiosity. Large themes fascinated him and he wrote about them at length: reflections on poetic creation and language; his vision of the

course of Western poetry from the enthusiasm of Romanticism to the ironic vision of the modern avant-garde, in which he compared not only works in different languages but placed them against the background of other, non-Western poetics; his thoughts on modern culture, politics, and society, always emphasizing the need for a careful, critical outlook on the world. And he was excited by new scientific discoveries or intellectual inquiries; the latest theory on the Big Bang, debates about the nature of the mind or the decipherment of the Mayan script. . . . Then unexpectedly—and the idea of "unexpectedly" signaled by a sudden change of gesture or of manner marks my memories of him—his conversation would swerve toward unpredictable subjects: French erotic literature of the eighteenth century, the political maxims of an ancient Chinese scholar, medieval theories on love or melancholy.[7]

Here is the quintessential intellectual—excited about almost any idea, any theme, any notion, so long as its tentacles touch something significant in culture.

All intellectuals are in love with ideas; not all intellectuals are in love with truth. Some whom I am willing to call intellectuals do not even believe there is truth of any substantive kind. Everett Knight, for example, asserts, "The hunger for food may be satisfied, not that for the Truth, because there is none; and it is probable that the real revolution of our time is the discovery that while something can be done about hunger, nothing can be done about spiritual hunger."[8]

Christians need not be—are not!—so pessimistic. We will, therefore, have much reason to return to notion of the "love of truth," and will do so in chapters five, six and ten.

The Intellect as a Tumble Dryer

Intellectuals are dedicated to clarifying ideas, developing them, criticizing them. Fuzzy thinking is the bane of intellectuals. When they see an idea ill-conceived, poorly formulated, twisted out of shape by bile or bias, they bring it into focus, straighten it, examine its implications and attempt to determine how true or accurate it is in doing what it claims to do. When intellectuals find an idea clearly expressed, it is a cause for rejoicing. When they clarify a confused idea, they take pride in their work—sometimes of course too much pride, for sometimes they do not do for an idea as much as they think. Intellectuals are not always right, even when—especially when—they think they are absolutely right.

The intensity of the dedication to this task is fundamental. As Jacques Barzun says, "The analogy of athletics must be pressed until all recognize that in the exertions of Intellect those who lack the muscles, co-ordination, and will power can claim no place at the training table, let alone on the playing field."[9]

Intellectuals turn ideas over and over, seeing their implications, stacking them atop one another, arranging them. The intellect is a mental tumble dryer. Perhaps nothing so characterizes intellectuals as their perpetual mulling over an idea and its cohorts. Ideas can be arranged in an infinite variety of ways. Intellectuals know this and sometimes have a hard time stopping their perpetual rearrangement

---

**What a phantasmagoria the mind is and meeting place of dissemblables.
At one moment we deplore our birth and state and aspire to
an ascetic exaltation. The next we are overcome by the smell of some
old garden path and weep to hear the thrushes sing.**

VIRGINIA WOOLF
Orlando

---

long enough to release them to the public domain. There is always one more permutation to try. Recall Newman's description. He thought with pen in hand, says Ker, and the result was multiple drafts of his books before publication.[10]

When turning over ideas becomes a deliberate but unfocused act, it is called *lateral thinking* and can be a great stimulus not just to problem solving but to the emergence of new thought patterns, new paradigms and original ideas.[11] The creative intellectual raises such thinking to an art, but it is possible for the less intellectually endowed to do as well:

We possess the ability to see things and make things in patterns that have never existed before. We can gather materials, attitudes and patterns to interact randomly until a "fit" occurs and things not correlated before come together in a unique creation. Every human being can do this and does do this.[12]

The Intellect in Silence
Intellectuals sit silent while new ideas pop up and old ones seem to rearrange themselves. This aspect of the intellect is one of the most mysterious. We do not know where ideas come from. They often simply "pop up." There they are: we didn't have them before. We have them now. Gilbert Highet says it well:

> We are all cave men. The cave we inhabit is our own mind; and consciousness is like a tiny torch, flickering and flaring, which can at best show us only a few outlines of the cave wall that stands nearest, or reflect a dangerous underground river flowing noiselessly at our feet, so that we start back in horror before we are engulfed.[13]

We do not know very well how the mind works; but we know that passivity is its first law. Still less do we know how inspiration comes; but we can notice that it utilizes our unconsciousness more than our initiative. We go forward amid difficulties like a rider in the night; it is better to trust our mount than to pull unwisely on the bridle.

A. G. SERTILLANGES
The Intellectual Life

Or better, I think, when we start back in wonder. Philosophy and poetry have more in common than is usually thought: both begin in wonder.[14] On this score Josef Pieper is eloquent:

> *To perceive means to listen in silence*: . . . The invisible alone is transparent, and only in silence is hearing possible. Moreover, the stronger the determination prevails to hear all there is, the more profound and more complete the silence must be. Consequently philosophy . . . means: to listen so perfectly and intensely that such receptive silence

is not disturbed and interrupted by anything, not even by a question.[15]

Like the ancient and medieval philosophers Pieper distinguishes between *ratio* and *intellectus*. The former is "the power of discursive thought, of searching and re-searching, abstracting, refining, and concluding." The latter is "the ability of 'simply looking.'" Here "the truth presents itself as a landscape to the eye." As Heraclitus might say, the *intellectus* "listens-in to the being of things."[16] In full-fledged thinking both *ratio* and *intellectus* are involved.

We will return to this mysterious matter of the mind when we turn in chapter seven to the practical ways we can stimulate thought, or at least recognize when it is occurring. Here we need only note that the best and freshest thinking often takes place when

---

Thinking is the soundless dialogue that we carry on with ourselves in solitude. It does not directly yield knowledge as the sciences do, nor does it directly result in practical wisdom. It is always "out of order" and "contrary to the human condition." Thinking requires a withdrawal from the common-sense world of appearances; it is characterized by reflexivity and has a unique self-destructive tendency. It is like Penelope's web; it undoes every morning what it has finished the night before, and the metaphor that Arendt thinks is most appropriate to characterize the activity of thinking is the one that Socrates used—the metaphor of the wind.

R I C H A R D   B E R N S T E I N
"Thinking on Thought,"
The New York Review of Books

---

the mind is at ease, not trying to think but simply, say, *paying attention* or *reflecting*, not so much pursuing ideas down endless corridors as letting ideas pursue us, being receptive, letting reality come to us.

So the intellectual at work may indeed appear to both herself and others to be very much at leisure, a silent mental receptacle for ideas that emerge as if from nowhere.[17] These ideas enter, sign in, state their name and become players in the game of intellectual life. To the intellectual there is often in fact a genuine sense that it is a game that is being played.

The Intellect at Play

Intellectuals play with ideas, pun with their terminology, laugh at them. This may seem an odd characteristic to attribute to intellectuals. But if thinking persons do not have the distance from ideas that is necessary for humor, if they cannot laugh about what they think, they stand in grave danger of being ideologues. The ideologue's devotion to one central idea excludes any ability to see its potential flaws or any reasonable objections to it. The ideologue is a plague on intellectual life. The search for truth ends because it has been found— and bound. The mind of the ideologue is now locked tight, guarding the truth from creeping doubt, from being assailed by any alternatives that would call even part of it into question.

Better to play the role of the medieval jester who could "dispense with the usual proprieties because he was outside the social hierarchy."[18] The king's fool could tell the embarrassing, perhaps awful truth, with less fear of reprisal than if it came via the courtiers. Today this role is played by cartoonists with an intellectual bent and sometimes even by professors outside the corridors of power.

Lightness of heart was, according to many who knew him, a quality that Isaiah Berlin held in abundance. In the midst of complex intellectual prose Berlin's *joie de vivre* broke through: "He left the moral quality of his voice behind him, in the long tumbling paragraphs and the clauses within clauses of his best essays, and it is to these that we can turn when we need to remind ourselves what intellectual life can be: joyful, free of illusion, and vitally alive."[19]

The intellectual "delights in the pleasures of thinking," says sociologist Lewis A. Coser. "Indeed one test of a true education is that it sits lightly on the possessor. He knows better than anybody else how thin in spots is the mantle which others would pluck from him," chimes in literary scholar Jacques Barzun.[20] And farmer-poet-novelist Wendell Berry agrees: "By taking oneself too seriously one is prevented from being serious enough."[21] Reflecting on the vital life of many Catholic intellectuals, Mary Jo Weaver puts it well: "When the heart is rooted in God, the mind is free to play. Free to have fun."[22] Humor, punning, laughter: these foster humility. They lighten the load a true intellectual begins to feel when the burden of truth—disagreeable as much truth about the human situation is— becomes too heavy to bear. For the "truth" is that, save God alone, no person—intellectual or otherwise—has all the truth. The one who thinks so is not only insufferable but just plain wrong.

Some intellectuals, of course, do not yet have the truth they seek but are so devoted to it that they abandon their connection to the world and its personal relationships. Such is the case with what George Steiner describes as the "absolute scholar":

> The absolute scholar is . . . instinct with Nietzsche's finding that to be interested in something, to be totally interested in it, is a libidinal thrust more powerful than love or hatred, more tenacious than faith or friendship—not infrequently, indeed, more compelling than personal life itself. Archimedes does not flee from his killers; he does not even turn his head to acknowledge their rush into his garden when he is immersed in the algebra of conic sections. . . . The archivist, the monographer, the antiquarian, the specialist consumed by fires of esoteric fascination may be indifferent also to the distracting claims of social justice or familial affection, of political awareness, and of run-of-the-mill humanity. . . . Hence not only the legends that cluster about Faust, the tale of the man who sacrifices wife, child, home to the breeding of the perfectly black tulip (an old story told by Dumas).[23]

It is the ideologue who deserves all the anti-intellectual dismissals taken note of in chapter one. My father was right: "An intellectual [read ideologue] is indeed a person who is educated beyond his intelligence."

The Intellect as Battlefield
Intellectuals watch ideas clash, pick up the pieces and start over. No one knows the clashing noise of contradictory and incoherent ideas bet-

ter than the intellectual. Philosophies lie like dying soldiers on the pages of history. Aristotle bests Plato; Plotinus leapfrogs Aristotle to save Plato by transforming him. Augustine raids the neo-Platonic Plotinus and Manichaeans, then rejects the latter and transforms the former. Aquinas raids Aristotle and transforms his philosophy. These are not the sounds of ignorant armies clashing by night; they

---

Thinking is a tiring process; it is much easier to accept beliefs passively than to think them out, rigorously questioning their grounds by asking what are the consequences that follow from them.

L. SUSAN STEBBING
Thinking to Some Purpose

---

are the sounds of ideas launched by bows and cannons and missile launchers, fended off by shields and bucklers and pillboxes, or detected by radar and destroyed midair.

The intellectual battlefield is strewn with corpses. Then out of the barracks of the universities come new heroes, young intellectuals. Each one surveys the field, spies a corpse or perhaps a battalion of corpses, breathes new life into the bodies, and a new army forms. So arise the neo-Aristotelians, the neo-neo-Platonists, the neo-gnostics, the neo-scholastics. Freedom fighters or guerrillas—take your pick—from the ranks of the pseudo-intellectuals join the fray—the deconstructionists, the mere sociologists of knowledge, the post-modern brokers of power.[24]

So long as humankind exists "under the sun," so long as there is an open society where ideas are still allowed to be freely expressed, intellectuals will be there to stimulate, curb and redirect the flow of ideas. After the most devastating of intellectual disasters someone will be there to pick up the pieces.

The Intellect as Cautious Judge

Intellectuals judge ideas and withhold judgments about them. It is important to emphasize this dichotomy, sometimes paradox. Intellectuals must not draw their conclusions too quickly. Thinking takes time—

at least for most human beings. Unlike a giant computer that grinds
out inevitable answers according to program, intellectuals are both
limited and fallible. Bias, preconceived but erroneous ideas, hasty
skipping over relevant details, inordinate desire for a given out-
come, fear of the implications of an idea, unwillingness to accept the

---

Intellect is the broom with which to clear the mind of cant.

JACQUES BARZUN
The House of Intellect

---

consequences of correct reasoning: all these and more stand in the
way of the mind's reaching a worthy judgment.

True intellectuals, therefore, reach their conclusions with deliberate humility and caution. Again, Isaiah Berlin represents the best of
a type: "He was superbly unpretentious and unpretending."[25]

The Intellect as World Traveler

*Intellectuals bring ideas into contact with their counterpart in other sys-
tems of thought.* We no longer live in a unified world—socially, culturally or intellectually. We live in a pluralistic world.

**To think effectively is to think to some purpose. To pursue an aim
without considering what its realizations would involve is stupid:
the result may be fortunate but it cannot be wise.**

L. SUSAN STEBBING
Thinking to Some Purpose

In more specific religious terms, pluralism no longer means that
some of us are Baptists and others Methodists, or some of us are
Protestants and others Catholics. It now means that our next-door
neighbors may be Rastafarians on one side and purely secular, non-
religious folk on the other. Down the block they are building a
Hindu temple and across town a mosque. Our hairdresser may be
meditating each morning for twenty minutes on a seemingly meaningless mantra; our grocer sits in a yoga position for a half-hour

each evening; our boss takes New Age management training from the Forum.

Everywhere we turn we find someone with a view different from ours—each one contending that he or she is free to hold this view and quite content to let us continue to believe whatever we want. As Leon Wieseltier, literary editor of *The New Republic*, tells us: "The sidewalks are crowded with incommensurabilities. You live and work and play with people for whom your view of the world is nonsense, or worse."[26]

True intellectuals have a clear view of the panorama of worldviews; this allows them a breadth of perspective and enables them to see every idea in the larger context of new twenty-first-century alternatives. They will understand what the presuppositions of their own ideas really are and grasp as well those of others with whom they engage. They will have pondered such questions as, What is fundamental reality—God or nature, matter or spirit? What constitutes the basic character of human beings? What is their relation to fundamental reality? How can anyone know anything at all? What is the foundation of human morality? What, if any, is the meaning of human history?[27]

The Intellect as Celebrant and Servant

Intellectuals invite ideas to dine and have a ball. That's a bit metaphorical, a bit over the top, you say? What it suggests is that intellectuals revel in the whole process of thinking. It's a feast, not a fast. The ideas may have been recognized and cultivated in solitude, the ban-

---

Yes, the outer world—both visible and invisible—is ultimately a mystery.
So too is the other world we inhabit—the inner world,
the world of the mind. Not one of us knows what his own
mind can do, or will produce.

GILBERT HIGHET
Man's Unconquerable Mind

---

quet may be only private, but it won't seem that way. In the mind of an intellectual ideas take on a vibrant life of their own. Sometimes they play the music of the spheres, sometimes a monkish chant, sometimes the few and friendly chords of folk music. Sometimes they beat a jazz take-five rhythm or sound an improvised birdland wail. The life of the mind is not quiet.

Intellectuals suit ideas for service in workaday life. Intellectuals have often gotten a bad reputation for just this aspect of their work. Paul Johnson's description of the "intellectuals" in *Intellectuals* is a devastating diatribe against those publicly active thinkers in the past who he believes have led the Western world astray. But there are those who have had a much more beneficial effect. Think of some modern examples: C. S. Lewis, Francis Schaeffer, Jacques Ellul, Dietrich Bonhoeffer, all of whom served up a plethora of ideas that have improved our world.

In any case, intellectuals are not to be seen simply as armchair philosophers. In Richard Weaver's words, ideas have consequences. Intellectuals cannot help but be a part of the process by which ideas affect human life. Best they be true ideas applied appropriately, of course. And with that observation we begin to broach the subject of the next chapter.

V

THE MORAL DIMENSION OF THE MIND

WHAT IS A CHRISTIAN INTELLECTUAL?

I*n the previous chapter we focused on the intellectual matters of the* mind. By describing an *intellectual* proper I tried to convey the inner character of intellectual activity: how thinking feels, whether that thinking is directed toward good or evil, God or the self.

I said as well that this was dangerous to do. And it is, for in cordoning off the moral from the intellectual I may have given the impression that intellectual life is solely mental life—the passage of ideas in, around, through and out of the mind. This would be to view the mind as brain only and to see the brain as just a self-conscious computer. It would be to think that thinking about one's mind is like a hard drive coursing through its memory boards and moving around ones and zeros.

Our thoughts are more than mental synapses: "Our thoughts must be what we ourselves are."[1] We must take seriously these words of James Allen: "The aphorism, 'As a man thinketh in his heart so is he,' not only embraces the whole of a man's being, but is so comprehensive as to reach out to every condition and circumstance of his life. A man is literally *what he thinks*, his character being the complete sum of all his thoughts."[2]

Even if the content of our thoughts is not our character itself, as Allen says, it is the key to our character. To identify a person as an intellectual is to say little about his or her character. A list of people usually called intellectuals is enough to justify this conclusion: Blaise Pascal, Voltaire, Marquis de Sade, Samuel Johnson, Jane Austen, Karl Marx, Søren Kierkegaard, Matthew Arnold, John Henry Newman, Bertrand Russell, Jacques Ellul, Simone de Beauvoir, C. S. Lewis. It is the content of one's thoughts, including their moral dimension and the actions that have ensued from those thoughts, that reveals one's character. All are intellectuals proper. Each is a unique person with a distinct character. Only some would make good friends, and fewer yet have had an overall positive effect on the history of the world.

Moreover, as Christians, if we are prone to thinking simply because we can't stop or if we are called to a life of the mind through obedience to God, we ought not strive simply to be an *intellectual*. We must become a *Christian intellectual* or an *intellectual Christian*. What then would that be?

A Christian Intellectual

Let us return to the definition given at the end of chapter one:

> A Christian intellectual is everything an intellectual proper is but *to the glory of God.*

This definition is deceptively simple. It suggests that all we need to do is add the general concept of *Christian* to the secular concept of *intellectual*, and this will give us the concept of a *Christian intellectual*.

When I began to write this book, even when I first formulated the definitions of *intellectual* and *Christian intellectual* as given above, I thought I would be doing this. But I soon discovered that we cannot simply take the notion of *Christian* and add it to the notion of *intellectual* and achieve our goal. The entire concept of *intellectual* becomes transformed as the implications of "to the glory of God" are fleshed out.

Packed into the phrase "to the glory of God" are not only moral limits, kingdom vision and life direction but profound ontological and epistemological implications as well. As Christians we are to do

---

Love, whether it be the attraction of Truth, or pure, simple, elemental love, always opens up the intellect and gives it the freedom of genius.

ERNEST DIMNET
The Art of Thinking

---

all to the glory of God. As Christian intellectuals we are to think to the glory of God. A. G. Sertillanges, whose marvelous book *The Intellectual Life,* written in 1921, I have only recently discovered, puts it this way:

> An intellectual must be an intellectual all the time. What St. Paul suggests to the Christian: whether you eat or drink or whatsoever else you do, do all to the glory of God, must apply to the Christian in search of light. For him the true is the glory of God: he must keep it always in mind, submit to it in everything.[3]

We begin our discussion of the *Christian* distinctive with the moral dimension. We have already examined Newman as a model

---

Keep your soul free. What matters most in life is not knowledge, but character.

A. G. SERTILLANGES
The Intellectual Life

---

for Christian intellectuals. His two passions—for truth and for holiness—are for Christian intellectuals primary aspects of giving glory to God. When I discussed Newman, I put the passion for truth first. Here I put first the passion for holiness. The reason will become obvious.

A Passion for Holiness

Holiness is being set apart for the glory of God, for God's glory is his holiness, his set-apartness from all else, his Otherness. There is a deep sense in which God is Totally Otherly, so otherly, so transcendent, that we cannot begin to think of him as he is, for he is I AM. All our knowledge about him comes only because he chooses to reveal himself to us. Out of his Otherliness he speaks us into existence. We are not made out of him as if he emanated us. We are created, brought into being, by his word.

So first of all, to be holy is to be set apart for God's service. And second, to be holy is to be characterized by the character of God— that is by the image of God in which he made us. To the extent that

---

**Thought worth the name can never rise from a nasty growth.
. . . Good men generally think right.**

ERNEST DIMNET
The Art of Thinking

---

we are in God's image, we are holy. When the Word became flesh himself, he showed us what that image of God is like in its fullest expression. To have a passion for holiness then is to have a passion to be like Christ.

Since we find ourselves even at our best to be only broken images of God, we are in a fix we cannot fix. If we are to be fixed, it will be God who fixes us. And he does. But he does this not just by redeeming us through the death and resurrection of Jesus but through restoring us into his image.

A passion for holiness is a passion for God to remake us. This he does through gradual means, the means of grace, the disciplines of the Christian life: baptism, Holy Communion, worship, fellowship with other believers, prayer, study and meditation on him and his written Word, fasting, solitude, silence, service. We will not go into the details of these disciplines. There are many marvelous books that do that.[4] The point here is that a Christian intellectual cultivates a passion for holiness, a passion to become like Jesus.

In terms of our thought life, the apostle Paul unpacked the notion of holiness: "Whatever is true, whatever is noble, whatever is right, whatever is pure, whatever is lovely, whatever is admirable—if any-

---

And I will say further, that if there exists in a man faith in God joined to a life of purity and moral elevation, it is not so much the believing in God that makes him good, as the being good, thanks to God, that makes him believe in Him. Goodness is the best source of spiritual clear-sightedness.

MIGUEL DE UNAMUNO
The Tragic Sense of Life

In Augustine's view the incentive for so much learning is not then by any means mere mastery of knowledge for its own sake; such ambition "puffs up" the mind and makes it an object of idolatrous worship. What prompts earnest and excellent scholarship in the Christian is "fear of the Lord."

DAVID LYLE JEFFREY
The People of the Book

---

thing is excellent or praiseworthy—think about such things" (Phil 4:8). A passion for holiness will therefore result in a passion not only to know the truth but to do the truth.

A Passion to Know and Do the Truth

Aristotle got this right: "All men by nature desire to know."[5] He could have said, "All men by nature desire to know the truth," but he did not need to, for this was a given for him and his culture. Aristotle's notion of truth was also straightforward. By truth he meant "the self-revelation of reality."[6] A true statement states what is. But Aristotle missed a crucial biblical insight. He did not acknowledge the basic brokenness of human nature. The desire for knowledge is there, but so is the desire to hide from the implications of the truth.

For a Christian, therefore, there will be struggle not just with learning the truth we seek but with coming to know it on the nerve endings of our lives.[7] Yet it is only to those who are willing to do the truth that the truth itself comes. Virtue is rewarded by knowledge.

To charge the intellect with perpetual blindness so as to leave it no intelligence of any description whatever, is repugnant not only to the Word of God, but to common experience. We see that there has been implanted in the human mind a certain desire of investigating truth, to which it never would aspire unless some relish for truth antecedently existed.

JOHN CALVIN
Institutes of the Christian Religion

As Sertillanges says, "Truth visits those who love her, who surrender to her, and this love cannot be without virtue."[8] Or again: "The qualities of character have a preponderant role in everything. The intellect is only a tool; the handling of it determines the nature of its effects. . . . To judge truly, you must be great."[9]

E. Michael Jones and John Henry Newman agree: knowledge—that is, justified true belief—requires moral character. Jones writes:

> Far from being two mutually exclusive compartments hermetically sealed off from each other, the intellectual life turns out to be a function of the moral life of the thinker. Apprehension of the truth can only take place when the clamoring of the passions [self-centered desire] has died down. The mind is like a window. It is transparent only when it is clean. If it, through strenuous effort, catches some glimpse of the truth, then it is the truth that shines forth in that system and not the personality of the thinker.[10]

Jones draws the closest of relationships between the intellect and the moral life: the moral governs the intellectual. If we have a passion for holiness, we will have a passion for truth. And if we have a passion for truth, we will be rewarded by a knowledge of the truth. On the other hand, if we let our usual, baser human desires govern our lives, we will quite simply never know the deepest moral truths, or perhaps any truths at all that challenge us.[11] Jones concludes: "We can only know what our moral lives allow us to know. Only the pure of heart shall see God. Or as St. Paul puts it, 'The spiritual man

. . . can appraise everything, though he himself can be appraised by no one.' "[12]

What then happens to the intellect and its search for truth when self-serving desire dominates? Does the mind stop working? "The turning away from the truth at the behest of disordered passions does not mean that the mind will stop functioning; it only means

---

Truth is so obscured nowadays and lies so well established that unless we love the truth we shall never recognize it.

BLAISE PASCAL
Pensées

---

that that mind will not perceive the truth."[13] Worse, I would add: not only will the mind not perceive the truth, it will succumb to falsehood masquerading as truth.[14] Reality will slip through the mind's grid, leaving only the clotted dregs of error. Fr. Seraphim Rose sounds the warning: "Man's mind is supple, and it can be made to believe anything to which his will inclines."[15]

In *Degenerate Moderns* Jones shows how this principle ("we can only know what our moral lives allow us to know") works out in the lives and scholarly work of several modern intellectuals—for example, Margaret Mead.[16] In her classic study *Coming of Age in Samoa*, Mead either completely misunderstood the social system or fabricated her data (or both). In depicting the Samoa as "a paradise of free love"[17] Mead not only got the facts wrong but paved the way for dealing with her own feelings of sexual guilt.

> The general public—and Mead as well—was only interested in cultural relativism insofar as it sanctioned a certain attitude toward sexual mores. . . . Mead had turned anthropology into a powerful engine designed to soothe the troubled consciences of those who were interested in overthrowing the mores of Western, i.e., Judeo-Christian, civilization.[18]

Coming of Age in Samoa became a bestseller and has been considered a classic in anthropology. This shows, Jones says, "that the same need for rationalization permeated large segments of the culture it addressed. . . . The intellectual project of cultural relativism

---

But thinking is primarily for the sake of action. No one can avoid the responsibility of acting in accordance with his mode of thinking. No one can act wisely who has never felt the need to pause to think about how he is going to act and why he desires to act as he does.

L. SUSAN STEBBING
Thinking to Some Purpose

---

was rooted in sexual guilt."[19] Mead's "anthropology was, in effect, thinly rationalized sexual behavior."[20]

Jones draws from his critique of Mead some rather dire conclusions:

> The traditional manuals of moral theology have always claimed that one of the results of lust was a "darkening of the mind". Hatred of God is another. So intellectual life in the twentieth century is characterized by a vicious circle, oscillating between sexual and intellectual sins: sexual sin leads to bad science as a form of rationalization, turning one's back on the truth in the interest of ideology or self-will, which in turn leads to more dissolute behavior, which in turn leads to ever more ludicrous theories, until something like the Freeman book [an exposé of Mead's shoddy scholarship] comes along and the bubble bursts; whereupon the world says, in effect, well, we never really took her seriously anyway.[21]

Then Jones quotes the following verses from Romans 1:22-26:

> The more they called themselves philosophers, the more stupid they grew. . . . That is why God left them to their filthy enjoyments and the practices with which they dishonor their own bodies, since they have given up divine truth for a lie and have worshiped and served creatures instead of the creator. . . . That is why God has abandoned them to degrading passions: why their women have turned from natural intercourse to unnatural practices.[22]

Dangerous indeed it is to cordon off the intellect from a devotion to God and a passion for truth and holiness. Sertillanges says it well: "Purity of thought requires purity of soul; that is a general and undeniable truth. The neophyte of knowledge should let it sink deeply into his mind."[23] Long before this, John Henry Newman held a similar view. He wrote in a letter of 1869, "If there is a way of finding religious truth, it lies, not in exercises of the intellect, but close on the side of duty, of conscience, in the observance of the moral law."[24]

For Christian intellectuals it is not just thoughts about God that bring them into fellowship with God. As Newman says, it is true thoughts about anything:

> When men begin all their works with the thought of God, acting for His sake, and to fulfil His will, when they ask His blessing on themselves and their life, pray to Him for the objects they desire, and see Him in the event, whether it be according to their prayers or not, they will find everything that happens tend to confirm them in the truths about Him which live in their imagination, varied and unearthly as those truths may be.[25]

In ordinary matters, we understand this responsibility of knowledge quite well. We know certain mushrooms are poisonous. So we don't eat them. We know gunpowder explodes. So we confine it and direct its power to propel a missile to a target we choose. If we don't live by what we know about gunpowder, then we are likely not to be around. This principle works in spiritual matters too.

If we are bent on knowing the truth and are committed to obeying the truth as we come to know it (that is, if we are morally attuned), we can come to know truth about God and his world.

The Soul of the Christian Intellectual

I have reached a crucial point in writing this chapter. I don't know how to go on. Strange, you say? I agree. But I have a problem. I do not know whether what I have said above will have struck you as it strikes me—every time I think about it. The insight of the principle above should be shocking. Let me repeat it:

We only know what we act on.

Or:

We only believe what we obey.

If this does not shiver your timbers, I don't know what will. For is it not the common experience of all of us—you and I—that we do not incorporate the truth of these propositions in our lives? We say we know, but we do not do as we know. We say we believe, but we do not act like it.

Let me give you the brief assignment I was given almost thirty years ago. Take a sheet of paper and jot down five things that you believe about prayer. Afraid to take the test? Think I have something

---

Good thoughts are only good so far as they are taken
as means to an exact *obedience,* or at least this is the chief part
of their goodness.

JOHN HENRY NEWMAN
Diary

---

up my sleeve? I do: the same revelation I was given thirty years ago. So do it.

To encourage you to participate in this project, I am putting my next comments in an endnote. Do the assignment; then look at the note.[26]

Now answer this question: What do you know (or believe) about prayer?

I have never forgotten the lesson this assignment taught me, and I speak and think about prayer differently as a result.

Are you up to doing another assignment? This one I will merely sketch. You will know how to fulfill it. Read the Sermon on the Mount (Mt 5—7) or even the first few verses. Consider how you act in light of it. Can you still in all honesty say, *Credo,* I believe . . . ? Are you not knocked to your knees, saying to him in whom you say you believe, "I do believe; help me overcome my unbelief!" (Mk 9:24)?

**Now whosoever supposes that he can know truth
while he is still living iniquitously, is in error.**

ST. AUGUSTINE
De Agone Christiano

The shocking part of the simple principle that we only know (or believe) what we do (or obey) is that we do not act as if it were true. Its possible truth actually frightens us. Even knowing the truth of the principle only partially buffers the shock I had when I read the following remarks by Newman, as quoted by his biographer:

> As the Bible constantly teaches, "obedience to the light we possess is the way to gain more light." Nor must our obedience be anything other than unconditional: "till we aim at complete, unreserved obedience in all things, we are not really Christians at all."[27]

Miroslav Volf, speaking in light of the recent conflict in his Balkan country of origin, notes the propensity of Christians "who affirm the most strict understanding of scriptural authority but find zillions of ways of transgressing theologically and personally against it." It is not affirmation of the truth that is lacking. We need rather to learn "how biblical texts can shape lives in salutary ways, how they are fruitful texts, how they are texts one can live according to."[28]

In like manner, N. T. Wright distinguishes between a Christian and non-Christian New Testament scholar: "The Christian is prepared to say [when he or she reads the text], 'I don't like the sound of this, but golly, if this is what it really means, I'm going to have to pray for grace and strength to get that into my heart and be shaped by it.' "[29]

We are faced with a problem that is at once both intellectual and practical. How is it possible to speak meaningfully—as we do seem to speak—about not doing what we know we ought to do? How is it that knowing seems to be one thing and doing another? And how is it that they are the same thing? This is a puzzle that I have been trying to solve for a very long time. What follows is my current best attempt at a solution that is sound both intellectually and practically.

I will be begin by reviewing some of the biblical data.

The Biblical Data

Jesus sees belief and obedience as integrally related. The Gospel of John, for example, is permeated with this concept.[30] Nonetheless, the stunning Sermon on the Mount with its seemingly impossible demands ends with a recognition of a difference. Here it is assumed that in some sense one could hear Jesus' words (that is, one could understand what they mean) without doing them. That would make you foolish but still, sadly, quite human:

> Therefore everyone who hears these words of mine and puts them into practice is like a wise man who built his house on the rock. The rain came down, the streams rose, and the winds blew and beat against that house; yet it did not fall, because it had its foundation on the rock. But everyone who hears these words of mine and does not put them into practice is like a foolish man who built his house on sand. The rain came down, the streams rose, and the winds blew and beat against that house, and it fell with a great crash. (Mt 7:24-25)

And James, too, counsels, "Do not merely listen to the word, and so deceive yourselves. Do what it says" (Jas 1:22).

But if this is the case, then why do we not experience this close connection in our lives, and how can we understand what also seems to be true—that I do not always do what I say I know to be true or obey what I say I believe?

A Clarification

There are various ways of putting the seeming dichotomy I am dealing with: believing-obeying, hearing-doing, knowing-doing, theory-practice, orthodoxy-orthopraxy and wanting to do-not doing. These pairs of terms point to the same problem, but they are not quite identical. Lesslie Newbigin notes this as he contrasts two world-views—the classical and the biblical:

> The worldviews differ in respect to the roles of seeing and hearing. In the classical view, the true knowledge is vision, *theoria*. It is the vision of eternal truth. One therefore makes a distinction between *theoria* and *praxis*. One must first grasp the vision and then, in a second step, find ways of embodying it in action. Readers of the Bible will have noticed that these terms are totally absent. Because ultimate reality is personal, God's address to us is a word conveying his purpose and promise, a word which may be heard or ignored, obeyed or disobeyed. Faith comes by hearing, and unbelief is disobedience.[31]

Newbigin goes on to quote Dietrich Bonhoeffer, who is famous for emphasizing the connection between belief and obedience: "Only he who believes is obedient, and only he who is obedient believes."[32]

I agree with Newbigin: the key way the Bible speaks about the issue at hand is with the terms *belief* and *obedience* or *hearing* and *doing*. But *knowing* and *doing* are also involved.[33] It is perhaps true that Christian theology by using such terms as *orthodoxy* and, occa-

---

Knowing and doing, hearing and obeying are integrally connected for people whose convictions are truly and deeply Christian.

STEVEN GARBER
The Fabric of Faithfulness

---

sionally, *orthopraxis* has skewed the issue by suggesting a more classical division between *theory* and *practice*. Theory and practice do seem easier to see as separate. In any case, in what follows I will try to use *belief* and *obedience* as the focal terms.

A Division of the Soul
So then, back to the puzzle: Why do I not experience the equation of belief and obedience? Why do I often say that I believe what I do not embody with my life?

The usual answer is that I, all of us, really, are sinners. Our lives are split; our souls have two allegiances; we are inhabited, in the apostle Paul's terms, by the Old Man and the New Man (Rom 6:6; Eph 4:24). In other words, the answer is that there really is a difference between belief and obedience; they are not inevitably and invariably equated.

That seems fair enough. But that is not what puzzles me. What puzzles me is how the two (believing and obeying) can really be one, if we have both experience and biblical justification for seeing them as separable, as two. So I really want to examine how they can both be one and two.

I can put the issue in personal form: I am frustrated by the difference between what I say I believe and what I actually do. It is easy, for example, for me to say that I believe the Bible—that is, that what-

---

If a person does not become what he understands, he does not really understand it.

SØREN KIERKEGAARD
The Diary of Søren Kierkegaard

---

ever the Bible says I believe. Of course when I say that, I recognize that I do not know anywhere near all the things the Bible says. But I do think that I know a lot of what the Bible does say. I have read, reread, studied and restudied the Sermon on the Mount, for instance, and think I know pretty much what it says and much of what it means and what implications it should have for my life. Nonetheless, my behavior betrays me. Its demands are so stringent, I cannot seem to live by what it says.

Take a simple, gut-level example. Jesus makes an essentially ethical equation: ethically, lust is adultery.

> You have heard that it was said, "Do not commit adultery." But I tell you that anyone who looks at a woman lustfully has already committed adultery with her in his heart. (Mt 5:27-28)[34]

Moreover, I say that I believe this equation is true. Nonetheless, I still experience lust. If belief requires obedience, then how can I believe and not obey? Do I know that lust is adultery if I do not act as if I do?

A Companion in Misery

One thing is ironically comforting. I am not alone in experiencing such conflict. If my misery loves company, it gets it in the apostle Paul's explanation in Romans 7:14-24. There is a division among biblical scholars as to just who Paul is describing. Some say it is the unregenerate sinner, some say the regenerate believer still struggling with a strong propensity to sin, and others say the "Old Testament believer" who has not yet appropriated the life in the Spirit Paul describes in Romans 8.[35] But let us put aside any answer to this important hermeneutical question and consider the description itself, which is long, convoluted and repetitious. It reflects, I think, the knots in Paul's own soul at least in one time of his life, and surely it reflects my own twisted psyche. Here is my attempt to straighten out his comments in paraphrase:

> I do not understand myself. For what I want to do I do not do. Instead I do what I hate to do. I seem, on the one hand, to have the right desire—the desire to do good. But on the other hand, I simply don't do it. Surely when I behave this way, then it's not really me that is doing what I do. Something in me—a sinful nature—is doing what I know to be wrong. You see, the real me delights in God's law. The result is that a war is waging inside me.
>
> What a wretched man I am! Who will rescue me from this body of death?

There in a nutshell is the problem. Paul sees the puzzle not just as an intellectual poser but as a deep existential struggle in the soul. Regardless of whose voice Paul was speaking in, does not this description fit all of us today, even those of us who for a long time have thought ourselves to be "believers"? Granted, most of us can look back and see improvement—even great improvement—in resisting sin and following God's positive intention for our lives.

But who of us is completely free from the internal battle with our sinful nature?

To some extent it is still true: if we do not behave as we say we believe, or do not do as we say we know, we neither know nor believe. And if, then, we do not believe, we are caught in another existential conundrum: "Whoever believes in him [Jesus] is not condemned, but whoever does not believe stands condemned already because he has not believed in the name of God's one and only Son" (Jn 3:18).

Who will rescue us from this wretched situation? The apostle Paul has an answer: "Thanks be to God—through Jesus Christ our Lord!" (Rom 7:25). In Romans 8, the chapter that follows, Paul explains how Christ delivers us from the devastating split in our psyche.

Life in the Spirit

Christ frees "those who are in Christ" from the condemnation that otherwise justly comes to all sinners, that is, to everyone. We are no longer condemned for what we have done or even who we are as sinners. Now "those who live in accordance with the Spirit have their minds set on what the Spirit desires" (Rom 8:5). "The mind controlled by the Spirit is life and peace" (Rom 8:6). It is also obedi-

---

It is so difficult to believe because it is so difficult to obey.
SØREN KIERKEGAARD

---

ence to God's commands. As John Stott says, "Law-abiding Christian behaviour [is] the ultimate purpose of God's action through Christ."[36]

Stott untangles Paul's somewhat convoluted explanation of "walking according to the Spirit," explaining how we can follow the Spirit's promptings and yield to his control. He divides this explanation into *aspiration* and *mortification*.[37] First is *aspiration*, the positive act of setting our mind on the good and the true:

Our walk depends on our mind, our conduct on our outlook. As a man "thinketh in his heart (or mind) so is he" (Proverbs 23:7, AV) and so he behaves. It is our thoughts, ultimately, which govern our behaviour. . . . It is a question of our preoccupation, the ambitions which compel us and interests which engross us; how we spend our time, money and energy: what we give ourselves up to. That is what we set our minds on.[38]

So then, we are first to set our minds on those matters that are good—true, noble, right, pure, lovely, admirable, excellent or praiseworthy (Phil 4:8).

Second, we are to *mortify* our sinful nature, laying aside all sinful practices:

Mortification (putting to death by the power of the Spirit the deeds of the body) means a ruthless rejection of all practices we know to be wrong; a daily repentance, turning from all known sins of habit, practice, association of thought; a plucking out of the eye, a cutting off of the hand or foot, if temptation comes to us through what we see or do or where we go. The only attitude to adopt towards the flesh (sinful nature) is to kill it.[39]

Note that aspiration and mortification are not to be done once, after which one lives a sinless life. They are to be done daily. It is the spiritual disciplines of Bible reading, prayer, worship, fasting, Holy Communion, solitude and service (to name a few) that will keep both aspiration and mortification near the center of our daily lives. "Both," John Stott insists, "hold the secret to life in the fullest sense."[40] Both are central to the fulfillment of a passion for holiness.

The Practical Path to Becoming Whole

As I have mentioned, the path toward holiness through aspiration and mortification involves the traditional disciplines of the Christian life. Here I will make only a few particular comments about them. Many have written about them—most recently, and to me most helpfully, Dallas Willard, Richard Foster and Kathleen Norris.

If I understand what they say, I think that they would be in agreement with much of what I have written above. The disciplines are activities, but they are not for themselves; they are for soul making,

---

A purely mental life may be destructive if it leads us to substitute thought for life and ideas for actions. The activity proper to man is not purely mental because man is not just a disembodied mind. Our destiny is to live out what we think, because unless we live what we know, we do not even know it. It is only by making our knowledge part of ourselves, through action, that we enter into the reality that is signified by our concepts.

THOMAS MERTON
Thoughts in Solitude

---

and not just soul making but whole-person making. They are the ways God uses to remake us, to restore us into his image. When we are in his image, we truly *are* somebody.

The comments of Michael Casey in describing the especially thoughtful and deep way of reading Scripture called *lectio divina* suggests the hope that should fuel our journey:

> To live mindfully does not mean immediately becoming perfect. What is involved is an awareness of the truth of our being, shabby and fragmented as it is. Thus altered, we can invest our limited energies, not in massive programs of self-improvement, but in trying to perceive where God's grace is leading us and then following that impulse. If each step we take is God's choice then it will be both possible and fruitful, though not necessarily in the manner we imagine. We may have to live for years in a state of dissatisfaction with ourselves, but this is the price we pay for coming to a substantial reliance on the action of God. . . . Mindfulness is also a matter of deliberately thinking about the positive components of faith and allowing ourselves to be influenced by them.[41]

Our prayer should be that of the psalmist, "Give me an undivided heart, that I may fear your name" (Ps 86:11), our actions like those the apostle Paul commends: "We demolish arguments and every pretension that sets itself up against the knowledge of God, and we take captive every thought to make it obedient to Christ" (2 Cor 10:4-5).

The Moral Dimension of the Christian Intellectual

This long treatment of knowing and doing may appear to be a diversion from my attempt to define the term *Christian* as it serves as an adjective modifying *intellectual*. But if so, it will be because *doing* what one claims to know seems foreign to *knowing* itself. It is almost universally assumed that one can *know* without *doing*. Indeed, public intellectuals are notorious for their failure to live up

---

The knowledge of God is not absolute, abstract knowledge, a knowledge important in itself. It is not knowledge for its own sake. This is such knowledge as has a direction, which is good for something, which has thus no value in itself, which does not have, or no longer has, a law of its own. "So to know God as to give Him honor": this knowledge has no value except that of its object, its task, its goal: to honor God.

KARL BARTH
The Faith of the Church

It is man's glory to be the only intellectual animal on earth. That imposes upon human beings the moral obligation to lead intellectual lives. The slothful are blind to the glory and neglectful of the obligation.

MORTIMER ADLER
Intellect: Mind over Matter

---

to their stated moral values. But at least they can think of themselves as worthy intellectuals. They do not have to bear the burden of *doing* in order to lay claim to *knowing*.

Christian intellectuals, however, must not even pretend to hide behind such a dichotomy. There is a unity of knowing-doing, believing-obeying, orthodoxy-orthopraxy, theory-practice. Thinking Christians who do not do as they say are not *Christian intellectuals* at all. A Christian intellectual cannot escape the burden. Christian intellectuals are those whose intellectual lives are lived to the glory of God. They will *do* what they claim to *know*.

VI

PERFECTING
THE
INTELLECT

*THE
INTELLECTUAL
VIRTUES*

I*t is time to get practical. We have focused on the nature of a Christian* mind. We have examined Newman's definition of the "perfection of the intellect" and my concept of the Christian intellectual. This may seem to be an exercise in romanticism: surely the ideal is too high. We remember Newman's ecstatic utterance:

> [The perfected intellect is characterized by] the clear, calm, accurate vision and comprehension of all things, as far as the finite mind can embrace them, each in its place, and with its own characteristics upon it. It is almost prophetic from its knowledge of history; it is almost heart-searching from its knowledge of human nature; it has almost supernatural charity from its freedom from littleness and prejudice; it has almost the repose of faith, because nothing can startle it; it has almost the beauty and harmony of heavenly contemplation, so intimate is it with the eternal order of things and the music of the spheres.[1]

What folly to attempt the acquisition of such a mind! This way lies madness! The music of the spheres, indeed!

But then some of us who have studied English literature may remember another Victorian who wrote:

> Ah, but a man's reach must exceed his grasp,
> Or what's a heaven for?

Robert Browning was putting into the mouth of the artist Andrea del Sarto a principle del Sarto did not follow. Much to his regret, del Sarto had stuck with what he knew he could do. Contemplating his own art, he continued:

> All is silver-gray,
> Placid and perfect with my art: the worse![2]

If we stick with our self-imposed limitations, we will never know what we can do. The imperfect product of an intellect that stretches beyond what looks to be its limits may more glorify God than the perfect product of a mind turning like a lathe programmed for a simple spindle. Or, to change the image, the mind that puts out to fish the troubled seas may land a catch that would never nibble at a mind scudding along on the smooth water close to shore.

Yes, the human mind has limitations. Yes, humility must characterize our self-understanding. Yes, each individual mind has its own limitations. Only a few of us can rival John Henry Newman, let alone Augustine, John Calvin, Gertrude Himmelfarb, Simone Weil or whoever our favorite intellectual giant is. But none of us know how much our mind can stretch. We simply can't know what we can't know unless someone who knows we can't know tells us. God has done that, of course. He has told us that we cannot penetrate his mind to the depths.

> "For my thoughts are not your thoughts,
>   neither are your ways my ways,"
>   declares the LORD.

"As the heavens are higher than the earth,
  so are my ways higher than your ways
  and my thoughts than your thoughts." (Is 55:8-9)

But there is little else he has told us we cannot know, and there is, to be sure, very much that can be known. So we must not sell ourselves short whether as humanity as a whole or as individuals. Maybe, just maybe, we can hear at least an echo of the music of the spheres.

But how? Indeed, how? It's time to get practical. This and the following chapter will examine four phases in our answer to this question: virtues, disciplines, tips and blocks, remembering as we do so this marvelous insight of A. G. Sertillanges:

> Every truth is practical; the most apparently abstract, the loftiest, is also the most practical. Every truth is life, direction, a way leading to the end of man. And therefore Jesus Christ made this unique assertion: "I am the Way, the Truth, and the Life."[3]

The Intellectual Virtues

Nothing is more practical and more abstract at the same time than the virtues, for they are the motivating, energizing passions that fuel our action. First, an abstract definition:

> Virtues are dispositional properties, along with the concerns and capacities for judgment and action that constitute them. . . . Virtues are deeply embedded parts of our character that readily dispose us to feel, to think and act in morally appropriate ways as our changing circumstances require.[4]

Man's highest pleasure consists in acquiring and intensifying consciousness. Not the pleasure of knowing, exactly, but rather that of learning. In knowing a thing we tend to forget it, to convert it, if the expression may be allowed, into unconscious knowledge. Man's pleasure, his purest delight, is allied with the act of learning, of getting at the truth of things, of acquiring knowledge with differentiation.

MIGUEL DE UNAMUNO
The Tragic Sense of Life

Now the practical implications: Faced with the life of a new day—significant decisions or insignificant ones—what do I do? How do I decide to brush my teeth or shower? Habit certainly prevails here, but why these habits? Because our character—its virtues and vices—is compiled over a thousand previous decisions. Who we are—our Being, as discussed in the previous chapter—is formed and reformed as we decide this way or that. There is a symbiotic relationship between what/who we are on the inside and what we do on the outside. When we act unconsciously, we play out our virtues and vices from the inside out, and these actions tend not merely

---

The ethic of character is a centuries-old conversation about how we make sense out of our lives and order our existence. Its vantage point is that it is in beliefs expressed and shaped by behavior, characteristically, that the moral life is formed, individually and corporately. And so the first questions of ethics have more to do with how one lives than what one believes.

STEVEN GARBER
The Fabric of Faithfulness

---

to express but to confirm our character. When we act consciously—decide only after thinking about our decision—we deliberately set our character: we become thereby either more virtuous or, of course, less.

There is no argument, is there? We are as Christians to become more virtuous. So we are to act in such a way as to help mold our character to be more in line with who we really are—creatures made by God in his image. In terms of the virtues—especially the intellectual virtues—how does this play out?

The Structure of the Intellectual Virtues

In *Epistemology: Becoming Intellectually Virtuous* W. Jay Wood lists four types of intellectual virtues, each having to do with a different aspect of the intellectual life. While Wood does not himself chart these, the following schemata does:[5]

Acquisition virtues: passion for the truth	Application virtues: passion for holiness
inquisitiveness	will to do what one knows
teachableness	love
persistence	fortitude
humility	integrity
	humility
Maintenance virtues: passion for consistency	Communication virtues: compassion for others
perseverance	clarity of expression
courage	orderliness of presentation
constancy	aptness of illustration
tenacity	humility
patience	
humility	

There is no question which of these virtues are the more central, the more controlling, the more important. We have already discussed them many times. But they are linked and we must examine them again: *the passion for truth* and *the passion for holiness;* and they are set in the framework of *humility.*

A Passion for Truth

Christian intellectuals do not just love ideas; they love the truth. And love it they must, for as St. Gregory the Great wrote, "Truth is not known unless it is loved."[6] And Pascal and a host of other wise Christians have echoed this down through the ages.

> He who understands truth without loving it, or loves without understanding, possesses neither one nor the other.—Bernard of Clairvaux[7]

> Truth is so obscured nowadays and lies so well established that unless we love the truth we shall never recognize it.—Pascal[8]

> In love, and only in love, is real knowledge of the Truth conceivable.—Pavel Florensky[9]

Truth visits those who love her, who surrender to her, and this love cannot be without virtue.—A. G. Sertillanges[10]

Should this be odd—this connection between love and truth? Surely not in the biblical scheme. Jesus himself gave reasons why the religious leaders should believe that he is the One sent from God and why they don't. "I know that you do not have the love of God in your hearts," Jesus says. "I have come in my Father's name, and you do not accept me; but if someone else comes in his own name, you will accept him" (Jn 5:41-42). Their refusal to recognize him as the One sent from God is a clear indication of their lack of love for God. The issue is moral, not intellectual. A clear knowledge of who Jesus is follows from a love of God.

I have long been convinced that if one really wants to know the truth about God, if one really loves the truth, then more than a glimpse of that truth will come. So I often plead with students to read the New Testament, especially the Gospels, and ask God to show them the truth about Jesus. "Tell God that you want to know the truth so much that you are willing to do what you learn to be truth, to act on the implications, no matter how costly," I urge. "You may well have to change your life. You may find these changes costly. You may have to reconsider your plans for love and marriage. You may lose some friends. You may not get or even seek that

---

Truth is ever new. Like the grass of morning, moist with glistening dew, all the old virtues are waiting to spring up fresh. God does not grow old. We must help our God to renew, not the buried past and the chronicles of a dying world, but the eternal face of the earth.

A. G. SERTILLANGES
The Intellectual Life

---

high-paying job in a high-tech company. But if you are willing to follow the truth that much, you will find it in Jesus Christ."

Jesus said to those who had begun to believe that he was the One sent from God, "If you hold to my teaching, you are really my disciples. Then you will know the truth, and the truth will set you free" (Jn 8:31-32). Holding to Jesus' teaching doesn't mean just "reading the Bible" or "listening to sermons." It means obeying what Jesus says. The cost of finding the truth is obedience; the consequence is knowing the truth and being set free, free from all that separates us from God and final human fulfillment. Is it worth it? A thousand times over.

Truth and holiness demand the elimination of many typical human passions: passion for possession (materialism), passion for economic success (money), passion for pleasure (hedonism). Wendell Berry reminds us, for example:

> What a man most needs is not a knowledge of how to get more, but a knowledge of the most he can do without, and of how to get along without it. The essential cultural discrimination is not between having and not having or haves and have-nots, but between the superfluous and the indispensable.[11]

As Jesus said, "Whoever wants to save his life will lose it, but whoever loses his life for me and for the gospel will save it." Then Jesus counted the cost: "What good is it for a man to gain the whole world, yet forfeit his soul?" (Mk 8:35-36). Consider too those great, comforting words of Jesus, "Come to me, all you who are weary and burdened, and I will give you rest. Take my yoke upon you and learn from me, for I am gentle and humble in heart, and you will find rest for your souls. For my yoke is easy and my burden is light" (Mt 11:28-30). Finally, there is God's great promise to the Jews in exile in Babylon hundreds of years before Jesus: "You will seek me and find me when you seek me with all your heart. I will be found by you" (Jer 29:13-14).

The formula in the religious and moral realms is simple: If one loves the truth, one will do the truth one knows; if one does the truth one knows, one will be rewarded with more truth.

Putting the Formula to the Test

How practical these virtues are—the passion for truth and the passion for holiness! No one needs to tell us what *to do* about them. That we know, enough to be responsible for whatever it is we do about them—encourage them or suppress them.

So the first way to put the formula to the test is to obey what we know, yearn for knowing more so that we can obey more. A second way is to notice how the absence of the combination of these virtues

---

Wisdom is the integral comprehension of the truth: without love it cannot be attained, or at best barely attained.

THIERRY OF CHARTRES

---

leads to ignorance, arrogance, decadence and debauchery. The apostle Paul outlined this clearly in Romans 1:18-32.

> The wrath of God is being revealed from heaven against all the godlessness and wickedness of men who suppress the truth by their wickedness, since what may be known about God is plain to them, because God has made it plain to them. For since the creation of the world God's invisible qualities—his eternal power and divine nature—have been clearly seen, being understood from what has been made, so that men are without excuse.
>
> For although they knew God, they neither glorified him as God nor gave thanks to him, but their thinking became futile and their foolish hearts were darkened. Although they claimed to be wise, they became fools and exchanged the glory of the immortal God for images made to look like mortal man and birds and animals and reptiles.
>
> Therefore God gave them over in the sinful desires of their hearts to sexual impurity for the degrading of their bodies with one another. They exchanged the truth of God for a lie, and worshiped and served created things rather than the Creator—who is forever praised. Amen.
>
> Because of this, God gave them over to shameful lusts. Even their women exchanged natural relations for unnatural ones. In the same way the men also abandoned natural relations with women and were inflamed with lust for one another. Men committed indecent acts with

other men, and received in themselves the due penalty for their perversion.

Furthermore, since they did not think it worthwhile to retain the knowledge of God, he gave them over to a depraved mind, to do what ought not to be done. They have become filled with every kind of wickedness, evil, greed and depravity. They are full of envy, murder, strife, deceit and malice. They are gossips, slanderers, God-haters, insolent, arrogant and boastful; they invent ways of doing evil; they disobey their parents; they are senseless, faithless, heartless, ruthless. Although they know God's righteous decree that those who do such things deserve death, they not only continue to do these very things but also approve of those who practice them.

We read a passage like this, unrelenting in its dire warnings and predictions, and we wonder how anyone—including us—could be caught up in the slide to perdition. Yet we also reflect that we either are now or were once caught up in just such a slide. Only by the grace of God has the progress been halted. Only by the grace of God is the path of holiness beneath our feet. Only in the presence and power of the Holy Spirit can we walk that path.

Hating the Truth: A Culture in Decay

Love of truth brings obedience, holiness and further grasp of the truth. But the formula can also be cast in negative form: failure to do the truth brings hatred of the truth. David Lyle Jeffrey, in a brilliant essay, "Knowing Truth in the Present Age," rings the changes on this negative formula.

> When loving the truth is quite out of fashion, as it is at present, the very mention of the word can call up hatred. *Veritas otium parit*, said the Roman poet Terence—truth engenders hatred. The desire to flee truth is deep, deep in human nature, and that fact is not obscure to anyone.[12]

Jeffrey quotes Augustine's question:

> Why does truth call forth hatred? Why is Your servant treated as an

enemy by those to whom he preaches the truth, if happiness is loved, which is simply joy in truth?

And then Augustine's explanation:

> Simply because truth is loved in such a way that those who love some other thing want it to be the truth, and precisely because they do not wish to be deceived, are unwilling to be convinced that they are indeed being deceived. Thus they hate the truth for the sake of that other thing which they love, because they take it for the truth. They love truth when it enlightens them, they hate it when it accuses them. (*Confessions* 10.23)

Oh the self-deceiving ways of the human heart! Oh the desperate need for the grace of God! Oh the absolute need for humility for any of us who think we have the truth!

There is a subtle distinction here. On the one hand we must affirm that there is a truth, that it can be found, that by the grace of God who has made us in his image and wants us to know the truth, we can know the truth, at least some of it. On the other hand, we must recognize that we are fallen, subject to the perverted passions of all humanity. No perversity is finally foreign to us. Satan lies ever

---

Those who do not love truth excuse themselves on that grounds that it is disputed and that very many people deny it. Thus their error is solely due to the fact that they love neither truth nor charity, and so they have no excuse.

BLAISE PASCAL
Pensées

---

at the door seeking whom he may destroy, trapping us in our own nets of inordinate desire.

That infamous master of suspicion Nietzsche was, frankly, often right about our human frame: "The most common lie is the lie one tells to oneself."[13] Listen to Kai Nielsen, for example, justify his disbelief in the biblical God:

To say that a man has a purpose in the first sense [having a function or role to play in the world] is actually offensive for it involves treating man as a kind of tool or artifact. It is degrading for a man to be regarded as merely serving a purpose.[14]

God could not be good and make human beings with a purpose to fulfill, Nielsen says. Therefore either God does not exist (Nielsen's position) or God is not good. Of course, says Nielsen, there is a sense in which a person can have a purpose: one can have "goals, aims, intentions, motives and the like," and that is quite sufficient for a meaningful life. So Nielsen recapitulates the Fall in Eden, and so do we all when we put our desires for self-identity before our real identity as God's creatures.

Anti-intellectualism gives rise to the most extreme, the most morally deplorable, form of sloth. It is to be found in persons for whom the ultimate objectives in life are the maximization of pleasure, money, fame, or power and who, thus motivated, express their contempt for those who waste their lives in purely intellectual pursuits. It is almost as if they wished they did not have the burden of having intellects that might distract them from their fanatical devotion to nonintellectual aims.

MORTIMER ADLER
Intellect: Mind over Matter

Jean-Paul Sartre, one of the twentieth century's most well-known atheists, commented on his own experience at age eleven.

I don't know where the thought came from or how it struck me, yet all at once I said to myself, "But God doesn't exist!" . . . It's striking to reflect that I thought this at the age of eleven and that I never asked myself the question again until today, that is, for sixty years.[15]

Much later Sartre did construct a philosophic argument, proving to his satisfaction that God does not exist, but he admits that it was post facto. After his youth, he says, the possibility that God exists just never concerned him.

In my university work I once met a young man who was delighted beyond ecstasy that I could not prove to him that God exists. If God could not be proven by an argument, he felt free to do whatever he wanted.[16] He was off the moral hook. This student was fulfilling Nietzsche's stunning insight into the animosity between truth and desire. It explains why God as revealed in Jesus had to die and is given in the words of the "ugliest man":

> But he *had to* die: he saw with the eyes that saw everything; he saw man's depths and ultimate grounds, all his disgrace and ugliness. His pity knew no shame: he crawled into my dirtiest nooks. This most curious, overobtrusive, overpitying one had to die. He always saw me: on such a witness I wanted to have revenge or not live myself. The god who saw everything, *even man*—this god had to die! Man cannot bear it that such a witness should live.[17]

Thus does pride see truth, find it unacceptable and then kill it. To live in ignorance and delusion is easier. Oh who will deliver us from this body of death? We know the apostle Paul's response.

The Passion for Holiness
It should now be abundantly clear that the passion for holiness is so inextricably bound up with the passion for truth that while we can distinguish between them in theory, we cannot do so in practice. The passion for truth requires a passion for holiness, for the truth is that

---

Purity of thought requires purity of soul; that is a general and undeniable truth. The neophyte of knowledge should let it sink deeply into his mind.

A. G. SERTILLANGES
The Intellectual Life

God is holy and wishes us to *desire* to be so and, with his presence, to *be* so. The passion for holiness requires a passion for truth, for holiness includes being truthful, knowing and doing the truth. Our *being* what God wants us to be unites the two—truth and holiness—

so that in who we *are* and what we *do* there is no difference.

**The intellectual who is sincere says every day to the God of truth:
"The zeal of Thy house hath eaten me up."**

A. G. SERTILLANGES
The Intellectual Life

With the passion for truth and holiness leading the way, we can turn our attention to some of the other virtues outlined above. Most need no commentary.

Constancy, Patience and Perseverance

A. G. Sertillanges singles out three intellectual virtues: "You must bring to your work constancy which keeps steadily at the task; patience which bears difficulties well; and perseverance which prevents the will from flagging."[18]

Constancy. "Gutting it out" is the crude way of putting this virtue, but it captures the sense. When attention flags, when a short break doesn't work, when a longer one fails, gut it out. If you eventually have to abandon the project, let it be because the answer you seek is simply not available to human thought, or not yet available, or not available to you regardless of how hard you try. Only then may you feel free to stop trying.

I have certainly done that with a number of issues. The first theological/philosophical question I remember asking is, as far as I am concerned, insoluble: Why, if God wants all people to believe in him, does he not make it so they all do so? I was not yet in high school; I had no idea this was one of the all-time posers, a form of the freedom-determinism question in philosophy or the free will-predestination question in theology. I do now. I didn't solve it then; I haven't solved it yet. I've talked to some who think they have solved it; I don't think they have.

Is this perverseness on my part? Perhaps. With the good will I have brought to this question in the past, I don't think so. Is it mental incompetence? Perhaps. But the mentally incompetent do not know of their incompetence. So they (and maybe I with them) are stuck. Is it spiritual blindness? Perhaps. But the spiritually blind do not know of their blindness. So, stuck again. Is the question insoluble? Perhaps. But if it is, I can't know it, for I can only know what I do know, not what I can't know unless someone who knows tells me. So far God hasn't told me. Or I haven't heard. But if I haven't heard, it's as if he hasn't told me. Good grief! How do I get out of this mess?

In Russia in the 1840's it was common to carry on disputes throughout the night. At one time a controversy was raging at its height when someone suggested that the disputants have something to eat—where upon the critic Belinsky shouted out, "We have not yet decided the question of the existence of God and you want to eat!"

GEORGE B. DE HUSZAR
The Intellectuals

Constancy, in short, has limits. But from our standpoint they are indeterminate. We just stop trying when trying becomes too trying. Then sometimes, when we have taken the hard path, success arrives. Meditating on the reclamation of land long destroyed by thoughtless farming, Wendell Berry informs us that wrong is easy; gravity does the job. "Right is difficult and long," but it frees our mind to move from shadow to light. In being long, constancy may indeed be difficult; then comes the reward—the light of truth. At least at times. And when it doesn't, patience takes over.

Patience. Patience calms the spirit when constancy produces frustration.

Perseverance. Perseverance prevails even when patience gives up.

These three virtues—constancy, patience and perseverance: don't leave the false comfort of thoughtless existence without them. A further virtue is one that guards against the great potential for disappointment, if not despair.

Courage

Courage is a virtue that is required if we are to overcome the possible intellectual and emotional catastrophe that can befall any thinking person. If we begin to think about something we have not considered before, we may be disconcerted by what happens. Here is a principle capable of infinite illustration: Many of our cherished ideas are simply not true.

Let's begin with Santa Claus, a harmless childhood fantasy which when removed sometimes produces tears, sometimes a jaded though youthful "I thought so." The disappointment is not long-lasting. But when we have cherished ideas for years and years, from childhood through teens on into middle age, and we discover that we've been deluded, a few tears won't wash away the anguish. The challenge itself produces first shocked disbelief, then anger, then vilified rejection not only of the challenge but of the one who has begun to disabuse us of our error. We launch out with personal barbs and snide innuendoes; we poison the well.

In short, we often lack the courage to check out the challenge, to wrestle with the possibility that our own belief needs serious modification or rejection or replacement. But courage to do so is a virtue that must accompany us in developing our intellectual skills.

One is not really an intellectual unless one can say:
For me, to live is truth.

A. G. SERTILLANGES
The Intellectual Life

Such courage is, of course, a Christian virtue. Consider what it rests on: the existence of a God who knows the truth about everything and who wants us to know the truth as well. God does not want us ignorant, misinformed or deluded. He has told us that if we "hold to" his teaching, we will know the truth and the truth will set us free (Jn 8:32). Jesus was talking about the truth of his teaching, but it is just as true with the vast panorama of truths about the world. When we know what things are really like, we are free from their power to harm us as well as free to contemplate their beauty and employ their utility. As Mary Jo Weaver says, "The ability to combine belief and intellectual work is one of the hallmarks of a Christian intellectual. It means that, with a grounded faith, we can look at anything without fear."[19]

If our cherished beliefs are false, we do well to rid ourselves of them. It may take courage. It may trigger radical reassessment. It may change the course of our lives. But every pain of change will be followed by the joy of knowing and being known by him who is the way, the truth and the life. Sertillanges says, "Your most normal stimulant is courage. Courage is sustained, not only by prayer, but by calling up anew the vision of the goal."[20]

Courage is also needed if you discover something new or culturally different, something that proves odd to others but true to you. The problem is greater yet when what you comes to think of as true is not just odd but seen as "heretical" within your own "cognitive community." Sociologist Eviatar Zerubavel, himself "a member of a highly rationalistic, scientifically-minded society," says, "There may be potential Freuds and Darwins among us about whom we will never hear only because, unlike Freud and Darwin, they may lack the intellectual courage to voice their heretical views and thereby risk 'cognitive excommunication.' "[21] We might well think that the world would be better off without either Freud or Darwin, but it is a simple matter to substitute the intellectual heroes of one's own "cognitive community" to see that his point is well taken: there may be potential Luthers and Calvins, Newmans and Schaeffers among us who yet lack the courage to voice their views. May none of us be one of them!

The opposite problem, however, comes when courage to speak one's mind becomes arrogance. E. Harris Harbison says:

> There is always an irreducible egotism in most scholarship. Unless the scholar believes passionately in what he is doing, no matter how

far off the results or remote the audience or infinitesimal the apparent rewards, the job will never be done—or certainly not be well done.[22]

No wonder that arrogance is a likely charge to be levied against would-be intellectuals.

Humility

Humility is a virtue I felt forced to place in every one of Wood's categories—acquisition, maintenance, application and communication. Without it every virtue begins to become a vice. A passion for truth becomes a certitude that we have found and now possess it. A passion for holiness becomes self-righteousness.

Lack of humility—arrogance—is, in fact, one of the most frequent charges against intellectuals. Sometimes this charge cannot be avoided, being triggered by jealousy of another's seemingly relaxed life or brilliance of intellectual performance. If you are perceived as spending major blocks of time alone, you will inevitably be thought not only lazy but proud of your freedom to be lazy. This charge is hard to refute. So best not to do so directly. Let the rest of your life be more obviously spent serving others, and you may eventually find the comments less frequent.

The real problem, however, is not the charge that you are arrogant but the distinct possibility that you actually are. Self-examina-

---

The *humus* of humility is the good soil
in which the Word produces abundant fruit.

FATHER BERNARDO OLIVERA
"Lectio Vere Divina"

---

tion is always in order: "What do you desire? Vain glory? Profit? Then you are but a pseudo-intellectual."[23] We must take our cue from the great Christian intellectuals of the past: They knew "that the proud theologian was a living contradiction in terms."[24]

Philosopher J. Richard Middleton tells a poignant story of his sudden, unexpected bout of doubt, the onset of which came at the peak of his confidence in his intellectual ability. He had just written a successful book on the Christian worldview. He would now, he reflected, take on and solve the problem of evil. Finding that his powers of reason were not equal to the task, he plunged headlong into a despair it took years to transcend. He comments:

> It's not the childlike asking of questions or the honest admission of doubt that will get you into trouble with God. It's the unstinting belief, the confidence, the certainty that you—that I—have all the answers, either because we're smart, or because we're honest, or because we're scientific, or because we're Christians, or because we have a Reformational worldview.[25]

Beware the arrogance of a certainty resting on your own mental power: if there is certainty in our faith in God, it is not because we have naturally—or been endowed by God with—a fully perfected intellect.

We suffer from the sin of arrogance. That same arrogance causes others to suffer. Richard John Neuhaus issues a warning. Our very assurance that we as Christians are in possession of the truth has been and continues to be a barrier to others' learning the truth we claim to know:

> Few things have contributed so powerfully to the unbelief of the modern and postmodern world as the pretension of Christians to know more than we do. . . . If Christians exhibited more intellectual patience, modesty, curiosity, and sense of adventure, there would be fewer atheists in the world, both of the rationalist and the postmodern varieties.[26]

Leszek Kolakowski inserts a distinct note of realism when he discusses the responsibility of intellectuals:

> In the case of the intellectuals, the only specific matter they are professionally responsible for is the good use—that is, the upright and least misleading use—of the word. It is less a matter of truth than of the spirit of truth, since nobody can promise that he will never be mis-

taken; but it is possible to preserve the spirit of truth, which means never to abandon a vigilant mistrust of one's own words and identifications, to know how to retract one's errors, and to be capable of self-correction.[27]

Kolakowski continues: "The common human qualities of vanity and greed for power among intellectuals may have particularly harmful and dangerous results."[28] When you get an astounding insight into what looks to you like the truth, take two humility pills and call your friends for a reality check.

Describing the state of knowledge centuries ago, Thomas Aquinas said, "No philosopher has ever been able completely to know the essence of even a single fly."[29] He was right then. And Lewis Thomas is right in our age: "We do not understand a flea."[30]

The paradox of humility is that the more one strives to be humble, the less one succeeds.[31] So how is humility acquired? Listening to your friends respond honestly to your best thoughts is a relatively easy if painful way. But rereading the Sermon on the Mount is even better, if more devastating. Can you do so and remain proud? Immersion in Scripture, meditation on the mind and life of Jesus, active participation in a specific community of faith: these are the best ways to humility.

Virtues, Talents and Disciplines

It is important but sometimes difficult to distinguish between a virtue and a talent.

Talents are the abilities each of us is endowed with through nature by God. There is musical talent, physical talent leading to athletic ability, intellectual talent (some like my wife are very good at mathematics; some like me are not), language talent (ability to learn languages easily and quickly) and so forth. You name the skill and there is an attendant talent.

If you can't understand calculus enough to complete the exercises in a beginning calculus text, you have nothing to apologize for.

Well, at least I have nothing to apologize for. I hope! Lack of talent is not a moral flaw.

Talents can be developed by discipline, but only to a limited degree. Despite rigorous discipline, none of us can be as good as the best of us. Equal in talent we are not. God endows us with ability and we respond by developing it and using it in accord with the general principles we find in the Bible or our conscience or our community. Talents as such are neither moral nor immoral; they are simply our givens. It's how we develop and use them that counts.

Virtues can be even more developed than talents. Virtues are profoundly spiritual, because they mirror the character of God himself. Here too, discipline helps. It is not that the disciplines bring about salvation. That is by the grace of God alone. But God wants us more than "saved" into a future glory; he wants us to "work out our salvation with fear and trembling" (Phil 2:12). And that's what the spiritual disciplines do. The intellectual disciplines, as will soon be seen, overlap the spiritual disciplines to a large degree. What improves the whole person—body, soul and spirit—improves the mind.

Albert Edward Day, who notes that the apostle Paul relied on God for salvation, says this:

> But Paul was also a disciplinarian. "I beat my body to keep it in subjection." "They that are Christ's have crucified the flesh with its affections and lusts." "So fight I, not as one who beateth the air." "Mortify therefore your members which are upon earth." "Laying aside every weight and the sin which doth so easily beset us." "No man that warreth, tangleth himself with the affairs of this life." These are not the words of a man who scorned discipline.[32]

It is therefore to the intellectual disciplines we now turn.

VII

PERFECTING
THE
INTELLECT

THE
INTELLECTUAL
DISCIPLINES

A *brilliant thought, a solution to a problem, an intellectual insight* can come at any time. It can hit while you're driving, listening to music, praying in tranquillity, in ecstasy or even in anger. But these are unprogrammed, unprepared for and often quickly lost. If we want to develop the skills of a perfected intellect and enjoy the products of these skills in action, there are better ways of going about it.

There is, of course, no secret formula guaranteeing the perfection of the intellect, either in its skill in processing ideas and information or in its creative capacity to suddenly "have" a new idea or insight. "The process of discovery is *in general* nonrational," says William J. Wainwright.[1] But there are disciplines that can enhance whatever native abilities we have. We will examine five of them: solitude, silence, attention, lateral thinking and prayer. Following this is a reflection on Martin Heidegger's distinction between *calculative* and *meditative* thinking; this should deepen our grasp of why the intellectual disciplines are effective. Then we will open a grab bag of barriers to thought and tips for stimulating and enhancing thought.

Solitude: All Alone in the Light

The first requisite discipline is solitude. Of course thinking is done in groups, and it is caught from lectures, from public performances. But thinking itself—what goes on in our minds—is private.[2] And cer-

---

**Solitude is
not pain but ripening—
For which the sun must be your friend.**

FRIEDRICH NIETZSCHE
Dionysus Dithyrambs

---

tainly the ideas we pick up from reading or listening are best evaluated, weighed, pondered, linked up with other ideas in the quiet repose that solitude alone provides in measure.

So it is important to make a place for solitude to happen. For a person who is serious about a life of the mind, a den or its equivalent is an absolute necessity.[3] It must be a quiet place where spouse, children, friends and telephone do not interrupt. Keep the phone on the hook if it rings; let your answering machine take the message. It's probably someone selling aluminum siding anyway.

**Solitude is a deepening of the present,
and unless you look for it in the present
you will never find it.**

THOMAS MERTON
Merton: A Film Biography

Time in solitude is also important. Thinking cannot be rushed. Ideas spring to mind from the wellsprings of thought, and often they spring suddenly with what seems to be no preparation, no anticipation, just with apparent spontaneity. But for this to happen, time must be provided. Commenting on the attempt of some schools to hasten the educational process, Jacques Barzun writes:

> I favor acceleration, I am all for an end to dawdling and playing, but
> acceleration in matters of the mind must be internal, not physical; the
> aim must be intensity not speed. . . . To learn anything permanently
> he [a student] needs periods of intellectual loafing.[4]

Time in solitude is often time waiting. Nothing may seem to be
happening. There is here an analogy to the waiting we do as God's
children. The psalmists enjoin us to seek the face of God. We do.
Nothing happens. We wait. And that is what we are supposed to do.

> I wait for the LORD, my soul waits,
>   and in his word I put my hope.
> My soul waits for the Lord
>   more than watchmen wait for the morning,
>   more than watchmen wait for the morning. (Ps 130:5-6)

So in the act and art of thinking: we are alone with our thoughts, but
our thoughts are shallow. We seem to be getting nowhere. So we put
down pen, book, paper, and wait.

**If you seek solitude merely because it is what you prefer,
you will never escape from the world and its selfishness; you will
never have the interior freedom that will keep you really alone.**

THOMAS MERTON
Seeds of Contemplation

Only in solitude is this possible. We need not fear the stares of
others who see we have stopped typing, stopped taking notes,
stopped reading. Only we and God know that our waiting is active.
We are not asleep. We are ready to receive.

Silence: A Spider Spinning a Web

Solitude means silence. Of course you may wish to play music, but
resist the urge. Play it only when you are off-line intellectually. Any
noise, any music—Bach, rock or Bacharach—grabs your mind or your

subconscious and trails it along after it.[5] (As I write this, my wife is in my den talking on the phone to our daughter. It's driving me nuts!)

One third-grader's insight is on target: "Silence is spiders spinning their webs, it's like a silkworm making its silk. Lord, help me to know when to be silent."[6]

Another young girl reflected: "Silence reminds me to take my soul with me wherever I go."[7]

And Wendell Berry muses:

> Best of any song
> is bird song
> in the quiet, but first
> you must have the quiet.[8]

But it is A. G. Sertillanges, who has given me more help in this chapter than any other writer, who makes the most helpful suggestions:

> Do you want to do intellectual work? Begin by creating within you a zone of silence, a habit of recollection, a will to renunciation and detachment which puts you entirely at the disposal of the work; acquire that state of soul unburdened by desire and self-will which is the state of grace of the intellectual worker. Without that you will do nothing, at least nothing worth while.[9]

And why will you do nothing worthwhile? Because in Josef Pieper's words, "to perceive means to listen in silence: . . . only in silence is hearing possible":

> Moreover, the stronger the determination prevails to hear all there is, the more profound and more complete the silence must be. Consequently philosophy . . . means: to listen so perfectly and intensely that such receptive silence is not disturbed and interrupted by anything, not even by a question.[10]

On a more practical note, Ernest Dimnet suggests that even the solitude of insomnia and fasting can be turned to advantage:

> Insomnia, before ending in exhaustion, generally produces a lucidity which no amount of normal meditation will replace, and the vigils of

literary men testify to the fact. Prolonged solitude accompanied by a little fasting acts in the same way.[11]

Solitude and silence alone do not produce thought. Too often they simply produce sleep. I often get settled at my desk, notice that there are some undone projects on my to-do list (call Joe, write Mary, file lecture notes . . .) and slowly do them rather than plunge into a task requiring careful thought. Then when in solitude I have cleared these tasks from my desk, having done them or put the to-do sheet out of sight, I lean back in my chair . . . and realize I sure could use a

---

**We receive only when we are recollected;
only in silence is heard the beating of the heart of God.**

FATHER BERNARDO OLIVERA
"Lectio Vere Divina"

---

cup of coffee. So I get the coffee—which requires preparing the machine and waiting for the coffee to perk. Meanwhile thumbs twiddle. Then . . .

Ah, a cup of coffee, a clear desk, a quiet den (my wife having left to be with our grandson), now it's thinking time. So I lean back again and fall asleep. Solitude without attention is somnolence.

Attention: Suspended Thought

Dimnet can help us consider the discipline of attention: "Attention is less a gift than a habit, and the knowledge of this ought to encourage those who wish to live inside their own souls."[12] If Dimnet is correct, attention is cultivated: it is the "elimination, one after the other, or by one sweeping effort of all images foreign to a train of thought."[13] But Dimnet is surely wrong about one thing: "On the whole, concentration is a natural state which can easily be reproduced by simple methods."[14] Simone Weil has it right: "Attention is an effort, the greatest of all efforts perhaps."[15] But effort is not necessarily rewarded.

What is *attention* anyway? Eviatar Zerubavel gives us a technical definition from the standpoint of cognitive sociology: "*Attending* something in a focused manner entails mentally disengaging it (as a 'figure') from its surrounding 'ground,' which we essentially ignore."[16] Take playing chess. In one background are the goal and the rules of the game, in another the physical environment of the particular game being played—the board itself, the opponent, the people looking on, the stir in the room. But the focus of the stellar chess player is on this game now: the position of the men, the speculated

---

We may ignore, but we can nowhere evade, the presence of God.
The world is crowded with him. He walks everywhere *incognito*. And the
***incognito* is not always hard to penetrate. The real labour**
is to remember, to attend. In fact, to come awake.
Still more, to remain awake.

C. S. LEWIS
Letters to Malcolm: Chiefly on Prayer

---

strategy of the opponent, the possibilities for the next move, the implications of each of the possibilities that might lead to a capture of the opponent's king. The slant of light illuminating the board is not noticed. Such is attention when one knows to what one should attend.

But what is attention when one is thinking and does not know yet just to what one should attend? The advice of *The Art of Prayer* is spot on, as the British would say:

> When you undertake some special endeavor, do not concentrate your attention and heart on it, but look upon it as something secondary; and by entire surrender to God open yourself up to God's grace, like a vessel laid out ready to receive it. Whoever finds grace finds it by means of faith and zeal, says St. Gregory of Sinai, and not by zeal alone. . . . Our efforts will be rightly directed so long as we preserve self-abasement, contrition, fear of God, devotion to him, and the realisation of our dependence on divine help.[17]

The psychology of attention is complex. One can't simply pay attention by paying attention to paying attention. It does no good to "work" at paying attention, Weil says. Rather one must first stimulate desire:

The intelligence can only be led by desire. For there to be desire, there must be pleasure and joy in the work. The intelligence only grows and bears fruit in joy. The joy of learning is as indispensable in study as breathing is in running.[18]

The desire to know, to think clearly, to pursue ideas back to their sources and on toward their implications: this desire should not be

---

An intellectual must always be ready to think, that is, to take in a part of the truth conveyed to him by the universe, and prepared for him, at such and such a turning point, by Providence.

A .   G .   S E R T I L L A N G E S
The Intellectual Life

---

difficult for one who is called by God to think. For those who do not experience such a call, I can only say, pay attention to the call you do have. That call will of necessity require some kind of thinking— instrumental thinking if no other. Hang in there: the spark of desire for more than useful ideas may strike when you least expect it. Fan it into flames by following some of the suggestions in this chapter.

In any case, when effort fails and attention cannot be maintained, take a break:

Twenty minutes of concentrated, untired attention is infinitely better than three hours of the kind of frowning application that leads us to say with a sense of duty done: "I have worked well!" . . . If we concentrate with this attention, a quarter of an hour of attention is better than a great many good works.[19]

Weil's paradoxical description of concentrated attention is worth examining:

Attention consists of suspending our thought, leaving it detached, empty, and ready to be penetrated by the object; it means holding in our minds, within reach of this thought, but on a lower level and not in contact with it, the diverse knowledge we have acquired which we are forced to make use of. Our thought should be in relation to all particular and already formulated thoughts, as a man on a mountain

who as he looks forward, sees also below him, without actually looking at them, a great many forests and plains. Above all our thought
should be empty, waiting, not seeking anything, but ready to receive
in its naked truth the object that is to penetrate it.[20]

Notice: one abandons thought to think. Really? Yes and no. One
abandons one's preconceived ideas. One lets the reality penetrate
the mind. Attention lets the Word of Reality speak the word of knowl-

---

The great enemy of knowledge is our indolence.
A. G. SERTILLANGES
The Intellectual Life

---

edge. John Henry Newman noted this characteristic of genuine
knowledge.[21] Genuine knowledge is knowledge of the real, not simply a "notional" view but a grasp of that which is.[22]

In silence one can also abandon thought simply to be in the presence of God. Anthony Bloom describes this well:

> Inner silence is absence of any sort of inward stirring of thought or
> emotion, but it is complete alertness, openness to God. . . . As long as
> the soul is not still there can be no vision, but when stillness has
> brought us into the presence of God, then another sort of silence,
> much more absolute, intervenes: the silence of a soul that is not only
> still and recollected but which is overawed in the act of worship by
> God's presence; a silence in which, as Julian of Norwich puts it,
> "prayer oneth the soul to God."[23]

Our age is an age of words only. Commentary upon commentary,
intertextuality—one text understood only as what can be made of
earlier texts embodied and replicated in the present text. Postmodernism has penetrated our consciousness in such a way that all of
us—Christians too—are beginning to think that words are all there
is. Everything is notional; nothing is real. All reality is socially and
linguistically constructed reality. "I like to think of God as . . ." we
hear people say. To which the reply surely must be "I wonder what
God thinks of you thinking of him that way."

This rampant nominalism must stop. And one way to make it stop is to pay attention to what is there. Francis Schaeffer, with remarkable prescience, insisted that we worship "the God who is there," not just the god(s) of our imaginations, the god(s) solely constructed of our human words. When students would propose that there was no reality to anything one talked about, when they proclaimed that everything was just words, words, words, Schaeffer would suggest that a pot of tea be poured on their heads.

We worship the God who is Word. As Karl Barth has said, "Between God and the Word he speaks there is no difference."[24] God is Father: "If we call God Father, it is because he is Father in reality. . . . The divine truth precedes and grounds the human truth."[25] And Earl Palmer writes:

> We discover who Aslan is by what he does. Here C. S. Lewis is like Karl Barth. Barth says you cannot divide the words of Jesus from the work of Jesus. They're inseparable. We finally meet and know Aslan by what he does in creation. . . . What ultimate good says and does in the Bible is now the same thing in Lewis's theology. Redemption by Aslan is not a word spoken but an event that occurs.[26]

Being is prior to knowing, more important than knowing.[27] It is more important, for example, to be who you should be than to know that you are what you should be. Of course it is better to know what you are, for the knowledge of what you are is a part of what you are. If you are ignorant of what you are, you are less than if you know; if you are mistaken about what you are, you are not fully what you ought to be. But if you are what God wants you to be, it is still better to be unaware or mistaken about who you are than to be aware of what you ought to be but are not.[28]

Evelyn Underhill has put the matter well:

> We mostly spend [our scattered lives] conjugating three verbs: to Want, to Have, and to Do. Craving, clutching, and fussing, on the material, political, social, emotional, intellectual—even on the religious—plane, we are kept in perpetual unrest: forgetting that none of

these verbs have any ultimate significance, except so far as they are transcended by and included in, the fundamental verb, to Be: and that Being, not wanting, having and doing, is the essence of a spiritual life.[29]

In an age in which postmodernism's reduction of the real to a linguistic construct (whose disciplines are hermeneutics and semiology) and modernism's emphasis on knowing rather than being (whose disciplines are epistemology and natural science), it is time to reassert the biblical priority of being (whose disciplines are theology and ontology or metaphysics). It may have a misplaced signified, a perverted meaning, but the slogan used to enlist people in the military has the words right: "Be all that you can be." With the military, cannon fodder may be all one becomes, but with God, ah, that's another matter. God simply is: "I AM WHO I AM" (Ex 3:14). This He Who Is is the Word, the One Who Speaks, and when he speaks, he says, "Jesus Christ!" To pay attention first to God in Christ: this is the first task of the Christian thinker.

> Too many of us are thinking these days as the world thinks because we do not begin our thinking by thinking about God. Only by paying attention to God will we experience the ecstasy that leads to wisdom. Prayer is that work, that disciplined attentiveness.[30]

As we look at what attention involves, we see how quickly we move from considering a psychological function to contemplating the final ontological reality, God himself.

There is no exaggeration here. Attending to reality is finally attending to God—the final reality and the author of all created reality. But, says Sertillanges, truth is everywhere.

> The important thing for the man of truth is to understand that truth is everywhere, and that he is allowing a continuous stream to pass by him which might set his soul working. . . . Truth is commoner than articles of furniture. It cries out in the streets and does not turn its back on us when we turn our backs on it. Ideas emerge from facts; they also emerge from conversations, chance occurrences, theatres,

visits, strolls, the most ordinary books. Everything holds treasures, because everything is in everything, and a few laws of life and of nature govern all the rest.[31]

Oddly enough, we can learn to pay attention to the ordinary from Japanese haiku. Matsuo Basho's haiku, for example, have a marvelous way of getting us to attend to a reality—the thingishness of things—that we often miss.

Lateral Thinking

Through Simone Weil I have already introduced lateral thinking without the term itself.[32] That term comes from Edward De Bono. "Lateral thinking," he writes, "seeks to get away from the patterns that are leading one in a definite direction and to move sideways by reforming the patterns."[33] De Bono outlines four features of lateral thinking:

1. Recognition of dominant or polarizing ideas.
2. The search for different ways of looking at things.
3. A relaxing of the rigid control of vertical thinking.
4. The use of chance.[34]

First, as De Bono indicates, you reflect on and list the relevant assumptions that undergird your current approach to solving a problem—intellectual or technical. Let's say the problem is to find oil. You assume that it might be beneath the surface of a particular field. So you drill five hundred feet but find no oil. So you drill another hundred and another hundred and another, and still no oil.

Second, take a fresh look at the problem. Maybe your original assumption was wrong. Maybe you were drilling in the wrong field. Move the rig. Try again.

Third, think of other possibilities for supplying what is needed or reassessing the need itself. Maybe oil is not the best form of energy to develop. Maybe you should be working on solar power or hydropower or tidal power or . . . Maybe you should be figuring out how to get along without any form of power, based on the natural order. Maybe you should be learning to live without power. Maybe, maybe, maybe . . .

Fourth, let chance and circumstance provide alternate solutions. That's how radioactivity was discovered. Chance let a photographic

---

An active mind is constantly in search of some truth which for it, at the moment, is the representation of that integral truth to which it has vowed its service. The intelligence is like a child, whose lips never cease their *why*.

A. G. SERTILLANGES
The Intellectual Life

---

plate be exposed to invisible radiation. The Curies figured that out, and the rest, as they say, is history—nuclear power, which, of course, is itself a mixed blessing.

De Bono suggests "true purposeless play without design and direction," brainstorming and browsing "a general store, or an exhibition or even [sic] a library."[35] I would add the stimulus of travel, museums, foreign cultures, foreign friends.

Prayer: The Downy Wing of Truth

You may well have already noted that the conditions of solitude and attention mimic the requirements for prayer. Indeed they do. And prayer is a requisite for thinking well. There is not only prayer itself—the placing of oneself at the disposal of God with the expectation that he will not only hear and answer but make his presence known—but the content of one's prayer, which includes petition for creativity, clarity and insight. "Prayer is a disciplined dedication to paying attention," write John Westerhoff III and John Eusden. "Without the singleminded attentiveness of prayer we will rarely hear anything worth repeating or catch a vision worth asking anyone else to gaze upon."[36]

The openness to God that constitutes the background of prayer is the same as the openness to Truth and truths that constitutes the background to thinking well. Prayer may go beyond thought as one is lifted into the presence of God, but it is never contrary to thought, and the ecstasy that upon occasion accompanies the encounter with God lies close to the ecstasy in which some of our best thinking occurs:

> Every intellectual work begins by a moment of ecstasy; only in the second place does the talent of arrangement, the technique of transitions, connection of ideas, construction, come into play. Now, what is the ecstasy but a flight upwards, away from self, a forgetting to live our own poor life, in order that the object of our delight may live in our thought and in our heart?[37]

Coming to know—or being newly and forcefully reminded—of the truth of God in Christ automatically works on our emotions and will. The intellect begets emotions: "The Incarnation of Christ leads up to Communion, in which the Body, Blood, Soul, and Divinity of the Saviour are not separated," writes Sertillanges. And this we know. But then he adds, "The quasi-incarnation of God in being, of eternal Truth in every separate instance of the truth should also lead

---

You will never find interior solitude unless you make some conscious effort to deliver yourself from the desires and the cares and the interests of an existence in time and in the world.

THOMAS MERTON
Seeds of Contemplation

---

up to a heavenly ecstasy, instead of our absent-minded investigations, and commonplace feelings of admiration."[38]

Do we miss this in our thinking? If so, it is because we are not taking seriously the serious business we are about when we think well. As Sertillanges says:

> Profound work consists in this: to let the truth sink into one, to be quietly submerged by it, to lose oneself in it, not to think that one is thinking, nor that one exists, nor that anything in the world exists but truth itself. This is the blessed state of ecstasy.[39]

When truth takes possession of you and slips her downy wing beneath your soul to lift it gently and harmoniously in upward flight, that is the moment to rise with her and to float, as long as she supports you in the upper air.[40]

Who says thinking is cold and the thinker an iceberg? If the thinker is an iceberg, then let the *Titanic* loaded with the seekers of materialistic comfort and thoughtless ecstasy beware!

Insight from Heidegger

Heidegger distinguishes between *calculative thinking* and *meditative thinking*. The former makes up the bulk of human thinking; it operates to make ordinary life possible, of course, but also when we are engaged in problem-solving of almost any kind from mathematical to theological. "Calculative thinking computes. . . . [It races] from one project to the next," Heidegger writes.[41] And John Anderson comments, "In calculative thinking we deal with our things in our terms for our advantage"[42]

Heidegger worries that "the approaching tide of technological revolution in the atomic age could so captivate, bewitch, dazzle, and beguile man that calculative thinking may someday come to be accepted and practiced *as the only* way of thinking."[43] Today, decades later, we might agree that Heidegger's prophecy has been fulfilled, if it were not for the hydra head of postmodernism which, while not replacing calculative thinking with Heideggerdian meditative thinking, has confined it to the harder sciences and replaced it elsewhere with sheer hedonistic, emotive thoughtlessness in the secular world and New Age spiritobabble in religion.

In meditative thinking, on the other hand, the thinker is intimately linked with Being itself. Here the thinker is most unified not only with his or her own nature but with Being itself. Anderson comments, "In meditative thinking, man opens to Being and resolves for its disclosure. Such a resolve is not an exercise of subjective human powers; rather, it is taking a stand which reveals Being, a kind of dwelling in Being."[44]

Reading this as a Christian, one might think that Heidegger is giving to traditional Christian mysticism a philosophic foundation or, perhaps, seeing in Christian mysticism a philosophic dimension not developed in Christian theology. That, I imagine, could be true if by Being Heidegger meant what Christians mean by God. It is, in fact, this possible meaning that has encouraged me to skim the surface, if not penetrate the mysteries, of Heidegger's work.

Take his comments on meditative thinking as *waiting*. Heidegger says that in thinking we can either wait *for* or we can wait *upon*. In the former we know what we are looking for; in the latter we do not. Waiting *for* reminds us of Psalm 105:4: "Look to the LORD and his strength; seek his face always." We seem to know what we are looking for—the face of God. But when we realize that we have little idea of "the face of God," waiting *for* his face may be much more like waiting *upon* his face. In any case, it should remind us that whatever we receive from such waiting we receive as a gift: "In waiting [upon] we leave open what we are waiting for."[45] What we are then given is Being itself, in Christian terms God. Such thinking, Heidegger reminds us, is thanking.[46]

The notion of being given God, of having him encounter us in a gift of himself, is very attractive to spiritually sensitive Christians. It was so, certainly, to Moses. "Show me your glory," he asks, almost demands, of God (Ex 33:18). And after protecting Moses in a cleft of a rock, God passes by him, showing him only his back, for God's face will be too much for Moses to behold. Moses dare not be given what he demands.

This gives us pause. Red flags pop up as we read that in meditative thinking the thinker "dwells in Being." Yes, we recall the apostle Paul's frequent mention of being "in Christ." There is a sense in which a Christian—thinker or not—can and sometimes does seem to "dwell in Being." But there is also a severe limitation to what "dwelling in Being" can involve for a Christian. With Heidegger "dwelling in Being" involves the ontological collapse of the distinction between the human and the divine.[47] Not only is such "dwelling in Being" not possible, but the very thought that it could be is a temptation. The notion that one can, has or does "dwell in Being" in that sense is the ultimate illusion.

Still, given a Christian twist, Heidegger's description of meditative thinking seems apt. Heidegger, for example, goes on to describe meditative thinking as *releasement*. The thinker is released from attachment to representational thinking (the sort that fuels calculative thinking) and released to Being, that in which he comes to dwell. And since Being itself is "an openness" or "an opening," there is an openness to "what is beyond the horizon of such knowing."[48] There is, in short, more to reality, to Being, in both the sense of God himself and the "being" of his creation. Being is a mystery too deep to be exhausted by calculative thinking, meditative thinking or both together, in parallel or in series.

Barriers to Intensive Thinking

A host of demonlike barriers rise to keep us from thinking or from attending to our thought as best we might. Most of them are obvious, but naming the beasts will help us, if not slay them, corral and control them.

Noise. In our society, noise is almost ubiquitous. It would be nice if my house sat on a wooded lot and a trout stream ran through my backyard. It doesn't. The Burlington mainline between Chicago and San Francisco: that's what runs through it. But with closed windows, no problem.

Silence, let alone solitude, in most office situations is impossible. But the demon noise must be cast out. So how? A host of suggestions pop into mind. Escape to a library, especially a college or university library. Sad to say, students these days do not use them much except just before final exams. That still leaves over forty weeks for thinkers. Find a quiet room in a church. Commandeer a table in the back of a restaurant in the middle of the afternoon. Try a park. Some are hardly used during the day, especially when schools are in session.

I have been fortunate to live a few minutes from Morton Arboretum—a quiet forest with little-used trails and lots of benches and downed logs to sit on. It would be even quieter if it were not so near a busy interstate, but eight months of the year I can be in my car with the windows up. It's not a tomb, but it's quiet enough. And my walks after solitary sitting do marvels for my sense of life.

Sertillanges gives a vision of a perfect place to think:

> Ah, if one could work in the heart of nature, one's window open on a fair landscape, so placed that when one was tired one could enjoy a few minutes in the green country; or if one's thought was at a standstill ask a suggestion from the mountains, from the company of trees and clouds, from the passing animals, instead of painfully enduring one's dull mood—I am sure that the work produced would be doubled, and that it would be far more attractive, far more human.[49]

Compared with other places in the world, the places of human affairs, the abode of the thinker is a "place of stillness."

HANNAH ARENDT
"For Martin Heidegger's Eightieth Birthday"

Sound romantic? Of course. Still, with a little imagination and a few trials and errors, almost everyone can exorcise the demon noise. And it must be exorcised.

Interruptions. Try hard to secure blocks of time that will not normally be interrupted. Let the answering machine respond to phone calls. If certain people constantly interrupt you, help them understand that this time is precious—sacred. Ask them if they would bother you if they thought you were praying or worshiping. Well, thinking is honoring God with your mind. Thinking is worshiping.

Background music. Turn it off! Doris Lessing gives us good reason for this radical suggestion:

> What is happening now, as we know, is that everybody is assaulted by music from every direction and young people might spend years of their lives with very loud, thumping music going straight into their brains. Now music is in fact extremely potent, very emotional, and

has always been used by governments and authority to affect people. It has been used by churches very efficiently. It is used by governments when they send young men off to war hoping that they will be so tanked up on music that they won't mind being killed. Shamans use it all the time either for healing or for ecstatic purposes. People know that music is very powerful, but apparently we never acknowledge that. Has anyone who is responsible, teachers or educators, thought that this music could in fact damage a young person? It is my belief that a whole generation of young people, and soon it will be more than one, are emotionally disturbed because of music, which goes straight into the emotional centers.[50]

It is only in silence that the mind can function without being carried along, albeit subconsciously, by the often profoundly moving subtheme of whatever music is playing.

Society. Yes, one can think in groups. But it takes lots of orchestration. For the most part, thinking is a private matter. Let people know that you need solitude and silence. Insist that this be given you. Par-

---

**The man who locks himself up in private with his own selfishness
has put himself into a position where the evil within him will either
possess him like a devil or drive him out of his head.
That is why it is dangerous to go into solitude merely because you
happen to like to be alone.**

THOMAS MERTON
Seeds of Contemplation

---

ents, work this out with your children, wives with your husbands, husbands with your wives, lovers with your lovers.

"Society life is fatal to study. Display and dissipation of mind are mortal enemies of thought. When one thinks of a man of genius, one does not imagine him dining out."[51] Well, Sertillanges the Dominican is not a good authority on dining out. I can't imagine anyone, especially a man of genius, not dining out. I love to dine out not just for the food but for the community. Community, especially a community of faith, has a vital role to play in thought, but it's usually a secondary, critical role. Others call us to account for what we have thought. They have not thought of it in the first place. But what better time and place for calm communal reflection than conversation over after-dinner coffee?

Bias and preconceived ideas. Sometimes as thinkers we are deeply committed to notions that are actually false or at least highly misleading. We are fundamentally wrong, but without some sort of challenge we can't imagine that we are wrong. I have discussed above (pp. 135-36) one way of countering this—lateral thinking.

Another way is deliberately to argue against your own deep commitments, try to prove to yourself—if only for the sake of clarity and studied conviction—that you are mistaken. How well can you counter the argument? If you can't readily do so, perhaps you need to change your mind. I say *perhaps* because generally *perhaps* is a caution worth raising whenever one is considering changing one's mind, especially with regard to fundamental notions.

Rejection. There is a distinct possibility that what you think will be rejected. You may be rejected as well. There is a cost to count: thinking may leave you with fewer friends. There usually is a tradeoff; you will acquire new friends. Still, a sacrifice may need to be made. As Sertillanges says:

> When the world does not like you it takes its revenge on you; if it happens to like you, it takes its revenge still by corrupting you. Your only resource is to work far from the world, as indifferent to its judgments as you are ready to serve it. It is perhaps best if it rejects you and thus obliges you to fall back on yourself, to grow interiorly, to watch yourself, to deepen yourself. These benefits are in the measure in which we rise above self-interest, that is, in which interest centers on the one thing necessary.[52]

Tiredness. Get enough sleep. Don't expect to think well if you don't. Sure, have coffee or soft drinks handy, but don't rely on them to overcome lack of sleep. Exercise is a great stimulant to good thinking—not eighteen holes of golf or even nine, but a brisk walk for half an hour may do wonders.

Anxiety. This is a tough one. Some of our thinking involves deep existential issues. Some has to be done under pressure, especially that which relates directly to our employment. Little can be done about that. But everything safe (no special relaxation drugs) and possible (no relaxing of our genuine responsibilities) should be done to relieve the pressure.

Jesus said it best, of course: "Do not worry about tomorrow, for tomorrow will worry about itself. Each day has enough trouble of its own" (Mt 6:34).

The best atmosphere for creative thought is expectant tension. You don't know. You want to know. You have some handle on how to know. You go for it. Desire fuels excitement.

Tips: Oil for Mental Machinery

I will close this chapter with a few tips—oil for the mental machinery—I've found helpful in keeping the mind running.

Notebook. It seems a little thing, but it is important. Ideas come and go. Sometimes they have to be caught on the fly. Sertillanges has this to say:

> Very often, gleams of light come in a few minutes' sleeplessness, in a second perhaps; you must fix them. To entrust them to the relaxed brain is like writing on water; there is every chance that on the morrow there will be no slightest trace of any happening.[53]

Pascal testifies to the same thing: "Chance gives thoughts, and chance takes them away: no art to conserve them nor to acquire them. Thought escapes, I wish to write it; I write instead that it has escaped me."[54]

Well, some thoughts can be caught on the fly. Sertillanges's advice is on target:

> Have at hand a notebook or a box of slips. Make a note without waking up too fully, without turning on the light, if possible, then fall back into the shadows. To get the thought thus off your mind will perhaps help your sleep instead of disturbing it. If you say, I will remember, I *will* remember, that determination is more likely to interfere with your rest

than a quick jotting. Remember that sleep is a relaxing of the will.[55]

Snatching ideas from the darkness. Ideas often come at odd times. Perhaps the most productive time for ideas for me is early in the morning. *Nota bene:* I got the basic idea for this book while shaving. It became conscious to me first as the content of the first paragraph of chapter one. The second paragraph fell in place as my wife and I drove to our offices at InterVarsity Press.

I understand the philosophical quest as an existential experience centered in the core of the human mind, a spontaneous, urgent inescapable stirring of a person's innermost life.

JOSEF PIEPER
In Defense of Philosophy

Falling asleep and waking up are special times for the brain, apparently. Ideas, images, stories float up, surface; the mind becomes aware. Interesting, often fresh insights take shape. Capture the insights of these moments. Keep a pad ready.

Making a resolution. Here is a tip I have never used. But Sertillanges is right about so many things, I will close this chapter by quoting the final two paragraphs from *The Intellectual Life:*

> Having made up your mind to pay the price, engrave your firm resolution, today if you have not done so already, on the tablets of your heart. I advise you also to write it down in black and white, legibly, and to put the words before your eyes. When you sit down to work, and after praying, you will renew your resolve each day. You will take care to note down especially what is least natural and most necessary for you—for you, as you are. If need be, you will repeat the formula aloud, so that your word may be more explicitly given to yourself. Then add, and repeat with full certainty: "If you do that, you will bear fruit and you will attain what you desire. Adieu."[56]

VIII

THINKING
BY READING

When *Augustine was struggling emotionally with whether he* would be able to abandon his profligate lifestyle, he was reading the apostles with his friend Alypius. Augustine left Alypius and threw himself under a fig tree. "Suddenly I heard a voice from a house nearby—perhaps a voice of some boy or girl, I do not know—singing over and over again, 'Pick it up and read, pick it up and read.' "[1] What happened to Augustine when he read Romans 13:13-14 was sudden, dramatic and radically life-changing: "I had no wish to read further, nor was there need. No sooner had I reached the end of this verse than the light of certainty flooded my heart and all dark shades of doubt fled away."[2]

Augustine's conversion—his shift from merely believing that the Christian faith is true to being willing to act on that belief—changed history. It is hard to think of what the future of the Western world would have been without this great saint and doctor of the church.

To be sure, all reading is not of this type. Even to Augustine it happened only once. But reading that directs our thinking can have mighty power to change our lives. Thinking by reading thrusts in two possible directions: In the first reading directs thinking; in the second thinking directs reading.[3]

Reading Directs Thinking

In its primary thrust reading directs thinking. One begins to read, giving over one's mind to the text and the primary meanings that begin to form. When the text of a great work fully engages the mind, when the reader is so completely occupied with what is being read, the world of the text becomes the world of the reader.

All sense of clock time disappears. The mind of the reader becomes one with the mind not of the author—for the author has long since launched the text to go out on its own—but of the text.[4] At least that is what it feels like, for the reader is no longer feeling anything but what is prompted by the work. Of course the reader's imagination is active; of course what is imagined is different for each reader (or better, we assume it is different; we can't show this in any way, because the furniture of each mind is beyond the access

---

A Book
He ate and drank the precious words,
His spirit grew robust;
He knew no more that he was poor,
Nor that his frame was dust.
He danced along the dingy days,
And this bequest of wings
Was but a book. What liberty
A loosened spirit brings!

EMILY DICKINSON
Poems

---

of any other mind); of course the present realization of this mind is just that—the present realization. One is living in the text. It's a world set apart from the nonreading world of ordinary experience.

When people say that they love Jane Austen's *Northanger Abbey* or John Le Carré's *The Spy Who Came In from the Cold* or Agatha Christie's *What Mrs. McGillicuddy Saw*, they are talking about their private experience of being taken out of the ebb and flow of their mind into the ebb and flow of another mind. Unlike most of their waking moments, in the best of novels they are caught up in an ordered flow of thought: fascination and delight, expectation and fulfillment, intrigue and realization, a sequence of sensations ever leading them on through the text. Some books are, as critics say, page-turners.

Consider the opening paragraphs of *Zen and the Art of Motorcycle Maintenance*. Robert Pirsig paints a word picture that puts me on the motorcycle with the narrator and his young son. I am riding, I am seeing the redwing blackbirds scurry up from the hedges along the blue highway, as William Least Heat Moon calls the secondary roads that interlace Minnesota.

Granted, part of my mental picture draws on my own experience as a schoolboy walking the two and a half miles to and from my country schoolhouse. From the thickets by the empty gravel road, not always passable by car after a heavy rain, hosts of redwing blackbirds suddenly spring up. Bright dashes of red lit by the sun give character to the small, dark clouds of whirring wings. Crows have loud voices, a distinctive *caw . . (silence) . . caw* that could be heard all over the pastures; I don't remember much about the twitter of the blackbirds. But the flash of their beating wings seems as vivid in my memory as the oft-repeated experience itself.

Reading is directing thinking, but it cannot prevent the mind from automatically making links with elements of its own past. Alberto Manguel notes this: "Beyond the literal sense and the liter-

---

**He [her father] buys me many Books—
but begs me not to read them—
because he fears they joggle the Mind.**

EMILY DICKINSON

---

ary meaning, the text we read acquires the projection of our own experience, the shadow, as it were, of who we are."[5] And so I cast my mental shadow on the text, and the text itself becomes not dimmer but brighter. David Lyle Jeffrey, reflecting on St. Augustine, thus comments: "Reading, like writing, is unavoidably a contextualized activity, both synchronically and diachronically. We read *now*, others have read previously, and every text we read is a creature of the past—even if of a relatively recent past."[6]

So while my mind is captured by the world of Pirsig's novel, it is also being fed from the deep wells of memory. Yet as soon as the memory is revived, it recedes into the background. As I read the next sentence, I am again back with the narrator and his son, riding across Minnesota, South Dakota, Montana—hours and hours of miles and miles. Dark clouds appear on the horizon, deluge me with

---

**In the reading room . . . they are inside the books.
They move sometimes within the pages, like sleepers
turning over between two dreams.**

RAINER MARIA RILKE

---

my own memories of storms on the plains, memories of riding horseback while three thunderclouds rising rapidly from the western horizon pursue me as if they were the Father, Son and Holy Ghost. And so it goes, as Kurt Vonnegut puts it. Reading is imagining with my mind in tandem with the mind of the speaker of the text. I am his and he is mine.

Here's the rub. When reading directs thinking, one's mind is absorbed in the mind of another. Many have certainly thought that dangerous. Censorship stems from the fear that the innocent reader's mind will be manipulated, that reading the wrong books will be hazardous to one's own intellectual, religious or spiritual health—or the political health of the ruling party! In the South slaves were typically forbidden to learn to read; in the medieval church an Index of off-limit books was prepared and has been revised over the years.[7] The last edition was in 1948, but it has not been reprinted since 1966.[8] The attempts—usually unsuccessful—by worried parents to remove supposedly harmful books (such as *Catcher in the Rye* or *Huckleberry Finn*) from school and public libraries are legion. Removing offending books or even locking libraries won't help much. "Lock up your libraries if you like," wrote Virginia Woolf, "but there is no gate, no lock, no bolt that you can set upon the freedom of my mind."[9]

The foundational insight leading to censorship is, however, correct. Books are dangerous, because the best of them are powerful conveyers of ideas, points of view, moral persuasion and the like. It

---

**People can lose their lives in Libraries.
They ought to be warned.**

SAUL BELLOW

---

is their value, their ability to do that, that leads to their danger. Sertillanges, usually a firm guide, stumbles here:

> What you must principally cut down is the less solid and serious kind of reading. There must be no question at all of poisoning the mind with novels. One from time to time, if you like, as a recreation and not to neglect some literary glory, but that is a concession; for the greater number of novels upset the mind without refreshing it; they disturb and confuse one's thoughts.[10]

Sven Birkerts goes much further in capturing the penetrating character of books. The best, he says, "haunt from a distance":

> When a work compels immersion, it often also has the power to haunt from a distance. I don't just mean that my thoughts now and again turn to the characters and the story—though this, of course, happens all the time—I mean that I feel haunted. Just as in a true "haunt" one feels the presence of spirits from the "other side," so do I sometimes feel the life of the book suddenly invade me. As if, for a moment, that life were my life—the walls come down. This only happens with certain books, but when it does it feels like a gift, a freely given transcendence of self. I'm not sure how to explain it, except maybe as a kind of cognitive "short circuit," where some triggering association suddenly shunts my readerly preoccupations, my subliminal self, into the foreground. Or as a consequence of some linguistic alchemy that brings a portion of the book so vividly to life that it overwhelms the affective centers.[11]

So books are indeed dangerous. But so is every good gift from God, and books are one of his greatest. One book especially.

The one book to which we need not fear to yield up our very lives is the Bible. And it is one of the great contributions of the Christian

---

**If you read to read and not to have read,
then your reading is serene, restful, and disinterested.**

FATHER BERNARDO OLIVERA
"Lectio Vere Divina"

---

tradition to emphasize this book and to encourage its being read both intensively and extensively. If any reading ever should direct thinking, it is the reading of the Bible.

Lectio Divina

Though as a form of reading directed by thinking, *lectio divina* is ancient, I became aware of it only a few years ago. How I missed knowing about something so central to Bible reading is an embarrassment to me but not much of a mystery. Being raised Protestant and learning literary criticism through secular education and Bible study through InterVarsity Christian Fellowship explain most of it. For rich as it is in emphasis on techniques of reading that enhance understanding, the heritage of Protestantism and InterVarsity is almost exclusively rational and pragmatic. Three basic questions are asked of any text: (1) What does it say? (2) What does it mean (first and foremost a question of the intentional meaning of the author to the first intended readers or listeners)? (3) What does it signify for my life (i.e., what does God want me to learn and to apply from this?)?[12]

Granted, applying this approach with rigor (and I was encouraged to do so) often resulted in responses that were more than purely intellectual. Having read Scripture, having understood it basically if not deeply, and having obeyed its implications for my life often led to a sorrow for my sins, repentance, prayers of thanksgiving for God's forgiveness, gasps of awe of God and his creation, worship both private and corporate. Bible reading under this general pattern has been life-giving, even life-transforming. I thank God for the instruction I have been given in this way of reading Scripture. Moreover, I have sometimes practiced *lectio divina* without knowing I was doing so. The Word of God, read carefully, works its own way with the reader. But *lectio divina,* a form of reading that was developed in the Middle Ages, pays attention to the ways it does so and enhances the likelihood that readers will really hear God speak to them. During a sabbatical from lecturing and editing I learned what it was first by doing it and then by reading about it.

So what is *lectio divina?* And how does such reading direct thinking? As I understand it now, *lectio divina* is not a technique but an atmosphere or ambience within which specific actions take place. As

---

With regard to literature, a fundamental observation must be made here: in the Middle Ages, as an antiquity, they read usually, not as today, principally with the eyes, but with the lips, pronouncing what they saw, and with the ears, listening to the words pronounced, hearing what is called the "voice of the pages." It is a real acoustical reading; *legere* means at the same time *audire*. . . . Most frequently, when *legere* and *lectio* are used without further explanation, they mean an activity which, like chant and writing, requires the participation of the whole body and the whole mind.

JEAN LECLERCQ
The Love of Learning and the Desire for God

Michael Casey says in his excellent study *Sacred Reading,* "Reading the Scriptures is the opposite of self-programming or any kind of brain washing. It is allowing God to speak to our hearts, minds, and consciences."[13]

We will take up the elements of *lectio divina* one by one, but they should not be seen as necessarily sequential. Eugene Peterson calls them "moments that continuously recur and are repeated in random order."[14] Note, by the way, that what immediately follows here is my understanding of *lectio divina* lifted from its medieval and monastic context. We will look at relevant aspects of its medieval context afterward.

Preparation. First, have a plan of reading that will extend over a period of time, say, a month or more. There are no better or worse passages of Scripture to read. The selection, however, should not be haphazard. Following an entire book of the Bible is one excellent way of ordering one's reading. Another is following readings laid out by a guide such as *A Guide to Prayer for Ministers and Other Servants*, by Rueben P. Job and Norman Shawchuck. This is the book my spiritual director gave me at the beginning of my recent sabbatical. Job and Shawchuck select one psalm to be read every day over the period of a week.[15] That exposes the reader to fifty-two psalms every year and promotes a deep engagement with each one. It is deep engagement that is the key to *lectio divina.*

Second, it is necessary to find a place where one can regularly be alone and quiet. I have been fortunate to have a room in my home where this is possible. Still I find the Morton Arboretum, a ten-minute drive from home, more conducive to silent attention. In cold or inclement weather the car itself is my prayer chamber.

Third, it is vital to approach one's reading in the right spirit. Prayer, a specific verbal request to God that he meet us as we read his Word, is, while not strictly demanded, very helpful in putting us in a receptive frame of mind. This receptivity will increase during the reading itself. No specific words are best, but here is a prayer suggested by Job and Shawchuck:

> Lord, you have promised to meet those who seek your face. Come now and reveal your presence to me as I make myself present to you. In the name of Jesus Christ my Lord. Amen.[16]

This prayer acknowledges that our reading of Scripture is not for sheer intellecual information but for an encounter with God. Michael Casey puts it well:

> What are we doing in *lectio divina?* We are seeking God. We are hoping to hear God's voice and do God's will, but we are operating in search mode. We have not yet attained the goal of our ambition, and so our reading is fundamentally an expression of our desire for God.[17]

With heart and mind attuned to listening, we are ready to begin.

Attentive reading aloud. We start with simple, quiet, attentive, reading of the Scripture itself. Following the practice of the Benedictine monks, we read the passage aloud.

Even though we are alone, mouthing the Word of God makes it and the author, the Spirit of God, seem more present. This is, of course, no mere *seeming*. The Holy Spirit is always present. It is we

---

For the ancients, to meditate is to read a text and to learn it "by heart" in the fullest sense of this expression, that is with one's whole being: with the body, since the mouth pronounced it, with the memory which fixes it, with the intelligence which understands its meaning, and with the will which desires to put it into practice.

JEAN LECLERCQ
The Love of Learning and the Desire for God

---

who are absent from him. Oral reading helps us realize in ourselves the reality that is already present. Jean LeClercq says,

> [*Lectio divina* results in] a muscular memory of the words pronounced and an aural memory of the words heard. The *meditatio* consists in applying oneself with attention to this exercise in total memorization; it is, therefore, inseparable from the *lectio*. It is what inscribes, so to speak, the sacred text in the body and the soul. . . . To meditate is to attach oneself closely to the sentence being recited and weigh all its words in order to sound the depths of their full meaning.[18]

The medieval monks read aloud even in the presence of others.[19] "Of John of Gorze," for example, "it was claimed that the murmur

---

Lectio divina is a technique of prayer and a guide to living. It is a means of descending to the level of the heart and finding God.

MICHAEL CASEY
Sacred Reading

---

of his lips pronouncing the Psalms resembled the buzzing of a bee."[20] When we are alone, the lips should not, I think, just buzz but pronounce the words with the meaning and force they would have if read aloud publicly. We then hear "the voice of the pages."[21]

There is indeed a public form of *lectio divina* still practiced in Benedictine monasteries. In some monasteries at each meal the monks eat in silence while one of them reads aloud. The whole psalter is read in this manner every three or four weeks. In other monasteries the psalter is read and sung during the offices. During meals spiritual classics or even secular books are read.

Attentive rereading in silence. Rereading is a vital part of any good reading; it is especially so for *lectio divina.* "The word of God is living and active" (Heb 4:12). When we are exposed to it through attentive reading, it penetrates our minds and reaches our hearts and the seat of our will. Our reading itself does not transform us, but God transforms us through our reading. This is my testimony and the testimony of all who read Scripture to meet God.

Rereading means, first and foremost, reading over and over again. But then this further reading sets up the circumstance for exegesis, careful attention to the *literal* meaning (that is, the meaning intended by the text or, better, writer of the text). "Exegesis," says Eugene Peterson, "is the furthest thing from pedantry; exegesis is an

---

Our sacred reading is not merely for the moment. We read for with the purpose of evangelizing our lives—just as we eat not only to enjoy the taste of food but to nourish our whole body and generate sufficient energy to implement our ambitions.

MICHAEL CASEY
Sacred Reading

---

act of love."[22] For this all the tools of reading I was taught through InterVarsity should be brought to bear by all of us who have been able to read this far in the present book. And all the more technical tools of the profession of biblical scholarship should be used by those trained to do so.

What had been missing from my own reading of Scripture was the rereading. I was encouraged by my spiritual director to conduct my daily devotions through Job and Shawchuck's guide. But there was too little Scripture to read, too few attendant readings from the great saints of the past. I was committed to spend an hour in devotions, but I could usually do everything suggested in thirty minutes.[23] I am not a fast reader, but still my director's instructions forced me to slow down, to leave empty spaces for quiet alone, for wakeful attending to the text or to the woods or den where I sat. I am convinced it was in the slowing down, the letting happen what would happen, that God worked changes I had hoped for for years—patience, openness, renewed, even new, willingness to obey what I was reading, rejuvenation of mind and heart.

During this hour I deliberately did not ask the typical InterVarsity questions of Scripture. I just let the words work their work. The hour consisted of simple attention to the text, the reading of excerpts from spiritual writing, and prayer. Nothing more. The more intellectual aspects of attentive reading, what passes for exegesis when I study the Bible, were left for other times in the day.

When the time for intense exegesis comes, however, one must not think of it as divorced from *lectio divina*. As Gordon Fee passionately proclaims: "Hence the aim of exegesis: to produce in our lives and the lives of others true Spirituality, in which God's people live in fel-

---

**Lectio Divina is not, as a rule, immediately gratifying. It is an active
and passive process of long duration. One does not reap the day following
the sowing! The worm is not instantly transformed into a butterfly!**

FATHER BERNARDO OLIVERA
"Lectio Vere Divina"

---

lowship with the eternal and living God, and thus in keeping with God's own purposes in the world."[24]

Entering the world of the text. This is Eugene Peterson's phrase describing *meditatio*. While we are attentively reading, both as we absorb the text and as we study it, we can be entering its world. If we are just interested in a "scholarly"—abstract and impersonal— understanding, we may get only that. But that will not be exegesis in the mode of *lectio divina*. As Peterson says, "This text is God-revealing—God creating, God saving, God blessing."[25] We lay ourselves open to the text to hear God in it, first listening and hearing God speaking to those original listeners, then hearing the Word for us.

> Meditation is the prayerful employ of the imagination in order to become empathetic with the text. . . . Meditation is not intrusion, it is rumination—letting the images and stories of the entire revelation penetrate our understanding. By meditation we make ourselves at home and conversant with everyone in the story, entering the place where Moses and Elijah and Jesus converse together.[26]

As we enter the world of the text and hear God speak to us, we automatically have much to say in response. But our first response is more likely to be surprise and awe, the dawning of recognition, the seeing of things not seen before, the hearing of God as if he were present, which, of course, he is. Prayer then comes as naturally as "the force that through the green fuse drives the flower."[27]

Prayer. Indeed, prayer is a major element of *lectio divina*. In fact, Casey calls *lectio divina* itself "a technique of prayer and a guide to living."[28] It is in prayer that we "answer" the Word of the Lord. And we can do so in any words that fit our honest response. We need not erupt immediately in words of praise. We may have much too much

---

**If you allow yourself to be possessed by the Word,
you will hear even his silence.**

**FATHER BERNARDO OLIVERA
"Lectio Vere Divina"**

---

other stuff on our minds. God's word is a "double-edged sword," piercing us, dividing our Old Man from the New. Words of frustration and anger are often the best words because they are the truest.

Here the psalms are our very best guide. These are the answering words of Israel—its prophets, kings and people—to their own *lectio divina*, their experience of the holy God. There is, I think, no emotion not present somewhere in this glorious collection of poems, prayers and exclamations of worship. Read them with attention; pray them with understanding.

> Prayer is the way we work our way out of the comfortable but cramped world of self into the self-denying but spacious world of God. It's getting rid of self so that we can be all soul.[29]

Reentering the ordinary world. With prayer we are already in the ordinary world, the ordinary world illuminated by the world of God's Word, finally the only world there really is. Prayer builds the bridge we cross each time we contemplate the Word of God and are returning to the workaday world.

The proof of the *lectio divina* actually comes at this point, for it is how we live in the ordinary world that demonstrates whether we have lived in the world of Scripture. Hearing demands doing. Being,

---

We read the Gospels not merely to get a picture or an idea of Christ but to enter in and pass through the words of revelation to establish, by faith, a vital contact with the Christ Who dwells in our souls as God.

THOMAS MERTON
Seeds of Contemplation

---

as we saw in chapter five, is the state in which our knowledge is embodied in action, our belief in obedience, our theory in practice. As Peterson says, "For most of us it takes years and years to exchange our dream world for the real world of grace and mercy, sacrifice and love, freedom and joy."[30] But many of us *have* years and years. May whatever years we have left be characterized by *lectio divina!*

The Medieval Context of *Lectio Divina*

The above description of *lectio divina* is not strictly historically accurate. In the Middle Ages academic exegesis, which I have included as a part of *lectio divina*, was considered not only as distinct from it but in contrast to it. In fact the whole intellectual enterprise that I have been encouraging throughout the present book is often rejected by the strongest proponents of *lectio divina*.[31]

In his excellent study of medieval monasticism, Jean LeClercq contrasts the monastic and the scholastic subcultures. The former emphasized interior spirituality, prayer, the search for the presence of God in the cloistered community. The latter emphasized academic study, disputation, acquisition and employment of secular literature and philosophy as aids to biblical interpretation, Christian theology and the search for truth in general. A broad range of contrasts can be charted:[32]

Monastic	Scholastic
cloisters	schools
lectio divina	*disputatio* or *quaestio*
spirituality	learning
interior	exterior
contemplative	active
love	knowledge
sanctity	disputation
Scripture	philosophy
experience	reflection
admiration	speculation

Teachers in each of these modes can also contrasted:

Monastic	Scholastic
St. Benedict	Abelard
St. Bernard of Clairvaux	Peter Lombard
St. Francis of Assisi	St. Thomas Aquinas

If the monastic subculture tended inevitably toward a world-denying asceticism, the scholastic subculture affirmed the world, especially its intellectual preoccupations.[33] Jacques Le Goff describes the scholastic method. First came a scholastic *lectio:*

The basic scholarly method began with a commentary on a text, the *lectio*, an in-depth study beginning with a grammatical analysis which gave the letter (*littera*), advancing to a logical explanation which provided the meaning (*sensus*), and ending in an exegesis which revealed the text's content of knowledge and thought (*sententia*).[34]

Then came commentary, debate and dialectics:

But commentary gave birth to debate. Dialectics enabled one to go beyond the understanding of a text to deal with the issues it raised, and diminished it in the quest for truth. An entire problematics replaced the exegesis. Following the appropriate procedures, the *lectio* developed into the *questio*.[35]

As a result we have the birth of the modern "university intellectual":

The university intellectual was born from the moment he "questioned" the text which then became only a support, when from a passive reader he became an active questioner. The master was no longer an exegete, but a thinker. He gave his solutions, he created. His conclusion of the *questio*, the *determinatio*, was the fruit of his thought.[36]

Le Goff concludes: "Thus scholasticism developed, the mistress of rigorous, stimulating, original thought with obedience to the laws of reason."[37] In biblical study, therefore, the complete vulnerable openness to the text, the totally receptive attitude is replaced perhaps not quite yet by doubt or suspicion but by an intellectual curiosity seemingly divorced from personal participation. As Le Goff describes the situation, abstraction was a major temptation of the thirteenth-century intellectual: "Attached to abstract and eternal truths, the scholastic risked losing contact with history, with what was contingent, moving, evolving. . . . One of the great pitfalls of the scholastic intellectuals was that of forming an intellectual technocracy."[38]

Here thinking directs reading—with a vengeance. When that attitude dominates, cold scholasticism (of the worst sort) sets in. The reader becomes an intellectual not to the glory of God but to the glory of human reason and, eventually, to the glory only of himself or herself.

We see again: the more things change, the more things stay the same. In the Middle Ages the state of Bible reading—and the intellectual realm in general—parallels our own. It is rare for us to see heart and mind brought together. Thus we marvel at the towering figure of St. Augustine, who struggled his entire life with the pull of the intellect and the pull of the heart but over his lifetime represents as well as anyone ever has the integration of the two.

Of course if the thesis of the present book is true, heart and mind are already together in the way God has made us. Whatever we are, we are in fact one in our *being*. This was the point of chapter five: *being* brings together knowing and doing, belief and obedience, for good or ill; for Christ's disciples it will be eventually for good, of course. For when time shall be no more, our perfected, glorified *being* will bring together in a perfect harmony a perfected heart, mind, body—and every other aspect of our human nature. We would do well to get on with it now. Such integration is a major aspect of seeking first the kingdom of God. Here we embody the final phrase of our definition of the Christian intellectual: our intellectual life is lived to the glory of God.

Lectio divina, I conclude, is the most perfect form of reading directing thinking. But it is only to the Bible that we dare give such undivided loyalty. Reading anything other than the Bible demands that thinking direct reading.

When the mind wanders, when it is brought up short by being taken where it doesn't want to go, when suddenly it shouts no or says *Slow down, let me think about this,* the thrust of reading reverses: our mind must direct our reading. This time Sertillanges gives the wise word:

> A book is a signal, a stimulant, a helper, an initiator—it is not a substitute and it is not a chain. Our thought must be what we ourselves are. When we read, our masters must not be a goal for us, but a starting

point. A book is not a cradle, not a tomb. Physically we are born young and we die old; intellectually, because of the heritage of the ages, "we are born old; we must try to die young."[39]

So how should thinking direct reading?

Thinking Directs Reading

While thinking directing our reading is not the normal mode of reading, it is the normal mode of studying. It is the mode of the scholar mining a text for its information, perspective, reflection, insight, but always alert for what it wants, what fits with its own thoughts, what does not and why not. Thus the scholar, the serious student, usually moves slowly through the text, underlining the passages that seem significant, making notes in the margins, writing minidissertations at the heads and feet of pages, interacting with the

---

The critic argues his distance from and towards the text. To "criticize" means to perceive at a distance at the order of remove most appropriate to clarity to *placement* (F. R. Leavis's term), to communicable intelligibility. The motion of criticism is one of "stepping back from" in exactly the sense in which one steps back from a painting on a wall in order to perceive it better. But the good critic makes the motion conscious to himself and to his public. He details his recessional steps so as to make the resultant distance, the elucidative measure, the prescriptive perspective—distance entails "angle" of vision—explicit, responsible, and therefore open to argument.

GEORGE STEINER
"Critic/Reader"

---

ideas, the metaphors, parrying the thrust of the writer—in short, not just making the book his or her own but drafting his or her own "book." The presumption is that that book will be a better one than the one being read because it incorporates the "truth" of that book minus the errors it has made, plus the new formulations that the mind arrives at in the process of directing the reading.

The point is this: We read not just to listen to what others say and to discern what others think; we read to learn the truth, to know and participate in the reality God has created, not the reality only imagined by others. Failing to proceed toward this goal of reading puts us among those Josef Pieper dubs "that modern type of philosopher who, instead of discussing his true subject, reality, discusses something quite different, the philosophies."[40] Pieper aptly quotes Aquinas: "The study of philosophy does not mean to learn what others have thought but to learn what is the truth of things."[41]

How does thinking direct reading toward truth as the end? Let's take the book I am reading as I write this chapter. I read the opening

---

The dualities which I have cited, and many others implicit in the argument, can best be subsumed under one fundamental antithesis. The critical act is a function of the ego in a condition of will. . . . Consciously or not, the critic competes with the text or art before him.

GEORGE STEINER
"Critic/Reader"

---

lines of *Ruined by Reading: A Life in Books,* a book whose author, Lynne Sharon Schwartz, I do not ever remember reading before. I bought the book, first, because I am studying reading in order to write this chapter. Moreover, I was intrigued by its title. Then too

---

The critic is *judge* of the text. The reader is *servant* to the text.

GEORGE STEINER
"Critic/Reader"

---

there was the blurb on the front cover: "Ferociously intelligent . . . Schwartz obeys the laws of gravity, but also manages to float free of the Earth at times, and almost to fly." I've never heard of the blurb writer either: Fredrick Busch in the *Los Angeles Times Book Review.* But its verbal nonsense reminds me of the howlers in the descriptions of Scriabin's preludes that I just read a few days ago.

> *Etude No. 6, in A major,* is a willowy study in sixths, a tone-picture of sylphlike cavorting in a lush meadow. *Etude No. 7, in B-flat minor,*

marked *presto, tenebreso, agitato,* is a sinister chariot ride across the dried out bed of the river Styx.[42]

When I read this blurb to my son, a pianist and, like me, a lover of Scriabin's piano music, he shook with laughter. I joined him. On a clear day blurbs like Busch's could fog up a clear mind. Still, Schwartz's title alone was enough to free my pocket of the list price minus 10 percent.

So how does *Ruined by Reading* begin?

> Rarely does the daily paper move me to re-examine my life. But a recent *New York Times* piece quoted a Chinese scholar whose "belief in Buddhism . . . has curbed his appetite for books." Mr. Cha says, "To read more is a handicap. It is better to keep your own mind free and to not let thinking of others interfere with your own free thinking." I clipped his statement and placed it on the bedside table, next to a pile of books I was reading or planned to read or thought I ought to read.[43]

As soon as my mind catches the drift of these opening lines, it disengages from the text and is off on its own. *Shades of Zen,* I think: *there is no mindset more different from mine.*

One must be an inventor to read well. . . . There is then creative reading as well as creative writing. When the mind is braced by labor and invention, the page of whatever book we read becomes luminous with manifold allusion. Every sentence is doubly significant, and the sense of our author is as broad as the world.

R A L P H   W A L D O   E M E R S O N
"The American Scholar"

I pause, take out a pen and draw a line in the margin. This could be a quotation to head the chapter in the book I am writing: it states the reverse of my opinion. Then as I read on, other thoughts, triggered by the text but not totally in line with it, rise to consciousness. I underline phrases and clauses, like "readers are thrill-seekers" and "only language thrills," ideas that are congenial but overstated. *I am reading a journalist, not a philosopher,* I think. But that's okay. All things in their season, and I am on vacation, a time for journalists and not philosophers, at least not Kant or Hegel—maybe Plato or Kierkegaard, and certainly Pascal, who always delights while he teaches.

By the end of the vacation, the book was read, passages were underlined, notes were jotted in the margin, the book was stacked among many others to be reexamined when I continued writing the chapter—which, by the way, was eight months later. Many other books had intervened, and I read them with, I trust, the attention they deserved. Some of them were stacked up waiting for me to choose one or two to further illustrate how thinking directs reading.

**Therefore, in reading profane authors, the admirable light of truth
displayed in them should remind us, that the human mind,
however much fallen and perverted from its original integrity, is still
adorned and invested with admirable gifts from its Creator.**

JOHN CALVIN
Institutes of the Christian Religion

I will get to some of them a bit later in this chapter. But first I want to describe a deliberate program in which thinking directs reading.

Reading Worldviewishly

Since the early 1960s I have been reading books in terms of the worldview they primarily embody. Doing so is a way of discovering how an individual author views the world or what philosophy the characters and stories he or she writes display, promote or vilify. In other words, it is one deliberate way in which thinking can direct reading. Reading worldviewishly involves not just a vicarious experiential participation in the world of the book but a standing over against the work and asking the critical questions that must be considered as a reader takes on the task of searching for the truth. I have already written at length about worldviews in *The Universe Next Door* and about reading worldviewishly in *How to Read Slowly*.[44] So my remarks here will be relatively brief.

Essentially, reading worldviewishly involves reading with an eye for the explicit and implicit way the work answers the following questions.[45]

1. What is prime or fundamental, reality—the really real? Possible answers include God, or the gods, or the material cosmos.

2. What is the nature of external reality, that is, the world around us? For example, is the world created or autonomous; chaotic or orderly; matter or spirit; part of us or apart from us?

3. What is a human being? Answers include a highly complex machine, a sleeping god, a person made in the image of God, a "naked ape."

4. What happens to a person at death? Do people become permanently extinct, or are they transformed to a higher state or reincarnated?

5. Why is it possible to know anything at all? Sample answers include the idea that we are made in the image of an all-knowing God or that consciousness and rationality developed under the contingencies of survival in a long process of evolution.

6. How do we know what is right and wrong? Are people made in the image of a God whose character is good; or are moral laws written into the nature of the universe; or are right and wrong determined by human choice alone or what feels good; or is the moral sense simply developed under the aegis of cultural or physical survival?

7. What is the meaning, if any, of human history? To realize the purposes of God or the gods, to make a paradise on earth, to prepare a people for a life in community with a loving and holy God?

Not every essay, novel or poem contains the answers to these basic questions, but the more significant the work that one is reading, the more all of these questions will be addressed or answers to them assumed. Moreover, the more intently our reading directs our thinking, the more easily we can answer these questions later when our thinking directs our reading.

Take Saul Bellow's novel *Mr. Sammler's Planet*. An initial reading reveals that its 284-page paperback version is crammed with reflection on every one of the seven questions. A second, more reflective reading brings to the fore numerous passages that are relevant to an examination of the worldview of the novel. Here I will explore only three of these.

But first a quick overview of the novel. The story concentrates on a few days in the life of Artur Sammler, who is seventy years old. The time is *now* (1969 is the original publication date), the place New

---

Every person carries in his head a mental model of the world—
a subjective representation of external reality. . . . The mental model
must be seen not as a static library of images, but as a living entity,
tightly charged with energy and activity.

ALVIN TOFFLER
Future Shock

York City. Around Sammler are a handful of skillfully portrayed minor characters, each of whom takes Sammler as a point of reference. The plot is slight, for the action follows Sammler as he comes to terms with the impending death of his nephew, Dr. Elya Gruner, a man about his own age. The story ends with Dr. Gruner's death and Sammler's final prayer for Gruner's soul.

The real heart of the story, however, is not what Sammler does in these few days; it is who Sammler is and what he has done (much of this comes by means of stream-of-consciousness flashback as Sammler thinks about himself, his past, and his present New York circle of friends and relatives). In themes and symbols the novel is incredibly rich and complex, for Sammler's life is an analogue of seventy years of Jewish consciousness. Born in Poland, Sammler worked as an intellectual journalist, living in England during the 1920s and 1930s and supplying articles for Warsaw papers. Back on the Continent in 1940, he, his wife and other Polish Jews were lined up, shot and left for dead in a mass grave. But Sammler escaped, hid in a tomb and was eventually brought by Dr. Gruner to New York as a displaced person. Here he and his daughter, who had escaped earlier, continue to live supported by the generosity of his nephew and benefactor.

None of this is, of course, known when one begins to read the novel for the first time. Rather, the details of character and past action unfold gradually till, when we reflect on the whole novel, the shape of Mr. Sammler's world becomes clear and his worldview lies open to examination. Then, as we further examine the opening paragraph and our thinking directs our reading, we see what we could not see the first time through, a rich prelude of description and ideas that opens the great symphony of the novel. Here is that opening paragraph:

> Shortly after dawn, or what would have been dawn in a normal sky, Mr. Artur Sammler with his bushy eye took in the books and papers of his West Side bedroom and suspected strongly that they were the wrong books, the wrong papers. In a way it did not matter much to a man of seventy-plus, and at leisure. You had to be a crank to insist on being right. Being right was largely a matter of explanations. Intellectual man had become an explaining creature. Fathers to children, wives to husbands, lecturers to listeners, experts to laymen, man to his own soul, explained. The roots of this, the causes of the other, the source of events, the history, the structure, the reasons why. For the most part, in one ear and out the other. The soul wanted what it wanted. It had its own natural knowledge. It sat unhappily on superstructures of explanation, poor bird, not knowing which way to fly.[46]

Later in the novel we learn why the opening line mentions "one eye," why Sammler is reflecting on his books, why he is concerned about the inability of explanations to adequately address the vital issues of life. Even at a first reading we may suspect that the novel will have a lot to do with how Sammler "views" the world and his relation to it. On the following page we learn that Sammler now has only one good eye and that he protects it by always wearing "smoked glasses." And a few pages later the theme of "explanations" resurfaces:

> Arguments! Explanations! thought Sammler. All will explain everything to all, until the next, the new common version is ready. This ver-

sion, a residue of what people for a century or so say to one another, will be like the old, a fiction. More elements of reality perhaps will be incorporated in the new version. But the important consideration was that life should recover its plentitude, its normal turgidity. . . . Alert to the peril and disgrace of explanations, he was himself no mean explainer.[47]

Here Sammler's historicism, his notion that worldviews come and go as time passes, emerges. Truth changes with time. What one wants is stability, a stability possible only with the soul, not with the intellect. Yet because he himself is "no mean explainer," he is always on the alert for the explanation of why there is no explanation. To satisfy his longing he turns to the Christian mystic Meister Eckhart, who leads him toward reality by meditation on the Sermon on the Mount.[48] By the end of the novel, Sammler has made his peace with reality. His prayer over the body of his dead nephew ends with the consolation that Dr. Gruner had "met the terms of his contract. The terms which, in his inmost heart, each man knows. As I know mine. As all know. For that is the truth of it—that we all know, God, that we know, that we know, we know, we know."[49]

I have quoted only three of many passages that deal primarily with only one worldview question: Why is it possible to know anything at all? There are many, many more on this issue. Moreover, with further analysis it is easily possible to answer all six of the other questions. In very short form, here are the answers: (1) Ultimate reality is a personal God; (2) the external universe is his creation; (3) human beings are his creatures free to act, responsible for their actions, and finally accomplishing the goal God has for them; (4) there would seem to be some life after death, but its details are obscure; (5) one knows finally not by the intellect but by an intuitive grasp of reality; (6) God is the foundation of good, but good and evil are so mixed in this world that no person can extricate one from the other; (7) history is proceeding along a path toward an end known by God but not humans.

It is, of course, a travesty to say that *Mr. Sammler's Planet* is "about" this worldview. No, the novel is "about" Mr. Sammler and his internal world set in the external world of the middle years of the twentieth century. The worldview we examine is its backdrop, a very important one to the novel and to our own search for "explanations"—true ones! For as our thinking directs our reading, we face ourselves as well as the novel. Is Sammler right about "explanations"? Is Meister Eckhart to be preferred over, say, Thomas Aquinas? Is truth utterly historical, finally almost fictional? Do we all *know* what our contract with reality is? Do we all fulfill that contract? In reflective reading, dozens of questions related to the other worldview questions also pose themselves. Is Sammler's God the God who is there? Is reality as turgid as Sammler thinks?

Good novels, good poems, deserve careful reading. *Mr. Sammler's Planet* is a good novel. Great novels, great poems, deserve *very* careful reading. By their power to create a "secondary" world in which, if we pay attention, we can enter and live, they provide for us windows on the "primary" world of everyday experience. We do not give ourselves to them in *lectio divina* as we do to Scripture, but we give ourselves to them in *lectio secularae*, knowing that when we emerge from the worlds of literature created by God's creatures, we emerge as God's creatures in the world God has created. His is the real world he has made knowable to us in part by enabling us to enter the world as understood by others. Thinking by reading therefore includes both reading directed by thinking and thinking directed by reading. The second completes the task begun by the first.

Ones Among the Many

Which books—or magazines or journals—to read is always an issue. When I first visit a great bookstore—say Eighth Day Books in Wichita or Blackwell's in Oxford—I am exhilarated. So many of the books I have always yearned to read are there. What a joy! But before I leave, a mild form of despair creeps over me. I will never have the time.

So choice, choice. I feel like Sartre's existential *l'homme* (I can't use the English equivalent, can I?): a useless passion condemned to be free. Then I perk up. *Ah! but there's heaven!* Heaven will be a place that fulfills my longest longings. Either I will have time to read all the books that I have not read before or I will receive something even better. This, of course, does not relieve me from the task of choosing. So how to choose?

When Søren Kierkegaard moved to his own lodgings, his father paid his considerable debts, the largest of which was the equivalent of $794 "for books and bookbinding."

W A L T E R   L O W R I E
A Short Life of Kierkegaard

Some principles are obvious: read the best books available on the topics that are most relevant to your call in life. Here Sertillanges is again helpful:

> Read only those books in which leading ideas are expressed at first hand. These are not very numerous. Books repeat one another, water one another down, or contradict one another, and that too is a kind of repetition. On examination we find that discoveries in thought are rare. The old stock or rather the permanent stock of ideas is best.[50]

Sertillanges is rather romantic in his description of what these best books give us, but his idealism is energizing:

> Contact with writers of genius procures us the immediate advantage of lifting us to a higher plane; by their superiority alone they confer a benefit on us even before teaching us anything. They set the tone for us; they accustom us to the air of the mountain tops. We were moving in a lower region; they bring us at one stroke into their own atmosphere. In that world of lofty thought, the face of truth seems to be unveiled; beauty shines forth; the fact that we follow and understand these seers makes us reflect that we are after all of the same race, that the universal Soul is in us, the Soul of souls, the Spirit to whom we have only to adapt ourselves in order to burst into divine speech,

since at the source of all inspiration, always prophetic, there is "God, the first and supreme author of all one writes."[51]

Then, too, Sertillanges's caveat is always to be remembered:

> The source of knowledge is not in books, it is in reality, and in our thought. . . . It is not what a writer says that is of first importance to us; the important thing is what *is*. . . . In any case the principal profit from reading, at least from reading great works, is not the acquisition of scattered truths, it is in the increase of our wisdom.[52]

The first principle is really the only genuine principle. Reading beyond what we know is relevant to our task in life is impossible to program. We do not know what we do not know. That especially includes the content of all those books that remain in the bookstore or library when we leave.

It may be best here to argue from biography, dangerous as that is. So I will return to the stack of books that I brought along for a week overlooking Lake Michigan. I will also return to my description written as I then reflected on my choice. One book is John Henry Newman's *Apologia pro Vita Sua*, a lot more interesting than its title suggests but nonetheless with its nineteenth-century manner proba-

---

Publishers, as everyone knows, fear nothing so much as the publication of a book, since, according to Lem's Law, "No one reads; if someone does read, he doesn't understand; if he understands, he immediately forgets"—owing to general lack of time, the oversupply of books, and the perfection of advertising.

STANISLAW LEM
One Human Minute

---

bly not one I will read at the lakeside. I am more likely to dip into his *Prayers, Verses and Devotions* or Newman scholar Ian Ker's *Newman on Being a Christian*.

Another book I have brought is Kathleen Norris's *The Cloister Walk*, a sheer delight with clear, quiet, reflective prose designed to set my mind in paths of righteousness—not a mean feat to accomplish with my mind. When I arrive, I'm about halfway through, savoring it, hoping it will last longer than her earlier and, to my mind, better book *Dakota*. That one scared up so many redwing blackbirds, I longed for it not to stop. But it did, and I went on to *The Cloister Walk*, where I now tread with more measured steps. If Norris cloys—heaven forfend!—I can switch to Henri J. M. Nouwen's *Creative Ministry*, a book the cover blurb describes as being "about the lifestyle of every Christian."

There is, of course, the book I started last week, Richard Weaver's *Ideas Have Consequences*, a work well known by people with an interest in cultural history. Its first sentence sets the tone: "This is another book about the dissolution of the West."[53] That's a rather forbidding

---

Altogether, I think we ought to read only books that bite and sting us. If the book we are reading doesn't shake us awake like a blow on the skull, why bother reading in the first place? So that it can make us happy, as you put it? Good God, we'd be just as happy if we had no books at all; books that make us happy we could, in a pinch, also write ourselves. What we need are books that hit us like a most painful misfortune, like the death of someone we loved more than we love ourselves, that make us feel as though we had been banished to the woods, far from any human presence, like a suicide. A book must be the axe for the frozen sea within us. That is what I believe.

FRANZ KAFKA
letter to Oskar Polak

---

opening, and the first two chapters do not belie the opening salvo. I may not read much of this book on vacation. Still, one day soon I will take it up again.

I also have with me two novels by Shusako Endo: his first, *The Girl I Left Behind*, and one of his more recent, *Deep River*, which I understand is a late-in-life rewrite of the first. I will read them in order, this week or whenever. Endo is a Japanese novelist, a Christian who struggles in most of his novels with the presence of Christianity in a country that bogs down in fever swamps any attempt to spread the gospel.

I have read most of his novels, but *Silence* was the first—an excruciating story of Christianity's initial entrance into Japan in the late sixteenth and early seventeenth centuries. *Silence* twists the mind and the emotions as it poses the most painful dilemma any Christian could ever face. A missionary priest who oversees the spiritual lives of young Japanese converts is arrested and imprisoned by the shogun for propagating the faith. He is not tortured physically, but his Japanese parishioners are. They are hung upside-down over a dung pit; their wrists are slightly cut, and they slowly bleed to death. To secure their release, all the priest has to do is step on an icon of Jesus, thus recanting his faith. What is he to do?

He could, one might suggest, pretend to recant, step on the icon and get the Christians released. But if he does that, the Christians will not realize he has dissembled for their benefit and will lose their faith. There seems to be no right answer. To read the novel is for one's mind to track with the priest's mind as he considers and makes his decision. It is also to step outside this mind, view the dilemma for oneself and, if you are like me, not to find a solution—rational or otherwise. I will not now reveal how it comes out. That would be to deny my readers of being Endo's best readers, the naive who lose their naiveté about a major evil perpetrated in the past.

But I do recommend, and that most highly, that shortly after reading *Silence* one reads Endo's *The Samurai*, a novel dealing with the same period in Japanese history. Here a priest and a Buddhist samurai warrior discover on the nerve endings of their own lives that a God who suffers as the crucified Christ is the only kind of God worthy of worship, even if it means being martyred.

All of Endo's novels are psychological studies in character seen in the framework of the Christian worldview. So as I contemplate reading *The Girl I Left Behind* and *Deep River*, I do so with anticipation of both sorts of thinking by reading: my reading directing my thinking and my thinking directing my reading.

What is one to make of the disparate set of books I have brought to the lakeside? Does it suggest utter randomness? Is Lynne Sharon Schwartz describing my lack of plan as well as hers?

> I vacillate lengthily, and foolishly, over whether to read at random.... I like to cling to the John Cage-ish principle that if randomness determines the universe it might as well determine my reading too, to impose order is to strain against the nature of things. Randomness continuing for long enough will yield its own pattern or allow a pattern to emerge organically, incurably, from within—or so I hope.[54]

Indeed my selection looks random. But it's not. There are among the selections four books that relate directly to my current research project; two to spiritual formation, which after many years of faith I am now pursuing more intently; one to an ongoing interest in cultural critique; and two novels by one of my favorite writers (novels are always a ready relief from direct exposition). The stack of books appears a motley lot only to one who doesn't know me.

Yet there is a randomness too. Many books relevant to my interests lie unread, stacked on my desk or stuffed into the shelves behind my reading desk—the kind of books Schwartz describes as "books I was reading or planned to read or thought I ought to read."[55] Why did I choose these particular books? Maybe Schwartz is right: from randomness will emerge an inner pattern.

Certainly the random breaks into my book-buying habits. It is rare for me to leave a bookstore without a new book, often one I had no notion of buying when I entered. Books don't exactly fall from the shelves and into my hands, but they attract my attention by their cover, their title, their author, their subject, and I am a goner. Book reading is often random as well. Books I buy on a sudden whim or "discovery" I sometimes read before ones that have been long awaiting my attention. But the newer books just as often get put on the waiting shelves and, when space gets too tight, get moved to some relevant shelf in my library. There is bit of mystery about my reading, a mystery with a source. As Schwartz says, "Perhaps randomness is not so much random after all. Perhaps at every stage what we read is what we are, or what we are becoming."[56]

There is often a paradoxical meandering order to thinking by reading: one thought, one book, leads to another and that to another and another till where one began is almost forgotten. There is a stream of consciousness that flows willy-nilly, and unless we take care, we are borne along like rafts on a subconscious river that has little explicit direction.

When we wake from reverie, then, it's time for intention to take charge, time for thinking to direct reading till it can safely abandon itself to the reading and be borne along by a strong-willed text to a destination we don't mind getting to.

A Reader's Prayer

Reading takes us places. Sometimes they are places we should not go. Sometimes they put us so in touch with reality that we can only pause in silent reverence. In any case, we can do no better than to yield our reading to the direction of our Lord, as does John Baillie:

> Leave me not, O gracious Presence, in such hours as I may to-day devote to the reading of books or of newspapers. Guide my mind to choose the right books and, having chosen them, to read them in the right way. When I read for profit, grant that all I read may lead me nearer to thyself. When I read for recreation, grant that what I read may not lead me away from thee. Let all my reading refresh my mind that I may more eagerly seek after whatsoever things are pure and fair and true.[57]

JESUS
THE
REASONER

*T*he gasps could be heard in any part of the room. The speaker had just said, "Jesus is the smartest man who ever lived."

Few, if any, of his listeners were prepared to hear that. But having heard it, having thought about it, having tried to find some way reasonably to disagree, no one was prepared to object. The stunned audience remained alert for some time.

Jesus the Intellectual

I was in that audience several years ago.[1] I was surprised then. Now I think I know why. If the speaker had said, "Jesus is the wisest man that ever lived," we would all have thought, *Of course, ho-hum,* and continued our half-attentive reverie. We all held advanced academic degrees. We were all InterVarsity staff, engaged in ministry to graduate students in major universities around the country. We affirmed and knew Jesus not just as Savior and Lord but as indeed the wisest man who ever lived. Over and over we had read his words in the

Gospels, we had seen them come true in our own lives. We could answer the critics who said, "Jesus never lived or never said such words or didn't mean what we take them to mean." And we would more than agree with the idea of Jesus being the wisest man who ever lived. But those were not the words we heard.

We heard Dallas Willard, professor of philosophy at the University of Southern California say, "Jesus is the smartest man who ever lived."[2]

So why were we so surprised? The main reason is not hard to see. The fact is, most of us did not think of Jesus as smart.[3] University people are smart—professors first, of course, especially at the prestige universities; then graduate students at these universities; then undergraduate students at the same universities—and so on down the intellectual pecking order. Scientists are smart, especially those who have won the Nobel Prize for their astounding insights into the workings of the universe. Einstein! Need I say more? A few writers are smart, like Dostoevsky or Shakespeare or Dante. A few independent intellectuals are smart: philosophers like Socrates, Descartes or Pascal. But Jesus was not smart. He was wise.

Wisdom does imply some smarts, of course, but not necessarily university-level brains. My grandfather was wise. St. Francis of Assisi was wise. And Jesus was wise. But the "smartest" man who ever lived? It doesn't sound quite right.

I don't know what went through the shocked minds of my colleagues. I do know what I realized: Dallas Willard, himself both a smart and a wise man, was smart enough to see what the rest of us had not: Jesus was the smartest man who ever lived.

Think about this along with me. What do we believe about Jesus? We believe that Jesus is the incarnation of the Logos, the Word of God (Jn 1:1-4). The Logos was in the beginning; he was with God in the beginning; he was God in the beginning. As the Logos, he was and is and always has been the ultimate, final intelligence of the Godhead, not just in the abstract but in the reality of Being itself/himself. As the preincarnate Logos he engaged in the process of creating not just the universe but "all things . . . things in heaven and earth, visible and invisible" (Col 1:16). He exhaustively knew the universe then and he knows it now. In him are hidden "all the treasures of wisdom and knowledge" (Col 2:3). As the Logos, Jesus is the ultimate foundation for human knowing—not just the knowing of Christians or the knowledge of God but the knowing of everything by everyone. When the world is judged, it will be by the One whose standard is perfect justice (Acts 17:31). With none of this are we surprised. This is traditional Christian theology.

But look what it implies. If Jesus is the incarnation of the Logos, how could he be anything other than the smartest man who ever lived?

Yes, but . . . I hear you think (now there's a trick!). We've forgotten about the incarnate part of the Incarnation. The Word became flesh. He left his home in glory and became Jesus. He took on human nature. He laid aside his omniscience for a time. The apostle Paul said that Jesus did not think equality with God a thing to be grasped (Phil 2:6). And Jesus himself told his disciples that he did not know when he was returning to earth (Mt 34:36). Only the Father in heaven knew that. Jesus asked people real questions, seemingly to elicit from them knowledge he did not have. "Who touched me?" he asked a crowd around him (Lk 8:45). When Jesus was on earth, he did not display a scientific knowledge of the world.

Perhaps the most poignant indication of Jesus' full humanity lies in his prayer in the Garden of Gethsemane. C. S. Lewis points this out:

> It is clear from many of His sayings that Our Lord had long foreseen His death. He knew what conduct such as His, in a world such as we have made of this, must inevitably lead to. But it is clear that this knowledge must somehow have been withdrawn from Him before He prayed in Gethsemane. He could not, with whatever reservation about the Father's will, have prayed that the cup might pass and simultaneously known that it would not. This is both a logical and a psychological impossibility. . . . But for this last (and erroneous) hope against hope, and the consequent tumult of the soul, the sweat of

blood, perhaps He would not have been very Man.[4]

Jesus was indeed very Man, but man in the concrete, not just the ideal Platonic form. He was a man of his time. In what we know of what he said, he did not even refer to the chief philosophers who had preceded him in Greece or the holy men of India. True, he knew, or at least thought he knew, the Hebrew Scriptures better than the scholars of his time. We certainly agree that he knew God personally in the profoundest depths of his being—intellectually and emotion-

---

We need to understand that Jesus is a *thinker*, that this is not a dirty word but an essential work, and that his other attributes do not preclude thought, but only insure that he is certainly the greatest thinker of the human race: "the most intelligent person who ever lived on earth." He constantly uses the power of logical insight to enable people to come to the truth about themselves and about God from the inside of their own heart and mind.

DALLAS WILLARD
"Jesus the Logician"

---

ally. A good case could be made that he is the cleverest and best storyteller who ever lived. And certainly one can find no moral philosopher, wise person or oracle who could top him in ethical insight. But he didn't know everything. He didn't show us he was the smartest man who ever lived—did he?

Let's do some imagining. Let's imagine that the incarnation occurred not a couple of thousand years ago. Let's say it occurred in 1972. We will have to grant some big, finally ungrantable assumptions. We will have to grant that the 1970s world he was born into is like the one some of us experienced—a world of nations, of advanced technology, of universities, of increasing democratic individualism. It is highly unlikely that such a world as ours would exist today if Jesus had not been born when he was. Christianity has had much to do with the intellectual background to the development of science and technology and the development of democratic individualism. But let's leave that aside for a moment and consider how the Logos become flesh might have behaved if he were twenty-eight years old in A.D. 2000.

Let's imagine that he was born into a nondescript American family above the poverty level. (Jesus actually was born to such a Hebrew family; on the basis of Mark 6:3 we see him as a practicing carpenter.) Let's say he grew up as a normal American boy, went to high school, then college and graduate school. Now at twenty-eight he is about to finish an advanced academic degree. (Remember, his own contemporary townspeople thought of him as a normal adult, the grown son of a local family [Lk 4:16-30].)

Now imagine Jesus as a graduate student in physics—the Word of God in the flesh doing math, reading academic journals, contemplating the formation of the cosmos, experimenting with string theory, reflecting on quantum mechanics. He has laid aside omniscience, let us say, but he is still a brilliant man. He has a human mind that is unfallen. That alone removes a major moral barrier to the acquisition of knowledge. Let's say you were his graduate adviser. How would you like to read his dissertation?

Or imagine him as a psychology major—the maker of human beings in his own image, completing his historical critique of psychology from Freud to Skinner.

Or imagine him as a philosophy major—writing his dissertation on warrant for belief in the existence of God.

Or imagine him as a literature major—the One who spoke the universe into being evaluating the antilogocentric theories of contemporary deconstructionists, or elucidating the novels of William Faulkner or the *Divine Comedy* of Dante.

These images boggle the mind.

We must be careful here, of course. I am not suggesting that Jesus possessed the content of the knowledge of twentieth-century physics or was aware of Derrida's critical linguistic theory. What I am saying is that Jesus as he walked the roads of Palestine was more intelligently aware, more intellectually capable, than anyone else of his time. String theory was understood by no one. If it had been relevant to Jesus' mission, no doubt he would have had access to this sort of knowledge. But it was not a factor in what he had to do. That is, he had the capacity for any modern notion, but these were not in his possession; he did not acquire this kind of knowledge. He was a man of his time.

It is, in fact, fair to argue that mere knowledge of the theories of modern science would lessen who he actually was. For without Newton or Einstein's physics Jesus walked on water, taught Peter to do so briefly, changed water into wine and stilled raging storms. As Willard puts it, Jesus was "master of molecules."[5] He had the kind of knowledge that allowed him by the power of the Spirit to do what needed to be done to accomplish his work on earth.

Every one of these pictures—Jesus as physicist, psychologist, philosopher, literary critic—is less than the Jesus we see in the Gospels, the One we meet in the quiet times of our devotions, the One we celebrate in our common worship. In picturing Jesus in this way we may come perilously close to reducing him to one of the "Jesuses" of the scholars associated with the Jesus Seminar—Jesus as a philosopher/cynic, a talking head, a wonderworker or a revolutionary. We must shy away from that. Jesus is not to be poured into the mold of our imaginations, even those supposedly based on the "assured results of biblical scholarship." Jesus is . . . Well, Jesus is human but finally incomparable in every way, intellectual included.

As Willard said in a lecture almost two years later, "If Jesus is Lord, how dumb could he really be?"[6] Of course Jesus is the smartest man, the most intellectual intellectual, who ever lived. How could we have ever thought otherwise?

Again, let me offer a caveat. I am intent on showing that the Jesus of the first century is the smartest man who ever lived, but for us as Christian thinkers today it is even more important to realize that it is the risen Christ with whom we now relate. In terms of our place in history, his earthly intellectual *capabilities* and *acquirements* are rooted in the omniscient, omnipresent, omnipotent risen Lord. It is on him we rely for habits of the mind. When we pore over the complexities of the subatomic structure, when we try to grasp the intricate grammatical forms of an unwritten language, when we struggle to understand our troubled psyches, the risen Christ is the One who knows the answers in infinite detail.

Still, seeing how Jesus showed his intelligence on earth can undergird our confidence not only in the infinite knowledge he now possesses but in the value of developing and using our intellect. As Willard says, "Paying careful attention to how Jesus made use of logical thinking can strengthen our confidence in Jesus as master of the centers of intellect and creativity and can encourage us to accept him as master in all of the areas of intellectual life in which we may participate."[7] So we turn to that.

Jesus the Reasoner

As the Logos, Jesus Christ is the epistemological foundation for our ability to reason. He is Jesus the reasoner. As the Incarnate Son of God, Jesus Christ is the prime example of how we should think. Who would not wannabe like him!

So let's return to the incomparable Jesus, the Jesus of the Gospels. If we investigate the way he is depicted in the New Testament, we can indeed see what we might have missed had we not done some imagining. We ask then: What did Jesus do when he thought? Well, that's hidden from us. But we can see what Jesus did when he spoke publicly, and that indicates for us what at least some of his thinking was like.

The Synoptic Gospels show us Jesus telling stories and making short, pithy comments. The Gospel of John shows him in long discourses, in some of which he uses ordinary human reasoning that follows the standard patterns of logic.

Before we look at these patterns of logic, however, we need to realize that we will be not be looking at the *ipsissima verba*—the very words of Jesus. Whether we are examining Jesus' words in the Synoptics or in the Gospel of John, we will be hearing these words in an English translation of Greek which itself is a rendering of Jesus' Aramaic language. Our assumption will be that this derivative form still embodies the essential patterns of Jesus' thought. Most traditional Christian scholars assume this, and so do many radical Christian and non-Christian scholars. There is really nothing else that can be done, given that there are few other sources for his sayings, and these other sources, like the *Gospel of Thomas,* are more than tainted by Gnosticism and quite unreliable.[8]

Actually, the fact that we have Jesus' words almost exclusively in Greek may be an advantage. If, as we believe, God has given us in the Gospels what we most need to know about Jesus, then not only are Jesus' words in Greek adequate for us, but so are his words in English or Swahili or Bantu or German. Truth about God is not the sole property of Hebrew or Aramaic. Even though we can learn much from studying Jesus' words as they appear in Greek, we are well justified in reasoning from the texts as we have them in English. That is what we will do here.

The Unexpected Jesus

What must strike any alert reader of the Gospels is the unexpected character of the Jesus who emerges from their pages. When we pay attention, there is an ever-renewed freshness to the Jesus we encounter. As we spend time away from the text, our image of Jesus fades. His striking, unique reality loses its sharp edge. He becomes more and more like a Norman Rockwell illustration, domestic, homey—a nice, rather wise man who lives down the block who each week comes to church to worship with us but not to call us to account.

But when we read the Gospels, we are struck with a towering figure who upsets us at every turn, alternately fascinating and frustrating, comforting and deeply disturbing at the same time. As we try to deal with this reality, we face both an intellectual and an existential task. Here is the Jesus of first-century time and space now becoming the Jesus of the present in the *kairos* of our own lived twenty-first-century moment. All our previous readings of the Gospels, all the comments of the scholars, all the meditations of the saints we have reflected on in our times of quiet devotion are called into question each time we read a Gospel afresh.

As we look at the mind of Jesus revealed through his encounters with people of his time, it will be helpful to keep this thought in the background of our consciousness: what Jesus did and said when he walked among us was utterly unexpected.

The revelation of his unexpected character begins with the annunciation of his birth, the astonishing events that ensued with the shepherds in Bethlehem, the adoration of the Magi, the escape to Egypt. The unexpected character of his mind begins to be revealed at age twelve, when for several days he astounds the rabbis in Jerusalem with his "understanding" (Lk 2:47). It is shortly followed (in the text, not the course of his life) by his profound insight and use of Scripture in answer to the devil (Lk 4:1-13). Jesus was no mere

---

Everyone of us forms an idea of Christ that is limited and incomplete.
It is cut according to our own measure. We tend to make ourselves
a Christ in our own image, a projection of our own aspirations
and desires and ideals. We find in Him what we want to find. We make
Him not only the incarnation of God but also the incarnation of
the things we and our society and our part of society happen to live for.

THOMAS MERTON
Seeds of Contemplation

---

cute kid; rabbis would not have spent so much time with him had he been only that. Knowledge of the Scriptures combined with a heart set on doing the will of the Father, as Satan's cleverest wiles failed to move Jesus from his mission.

Could Jesus have sinned? Many have asked that question. Willard's answer is simple and, I think, on target.[9] Yes, Jesus could have sinned, but he didn't do so because he was too smart. He knew better. Think about it: Why would he want to? Sin does not *free* a person. It binds a person.

When Jesus begins to encounter people of his own and surrounding villages, expectations are so shattered that threats to his very life become almost a daily matter. One story is told in Luke 4:14-30.

Early in his ministry he arrives in his hometown of Nazareth and goes, as is his practice, to regular sabbath service. He is handed the Scriptures to read; he finds Isaiah 61, reads the first two verses, hands the scroll back to the attendant, sits down to teach (the normal practice) and then declares that these verses describing the mission of the Messiah refer to him. At first his neighbors do not grasp what he has said: they speak well of him. Then, having given it some thought, they wonder: *Isn't this our neighbor's boy, Joseph's son?*

Jesus, as if to shock them even more, quotes an old proverb: "No prophet is accepted in his hometown." Then he likens himself to two of the greatest Hebrew prophets—Elijah and Elisha. They were also rejected by their countryfolk but accepted by foreigners: one from Sidon, the other from Syria.

We need to see how shocking this was. Imagine, for example, a young politician in Israel announcing in the Knesset that he is the long-awaited Messiah and that if the other politicians do not believe this, he will take his case to the PLO. Yasser Arafat will believe him. Or set it in a Christian context. Imagine a young college student coming home for the summer and announcing to his Baptist church that, first, he is Jesus returned as he said two thousand years ago and, second, if his old neighbors do not believe him, he will go to the Hare Krishna center across town; they will believe him. Can we then begin to understand why "all the people in the synagogue were furious," so angry that they drove Jesus out of town and would have pitched him off a precipice if he had not slipped through the crowd and escaped?

Over and over we see Jesus saying and doing the unexpected, even the outrageous. He lets a prostitute wash his feet with her hair, all the while telling his Pharisee host a clever story to show him that she is forgiven and he is not (Lk 7:36-50). He privileges repentant tax collectors and thieves over the hypocritical Pharisees (Lk 18:9-14; 23:43), children over adults (Lk 18:15-17), a poor widow over wealthy donors (Lk 21:1-4), a beggar over a rich man (Lk 16:19-31), servants over masters (Lk 22:24-30). When his family tries to see him but can't because of the crowd, he says that his disciples—those with him already—are his true mother and brothers (Lk 8:19-21). To be one of his followers, he says, a person must "hate his father, and mother, his wife and children, his brothers and sisters—yes, even his own life" (Lk 14:26). Healing people and justifying it from the law, he rejects strict adherence to sabbath rules.

Except for his treatment of the sabbath, the instances I have listed show Jesus' surprising character more than the workings of his mind. But in his treatment of the sabbath the cast of Jesus' mind becomes more evident. We turn now to examples of how Jesus argued: (1) *a fortiori* arguments, (2) arguments from evidence, (3) reasoning in dialogue and in direct conflict with others, (4) exegeting Scripture and (5) telling stories.

A Fortiori Arguments

Jesus frequently argued by analogy, more specifically by what is technically called *a fortiori* argument. An *a fortiori* argument takes the following general form:

> The truth of A is admitted.
> The support for B is stronger than the support for A.
> Therefore, the truth of B must be admitted.[10]

For example: if it is proper for a person to respect their pet cat, so much more is it proper for a person to respect, even love, their mother.

Jesus often used such an argument.[11] A peculiarly detailed example is found in John 7:21-23:

> I did one miracle [on the Sabbath], and you are all astonished. Yet, because Moses gave you circumcision (though actually it did not come from Moses, but from the patriarchs), you circumcise a child on the Sabbath. Now if a child can be circumcised on the Sabbath so that the law of Moses may not be broken, why are you angry with me for healing the whole man on the Sabbath?

The formal expression is as follows:

Premise A1: Circumcising a child on the eighth day is a proper act, even if the eighth day falls on a sabbath.

Premise A2: Healing a whole person is a more important life-giving act than circumcision.

Conclusion A: Healing a whole person is a proper act, even if it occurs on the sabbath.

Jesus thus challenges the religious leaders to act in accordance with their own understanding of the law; they already know—or should know—that healing on the sabbath is approved by God. At the same time, contained in his argument is an implied criticism of either their knowledge or their motivation. Jesus notes several times

---

Jesus' aim in utilizing logic is not to win battles, but to achieve understanding or insight in his hearers. . . . That is, he does not try to make everything so explicit that the conclusion is forced down the throat of the hearer. Rather, he presents matters in such a way that those who wish to know can find their way to, can come to, the appropriate conclusion as something *they* have discovered—whether or not it is something they particularly care for.

DALLAS WILLARD
"Jesus the Logician"

---

in this long passage that his critics have been trying to kill him (Jn 5:18; 7:19; 8:37, 40); now he says that to do this they are willing either to ignore or to remain ignorant of the law of God which they claim to accept as their own moral standard.

A second example regarding the sabbath comes in Luke 13:10-16, after Jesus has healed a woman "crippled by a spirit for eighteen years." The synagogue ruler is indignant:

"There are six days for work. So come and be healed on those days, not on the Sabbath."

The Lord answered him. "You hypocrites! Doesn't each of you on the Sabbath untie his ox or donkey from the stall and lead it out to give it water? Then should not this woman, a daughter of Abraham, whom Satan has kept bound for eighteen long years, be set free on the Sabbath day from what bound her?"

The form of this argument is quite simple:

Premise B1: It is proper to unbind and water an ox or donkey (which is thirsty for one day) on the sabbath.

Premise B2: A woman suffering from an illness (for eighteen years) is more worthy of relief than an ox or a donkey.

Conclusion B: It is proper to heal this woman on the sabbath.

In this case, the rightness of the argument was so obvious that "all his opponents were humiliated," while the ordinary people "were delighted with all the wonderful things he was doing" (Lk 13:17).

A third example of *a fortiori* argument comes in Luke 18:2-8, where Jesus encourages his disciples to persist in prayer:

He said: "In a certain town there was a judge who neither feared God nor cared about men. And there was a widow in that town who kept coming to him with the plea, 'Grant me justice against my adversary.'

"For some time he refused. But finally he said to himself, 'Even though I don't fear God or care about men, yet because this widow keeps bothering me, I will see that she gets justice, so that she won't eventually wear me out with her coming!'"

And the Lord said, "Listen to what the unjust judge says. And will not God bring about justice for his chosen ones, who cry out to him day and night? Will he keep putting them off? I tell you, he will see that they get justice, and quickly."

In syllogistic form this becomes:

Premise C1: An unjust judge will work justice if he is constantly asked.

Premise C2: God as a just judge will surely do better than an unjust judge.

Conclusion C: God will respond to persistent prayer quickly.

Multiple examples of such arguments abound in the Gospels.

Reasoning from Evidence

One way we reason is to give "reasons" why we take something to be true. That is, we make a case for our views. This is precisely what Jesus does in the fifth chapter of the Gospel of John. The Gospel of Luke reports a similar form of argument.

In John 5 Jesus is in a heavy dialogue with the religious leaders. It is the sabbath, and Jesus has just healed a man at the pool of Bethesda. When "the Jews" (John's designation for the religious leaders) hear of this, they take exception. They claim that it is against the traditional laws for healing to be performed on the sabbath. So Jesus explains his actions: "My Father is always at his work to this very day, and I, too, am working." In response the Jews "tried all the harder to kill him," for not only was he "breaking the Sabbath, but he was even calling God his own Father, making himself equal with God" (5:17-18).

Jesus does not challenge this conclusion. Instead he makes six further statements that, taken together, confirm that he is indeed doing precisely what they claim. A list of these reasons, paraphrased, makes this clear:

1. I do what my Father does—give life to the dead (5:18-25).
2. I judge as a representative of the Father (5:22).
3. If I am not honored, God is not honored (5:23).
4. The one who believes in me believes in God (5:24-27).
5. Like God, I have life in myself (5:26).
6. In God's power I always do what he wants (5:30).

With these claims Jesus strengthens the case against him, giving his opponents even more reasons for their conclusion. He is saying, in effect, "You are right. I am claiming to be equal with God." But he does not leave his critics without a rejoinder. He may be claiming to be equal with God, but that is because he really *is* equal to God, and they have had ample opportunity to see this for themselves.

He thus turns the table on his interlocutors by giving five reasons why his claim to divinity is true (Jn 5:31-45):

1. John the Baptist testifies to who I am (5:31).

2. The "works" that I do testify to who I am (5:36).

3. The Father testifies to who I am (5:37).

4. The Scriptures testify to who I am (5:38).

5. Moses testifies to who I am (5:40).

Jesus assumes that the religious leaders have had access to these reasons: They have heard John the Baptist's witness; they have seen what Jesus has done; they have—or claim to have—an insight into God's understanding; they have read the Scriptures; they accept Moses as their religious authority—perhaps their greatest religious authority, for he is the author of the Torah itself.

The Gospel of Luke shows Jesus using a similar type of argument. John the Baptist is in prison and has lost confidence in his own designation of Jesus as the Messiah. So he sends his disciples to Jesus to ask if he really is "the one who was to come" (Lk 7:20). Jesus responds by doing the *works* of the prophesied Messiah:

> At that very time Jesus cured many who had diseases, sicknesses and evil spirits, and gave sight to many who were blind. So he replied to the messengers, "Go back and report to John what you have seen and heard: The blind receive sight, the lame walk, those who have leprosy are cured, the deaf hear, the dead are raised, and the good news is preached to the poor. Blessed is the man who does not fall away on account of me." (Lk 7:21-23)

These *works* fulfill Isaiah 61:1-2, a text Jesus has already used in reference to himself (Lk 4:18-19).

Each of the reasons Jesus gives in John and Luke is rich in implication, but to further unpack them would take us beyond the point of this chapter, which is to demonstrate that Jesus often thought in ordinary human categories, that he used ordinary human reasoning to support his views—in this case his views about who he himself really is. The issue of Jesus' identity is also the subject of one of the most intense dialogues in the Gospels.

Jesus in Argument

Except for a brief aside (7:53—8:11), John 7—8 constitutes one sustained argument.[12] The setting is Jerusalem at the time of the Feast of the Tabernacles; his interlocutors are the "crowd" and the religious authorities (John simply calls them "the Jews"); and the major issue in these chapters is Jesus' identity. Who does Jesus think he is? And who is he really?

The entire sequence of this argument is immensely complex. Accusation and rejoinder, charge and countercharge all come in a seemingly seamless web. We will not examine the argument in detail; that would take us too deeply into biblical exegesis. Still, we can learn much by simply observing the character of the argument itself. The central claim of these chapters is Jesus' self-identification as One who has been sent by God to let the Israelites know who God is, what they should believe and how they should then live.

When Jesus begins to teach in the temple courts, he astounds the listeners: "How did this man get so much learning without having studied?" they ask (Jn 7:15). Had Jesus not studied? We do not have any direct reason to think he had any formal training, but with his performance at age twelve we have reason to believe that "study" itself was not foreign to him. In any case, his brilliance was easily recognized. Jesus, however, credits God as the source of his teaching. Moreover he says, "If anyone chooses to do God's will, he will find out whether my teaching comes from God or whether I speak on my own" (Jn 7:17).

In Jesus' "epistemology," doing God's will is integrally connected with "knowing" (coming to understand with confidence) whether Jesus' teaching is from God. If it is from God, the unstated assumptions—clearly pervading the Hebrew Scriptures—are that Jesus' teaching is true and that knowing (and doing) the truth is a prime value. That is why Jesus immediately charges the leaders with divorcing knowing and doing—that is, not being obedient to the law they accept as true and binding: "Has not Moses given you the law? Yet not one of you keeps the law" (Jn 7:19). As if this were not challenging enough, Jesus unveils their supposedly secret plans to kill him.

This they vehemently deny, making their own countercharge: "You are demon possessed" (Jn 7:20). Jesus ignores their charge and continues his own, accusing them of judging only by appearances, not seeking the truth. During the remainder of John 7—8, Jesus wrestles against the twisted forces of hypocrisy, illusion and deliberate, hardhearted refusal to see the truth. Some are convinced by Jesus; others want him arrested and put to death. But by the strength of his character and the power of his intellect, Jesus enters into the fray, calmly but passionately stating his shocking claims: "I am not here on my own, but he who sent me is true. You do not know him, but I know him because I am from him and he sent me" (Jn 7:28-29). "Whoever believes in me, as the Scripture has said, streams of living water will flow from within him" (Jn 7:38). "I always do what pleases him [the Father]" (Jn 8:29). Just as firmly and thoughtfully, he responds to their rejection of his self-identity. If we want to know and do the truth, it would seem impossible to read these chapters with anything other than a recognition of the depths of Jesus' intelligence.

The discourse reaches a climax in the middle of John 8. At this point, despite the rejection of many, "many put their faith in him," and so it is to them that he turns: "To the Jews who had believed in

---

It was a jealous Jehovah who really taught mankind the Law of the Excluded Middle: Greek formalization of logic (and geometry and grammar) probably would not have been sufficient of its own. Without a strong religious impulsion towards a single orderly world, and the consequent avoidance of opportunist, manipulative incoherence, the cognitive miracle would probably not have occurred.

ERNEST GELLNER
Postmodernism, Reason and Religion

---

him, Jesus said, 'If you hold my to my teaching, you are really my disciples. Then you will know the truth, and the truth will set you free' " (Jn 8:30-32).

If Jesus is the One whom the Father has sent to tell them how to live, then they should pay attention to what he goes on to say, and should act accordingly. That is only logical. But as is often the case in Jesus' dialogues, the unexpected happens. The "believers" immediately refuse to do this, first of all because it would mean that they would have to believe something unacceptable about themselves, to wit, that they are bound by sin. In the end, after Jesus has made his most "arrogant" claim ("Before Abraham was born, I am!" [Jn 8:58]), they become so furious with Jesus that they seek to stone him.

One could say that it is precisely Jesus' claim to intelligence—that is, to know what his audience does not—that gets him in trouble. But the more important point is that Jesus is "reasoning" with people just like us. He is assuming that his interlocutors can understand him and that if they wish to do so, they can come to understand and accept the truth about God, the truth about him and the truth about themselves. These two chapters (Jn 7—8) are indeed stellar illustrations of Jesus' mind at work.

Jesus as an Exegete

Jesus was a student of the Hebrew Scriptures as early as age twelve (Lk 2:41-52). By the time he reached maturity, he was a master. In the Sermon on the Mount (Mt 5—7) Jesus moves about in the Scriptures, not just interpreting them as the rabbis but speaking with great authority (Mt 7:29), implicitly claiming the same authority as the Scriptures themselves.

One of the common practices of the teachers of his time was interpretation of Scripture. Great pains were taken to do this, with scholars quoting earlier scholars, making further remarks of their own and, if their work was highly regarded by their peers, leaving behind a contribution to the tradition. So when controversy arose, the Scriptures and the traditions were consulted and used to test Jesus' teaching.

In Mark 12:13-34, the authorities ask him exegetical questions about marriage after the resurrection and the greatest commandment. These he handles easily. Then in verses 35-37 Jesus turns the tables and poses a question for them:

> How is it that the teachers of the law say that the Christ is the son of David? David himself, speaking by the Holy Spirit, declared:
>
> > "The Lord said to my Lord:
> > 'Sit at my right hand
> > until I put your enemies
> > under your feet.'"
>
> David himself calls him "Lord." How then can he be his son?

This is a traditional haggada-question, one involving the reconciliation of apparent contradictions in Scripture. In this case the question is, how can the Messiah be both David's son and David's Lord? The religious authorities are challenged to answer to this conundrum and can't do so. But later New Testament writers do (Acts 2:29-34; 13:39; Heb 1:5-13). As New Testament scholar William L. Lane says, "In these texts the prophetic promise to David [Ps 110:1] serves as the starting point for the proclamation of Jesus as the Savior whose resurrection and exaltation marked the fulfillment of the promise. Jesus is the fulfiller of Scripture, in this case, the promise to

---

Jesus himself is a profound student of the Scriptures.

E. HARRIS HARBISON
The Christian Scholar in the Age of the Reformation

David."[13] Jesus uses the conundrum not only to confound the authorities but to suggest to his disciples a text that will later help them interpret him as a fulfillment of prophecy.

Jesus' command of the Scriptures could be almost endlessly illustrated. Rarely would one find a casual quotation or one that did not relate specifically to a case in point. In his study of Jesus as logician, Willard chooses four for emphasis: Matthew 12:1-8 (on ritual law), Luke 20:27-40 (on the resurrection of the body), Matthew 5:29-30 (on the causes of sin) and Luke 20:42-43 (on the Messiah as David's son and/or Lord), a passage parallel to Mark 12:35-37. In each case, the brilliance of Jesus' understanding of Scripture stands out.[14]

Jesus the Storyteller

Everyone who knows anything about Jesus knows that he was a great storyteller, surely the greatest storyteller who ever lived. The longest of his stories—the parable of the prodigal son (Lk 15:11-32)—is short. The number of characters is minimal, usually two or three. But the form of his most intriguing parables is unique. These parables so engage the listener that the story is not really over until the listener responds.

Take the parable of the prodigal son. Members of the audience ("tax collectors, sinners and teachers of the law") realize that they are being depicted as characters in the story. The tax collectors and sinners are the profligate son who repents and is forgiven. The teachers of the law are the obedient elder brother who ends up rejecting his father. The elder brother will not be forgiven until he accepts his father as one who accepts his younger brother back into the family. The story as narrated ends with the elder brother still out in the field, overhearing joyous sounds of the celebration. But the story of the audience is not over. They still have the opportunity to come in to the feast. All they need to do is accept Jesus as One who accepts repentant outcasts. In all this Jesus is acting like his own heavenly Father. So if the "teachers of the law" reject Jesus as they have been doing prior to this story, they are rejecting the Father. This is a point Jesus elsewhere makes explicit: "He who listens to you listens to me; he who rejects you rejects me; but he who rejects me rejects him who sent me" (Lk 10:16).

The story I want to examine at length, however, is the parable of the good Samaritan. It is a stellar example of Jesus' peculiar storytelling art. In fact, it illustrates many of the elements of Jesus' character that we have already seen.

As noted above, Jesus often involves his audience in his stories.

This is nowhere more clear than in this parable. But who is his audience? Certainly his first audience is "an expert in the law," but there is a second audience as well. The setting of the parable gives us an insight into both:

> On one occasion an expert in the law stood up to test Jesus. "Teacher," he asked, "what must I do to inherit eternal life?"
>
> "What is written in the Law?" he replied. "How do you read it?"
>
> He answered: " 'Love the Lord your God with all your heart and with all your soul and with all your strength and with all your mind'; and, 'Love your neighbor as yourself.' "
>
> "You have answered correctly," Jesus replied. "Do this and you will live."
>
> But he wanted to justify himself, so he asked Jesus, "And who is my neighbor?" (Lk 10:25-29)

Note the character of the first audience: the lawyer's motive is not really to learn what Jesus had to teach him but rather to "test Jesus." *After all*, he thinks, *I'm the expert. Let's see if Jesus knows as much as I do.*

But Jesus, seeing his insincerity, immediately turns the tables and asks the lawyer what he thinks. Then he commends the lawyer for his technically correct answer, an answer drawn directly from the Hebrew Scriptures (Deut 6:4-8; Lev 19:18). But when Jesus goes one step further and says, "Do this and you will live," the lawyer realizes that Jesus' commendation contains a time bomb set to go off as soon as he and Jesus part company. The lawyer will have to live by his own answer to the question he asked! That is, he will have to love God totally and also love his neighbor.

In response the lawyer does not address the first commandment. This he knows cannot be contested. He cannot say, "But who is God?" without revealing an ignorance for which as an "expert" he would have no excuse. So he challenges the second commandment by asking that *neighbor* be defined. He now wants not just to test Jesus on his interpretation of the law but to limit the extent of the commitment to some convenient group, perhaps his own fellow Jews or maybe even those of his own social class.

Whatever the limits, though, it is clear that Jesus has called him to be responsible for his knowledge. Of course there is a problem. Loving others as we love ourselves—doing for them what we do for ourselves—is a task that is, quite frankly, impossible for any human being. We are fallen creatures. Even if we could love our neighbor as ourselves, we would not want to.

So wanting to get off the hook, the lawyer asks a somewhat more technical question about the law: "Just who is this person I am to love like myself?" Jesus has answered the lawyer's first question directly. He responds to the second question with the famous story:

> In reply Jesus said: "A man was going down from Jerusalem to Jericho, when he fell into the hands of robbers. They stripped him of his clothes, beat him and went away, leaving him half dead. A priest happened to be going down the same road, and when he saw the man, he passed by on the other side. So too, a Levite, when he came to the place and saw him, passed by on the other side. But a Samaritan, as he traveled, came where the man was; and when he saw him, he took pity on him. He went to him and bandaged his wounds, pouring on oil and wine. Then he put the man on his own donkey, took him to an inn and took care of him. The next day he took out two silver coins and gave them to the innkeeper. 'Look after him,' he said, "and when I return, I will reimburse you for any extra expense you may have.'
>
> "Which of these three do you think was a neighbor to the man who fell into the hands of the robbers?"
>
> The expert in the law replied, "The one who had mercy on him."
>
> Jesus told him, "Go and do likewise." (Lk 10:30-37)

Did Jesus answer the lawyer's question? No. It was the wrong question. The issue is not "Who is my neighbor?" but "Who am I to be?" You are to *be a neighbor,* and that means that everyone with whom you have contact is the object of your concern. Act like a neighbor. Let neighborliness characterize all your actions. Indeed at the end of the story, instead of being justified in his own and Jesus' eyes, the lawyer is back on the hook, swinging in the breeze.

Neat, we say to ourselves. *He deserves it. How dare he question Jesus like that! Doesn't he know better?* If that is the end of our deliberation on this parable, we leave our study worse than when we came.

But the dialogue Jesus has with the lawyer does not just show the insincerity of the lawyer. It attacks the fundamental way the lawyer views himself in society. And at that point the story begins to take on a more universal dimension—one that applies as much to us as to the lawyer. In other words, Jesus' story has a second audience—reader, you and me!

Let's look again, this time at the villains and the heroes of the story. The robbers of course are villains, but in the story they function only to set the context. The real villains are the people who pass by the victim—a priest and a Levite, both of them "good" folk, "religious" folk, pillars of the community.

The hero, on the other hand, is a Samaritan, from a Palestinian group of mixed Jewish and Assyrian heritage. They were so despised by the "pure" Jews that the Samaritan woman with whom Jesus talks in the Gospel of John is shocked when Jesus strikes up a conversation with her, "for Jews do not associate with Samaritans"

Jaroslav Pelikan tells of an old rabbi asked by his pupil, "Why is it that you rabbis so often put your teaching in the form of a question?" The rabbi shot back, "So what's wrong with a question?" Very often Jesus too deflected the question back in Socratic style, pressing the seeker toward a crisis point. His answers cut to the hearts of his listeners. I doubt I would have left any encounter with Jesus feeling smug or self-satisfied.

PHILIP YANCEY
The Jesus I Never Knew

(Jn 4:9). As we saw above, Jewish religious leaders in attacking Jesus once blurted out, "Aren't we right in saying that you are a Samaritan and demon-possessed?" (Jn 8:48).

To catch the force of Jesus' parable we need to see just how angry the lawyer—and any other normal Jewish person of Jesus' day—would be when Jesus chose to make good Jewish people the villains and a Samaritan the hero. But the choice was deliberate. What was at stake was neighborliness itself—second in importance only to loving God. Jesus could make his point best not by identifying neighborliness with the actions of God's chosen people but by selecting a man from the most unlikely social class. He thereby challenged the central core of the human heart—the lawyer's (and our) self-love, our inaccurate and unjust prejudice against other people. As one commentator puts it, "The parable is not a pleasant tale about a Traveler Who Did His Good Deed: it is a damning indictment of social, racial, and religious superiority."[15] If the lawyer were to follow the second of the great commandments—to love his neighbor as himself—he would have to completely reorient his attitudes to people around him.

We must not leave the parable without realizing that the story is about us as well as the lawyer. Put the story in modern dress. In place of the priest and Levite put the sorts of people we think highly of today—our religious leaders, the elders of our church, our social and even moral elite.

Then put in place of the Samaritan the outcasts of our social strata—

a bum on skid row
    (if we are working stiffs)
a mother on welfare
    (if we are upstanding suburbanites)
a broker on Wall Street
    (if we are simple-lifestyle Christians)
a feminist rabble-rouser
    (if we are opponents of radical feminism)
a male chauvinist
    (if we are biblical feminists)
a Palestinian
    (if we are Israelis)

an obnoxious fellow student
  (if we are college students)

Whoever is our least favorite kind of person—that's the Samaritan in the story for us. He or she is the one who proves neighborly. That's the one we should imitate.

Are we ready for this? Can we see through our prejudices? Does the story not tip us on our very heads? Isn't it like leaning over and looking at the world from between our legs? "Go and do likewise," we hear Jesus say. "Act like the one you despise, for the one you despise acts like God." Will we do it? Will we recognize neighborliness wherever we find it? Will we become aware that our own neighborliness extends no further than the nose on our face?

In their original setting, Jesus' parables often end without ending. This one does. What does the lawyer do? We don't know. It's up to him. When we read the parables, what will *we* do? It's up to us. The story of a parable gets finished on the action end of our lives. The story transforms us or it doesn't, but we write the ending. The picture is there before us, and Jesus says, "Go and do likewise."[16]

It is this characteristic—the open-endedness—of Jesus' parables that makes them such powerful teaching devices. If we submit ourselves to them, our minds will be discipled. If we write the right ending to them, our lives will be changed. There is no better way of opening our closed minds than to encounter Jesus in his parables.

A Foundation for Human Knowing

The ultimate foundation for human knowing is not the autonomy of human reason; it is not the autonomy of human experience. The ultimate philosophical and theological foundation for all human knowing is the Logos. The foundation is ontological: God not just as Being but as Reason or Meaning. And this Logos has an incarnate form—Jesus as "reasoner."

So Jesus is indeed a "reasoner"—yes, even an "intellectual." Granted, he did not emphasize this or call explicit attention to it.

Nor did he single out the "learned" as especially privileged. In fact in a moment of ecstasy he did the opposite.

> At that time Jesus, full of joy through the Holy Spirit, said, "I praise you, Father, Lord of heaven and earth, because you have hidden these things from the wise and learned, and revealed them to little children." (Lk 10:21)

This does not mean that to know the truth the "wise and learned" must lose their intelligence, that the intellectual must become an anti-intellectual. It means that everyone must first become, as children, receivers of God's revelation. Reception of God's gifts—intelligence itself and the content that comes through God's gracious revelation in the books of Scripture and nature—comes first. Augustine properly captures this with his principle: "I believe in order to understand."

The humility of Jesus, of course, did not preclude his intelligence. There was nothing wannabe about him. He was who he was, and as embodiment of the I AM, he had no need to wannabe anything else. I think it is helpful to see, however, that during his earthly life Jesus displayed all the intellectual virtues: a passion for truth, a passion for consistency, a passion for holiness and a compassion for others.

To charge the intellect with perpetual blindness so as to leave it no intelligence of any description whatever, is repugnant not only to the Word of God, but to common experience. We see that there has been implanted in the human mind a certain desire of investigating truth, to which it never would aspire unless some relish for truth antecedently existed.

JOHN CALVIN
Institutes of the Christian Religion

Look back at the chart of these virtues on page 110. Which of them does Jesus not model? Again, even humility applies. While affirming his own unique authority, Jesus did so humbly, deferring to his Father as his own authority: "My teaching is not my own," Jesus says at the beginning of the long discourse in John 7—8. "It comes from him who sent me" (Jn 7:16). Moreover, as he went out early in the morning to pray, he modeled both the spiritual and the intellectual disciplines: silence, solitude, attention, prayer. His dialogue with the lawyer along with the parable of the good Samaritan even counts as an example of lateral thinking: he shifted the false "legal" paradigm of the questioner to the true paradigm of the kingdom of God.

Our goal in this chapter has been, therefore, not only to recognize the divine Logos as the foundation for human reason but to see how that divine Logos in the incarnate Son of God embodies a model of the Christian intellectual. Christ the Logos is Jesus the reasoner. Would he not say to us as he did the "expert in the law," "Go and do likewise"?

X

THE RESPONSIBILITY OF A CHRISTIAN INTELLECTUAL

I *began the book with a confession: I was an intellectual wannabe.*
Almost fifty years have passed. As an editor I have had the privilege
of working with a number of genuine intellectuals, many of them
Christians with the highest dedication to our common Lord and
Savior. I have read, reread, studied and written about the works of
many, many more intellectuals, most of them self-confessed non-
Christians. In the past two years my attention to this dubious socio-
logical class has intensified. I think I am ready for another confession: *Being an intellectual is after all no big deal, nothing to particularly
admire or condemn.* Why? Because all Christians are called to be as
intellectual *as befits their abilities* and the work they have been called
to do. No one is called to be a sloppy thinker!

The Call to Intellectual Work
Whether or not one could be an intellectual is mostly not up to one's
choice. At least not for most people. An intellectual must be fairly

intelligent. Not all of us are. An intellectual must have access to an education. (This need not be formally academic. Think of Václav Havel or Eric Hoffer.[1] But it must include the possibility of wide and deep reading across a broad range of disciplines.) Many intelligent people have no such access. An intellectual must have unusual ability to communicate and access to publication. It is a sad fact that many intelligent people who can understand complex ideas do not know how to communicate them. Their writing is muddled, disorganized, bland and confused, utterly lacking in imagination and thus in zest. Many who can write can't, for a host of reasons, get published.

Thinking is everyone's business. Yet knowledge is power, and power entails responsibility. The free use of knowledge is a dangerous or meaningless phrase unless it connotes—like all liberties— activity controlled by responsibility.

GILBERT HIGHET
Man's Unconquerable Mind

Furthermore, and more specifically, an intellectual must have or develop all or most of those characteristics I listed in my original definition:

> An *intellectual* is one who loves ideas, is dedicated to clarifying them, developing them, criticizing them, turning them over and over, seeing their implications, stacking them atop one another, arranging them, sitting silent while new ideas pop up and old ones seem to rearrange themselves, playing with them, punning with their terminology, laughing at them, watching them clash, picking up the pieces, starting over, judging them, withholding judgment about them, changing them, bringing them into contact with their counterparts in other systems of thought, inviting them to dine and have a ball but also suiting them for service in workaday life.

No one can have all those traits just by desiring them or choosing to have them. Those who do have them start with abilities written into their nature over which they have had no control. These traits are nurtured or stymied by their environment. No one has much control over their environment and their nurture before adolescence. And try controlling it then!

When we consider the definition of a *Christian* intellectual, the matter is very different. Here we do have a large measure of control.[2] We are responsible to God for what we do with what we are given. First and foremost we are to become disciples of Christ, following him wherever he leads. It may not be where our native intellectual abilities would seem to be best employed. Evelyn Underhill notes:

> Henry Martyn, the fragile and exquisite scholar, was compelled to sacrifice the intellectual life to which he was so perfectly fitted for the missionary life to which he felt he was decisively called. . . . Things like this—and they are constantly happening—gradually convince us that the overruling reality of life is the Will and Choice of a Spirit acting not in a mechanical but in a living and personal way; and that the spiritual life does not consist in mere individual betterment, or assiduous attention to one's own soul, but in a free and unconditional response to that Spirit's pressure and call, whatever the cost may be.[3]

I do not wish to comment on the various ways God's guidance is available to us. Engaging in *lectio divina*, which I have already discussed in chapter nine, will go a long way toward helping each of us discern what it is God wants of us. But it certainly may be that what

---

In the end, the question of Christian thinking is a deeply spiritual question. What sort of God will we worship?

MARK NOLL
The Scandal of the Evangelical Mind

God wants is for you—or me—to be a Christian who delights in thinking, can do a good job of it and is called to play a distinct intellectual role as a Christian in the public arena.

Still, whether or not one's role is to be public, we are all called to use our minds as fully and as well as we can. In this sense everyone is to called to be an *intellectual*.

To the Glory of God

For those Christians called to the more rigorous life of the mind, recall the definition:

> A *Christian intellectual* is all of the above [description of an intellectual] to the glory of God.

Within this definition lies the core to discerning the responsibility of the Christian intellectual: *to the glory of God.*

What brings glory to God? More than any other theologian, Karl Barth has helped me understand the answer: "God does not need to make any fuss about his glory," he writes. "God is glorious. He simply needs to show Himself as He is, He simply needs to reveal Himself. That is what he does in man, His creature, in whom He wants to be reflected."[4] We, then, are the ones in whom God is glorified.

Really? Surely not, we may protest. Isn't that too much to ask? No. We are made in the image of God: we thus glorify God by reflecting the character of God in our *being*—the way we think and

---

The work of a professor is something to which some of us are called by God—in the classic sense of Luther and Calvin, such that if we did not do it, we would be acting disobediently.

NICHOLAS WOLTERSTORFF
"The Professorship as a Legitimate Calling"

---

act. The character of God is best seen in Jesus. Jesus was smart—the smartest man who ever lived. If we are smart, we glorify God in our smartness. Of course there is more to it than that. Of course Jesus was wise; so we must be wise. Jesus was good, loving, kind, compassionate; so we should be good, loving, kind, compassionate.

When we do not so glorify God, we are, says Barth, "inferior to brute beasts," for they fulfill their role of glorifying God simply by being created. Not to fulfill our role is our misery for us. Listen again to Barth: "Created to glorify God, we must know God so that we may and can glorify Him. . . . To glorify God, to live according to God, hence is a conscious act, an act of the will; in a word, a human act."[5]

How then does a Christian thinker "live according to God"? That is, what falls within the specific purview of the intellectual life that brings glory to God? Two fundamental matters are involved: learn-

---

The church needs scholars to assist her in the task of seeing precisely how the biblical vision applies to our present social realities and to assist her in the task of interpreting this social reality of ours.

N I C H O L A S   W O L T E R S T O R F F
"The Professorship as a Legitimate Calling"

---

ing the truth and telling the truth. We can see these two themes played out best, I think, when we see them resolved into one: *living in truth*.

Living in Truth

The phrase "living in truth" comes not from the Bible or Christian theology proper but from the profound reflection of Václav Havel, one of the twentieth century's most commendable intellectuals.[6] Though he rejects a specifically Christian faith, his essays and letters from prison reveal a basically theistic understanding of the transcendent foundation for morality. If there is today any moral conscience in international politics, it is to be found in him and his writings. Speaking before a joint session of the U.S. Congress, Havel challenged America's most successful politicians to accept their moral responsibility:

> The only core of all our actions—if they are to be moral—is responsibility. Responsibility to something higher than my family, my country, my firm, my success. Responsibility to the order of Being, where all our actions are indelibly recorded and where, and only where, they will be properly judged.

Havel's notion of *Being* is so similar to the Christian understanding of God that for all practical purposes this statement itself is Christian.[7] How effective Havel was may, I suppose, be judged by the subsequent actions of Congress. Living in the truth does not, however, measure success by its effectiveness in producing change in others. Living in the truth, like faithfulness, is its own success.

In one of the essays that contributed to his imprisonment as a political dissident, Havel introduces *living in truth* by telling the story of a greengrocer who one day does not display in his shop the

---

In its most original and broadest sense, living within the truth covers a vast territory whose outer limits are vague and difficult to map, a territory full of modest expressions of human volition, the vast majority of which will remain anonymous and whose political impact will probably never be felt or described any more concretely than simply as a part of a social climate or mood. Most of these expressions remain elementary revolts against manipulation: you simply straighten your backbone and live in greater dignity as an individual.

VÁCLAV HAVEL
"The Power of the Powerless"

---

slogan delivered with his onions and carrots.[8] It is not that he has paid any attention to what it and others like it say: "Workers of the world, unite!" He knows intuitively that it rests on a lie, but he has till now simply gone along with the instructions of the government—which he knows is not really the workers as the ideology proclaims. Like all ideologies, the "post-totalitarian" (Havel's term for the regime of Czechoslovakia in the 1970s and 1980s) ideology "is a specious way of relating to the world. It offers human beings the illusion of an identity, of dignity, and of morality while making it easier for them to *part* with them."[9] To succumb to ideology is to *live within a lie.*

Today, however, the grocer simply decides not to display the sign. He also stops voting in sham elections. He opts out of the system. For this he is relieved of his management job and posted to a warehouse outside the public eye; his salary is reduced and his vacation plans truncated; his children's education is put in jeopardy.

"His revolt is an attempt to *live within the truth.*"[10]

Living in truth in a totalitarian or even a post-totalitarian regime can be costly. But both before Havel's election as he languished in prison and after his election as he has continued to lecture to international audiences of politicians and fellow pundits, he exemplified and has called others to embody this life-form.

It is one of the tragedies of our world that there are so few intel-

---

The point where living within the truth ceases to be a mere negation of living with a lie and becomes articulate in a particular way is the point at which something is born that might be called the "independent spiritual, social and political life of society."

VÁCLAV HAVEL
"The Power of the Powerless"

---

lectuals like Havel. One thinks of Aleksandr Solzhenitsyn, and perhaps George Orwell and Albert Camus. But the twentieth century is mostly filled with antitypes, not anti-intellectuals but intellectuals who fail miserably in fulfilling the role of living in truth.

The Treason of the Intellectuals

Much of the anti-intellectualism noted in the opening chapter is justified. There has been a "treason of the intellectuals."[11] If the intellectuals of all ages have strewn much tragedy in their wake, the intellectuals of our age have strewn the most. Paul Johnson may be tendentious, but he is not completely misguided in his denunciation. In his tour-de-force *Intellectuals* Johnson picks the most reprehensible public thinkers and writers of the past two hundred years, holds them up to scrutiny and focuses on their peccadilloes, their most egregious errors of public judgment and the profound flaws in their personal character. He describes one of his antiheroes, for example, as "a comatose intellectual in supine posture."[12] Johnson's diatribe is echoed by more balanced analyses, such as those by Ernest Gellner, Tony Judt, Leszek Kolakowski, Archibald MacLeish and Thomas Molnar.[13]

The major charge against any public intellectual, though, seems to me to be whether he or she has tried to live in truth, which for intellectuals means both *learning the truth* and *telling the truth* as much as they are aware, or should be aware, of it. Judt and Kolakowski are only two of many critics who have pointed out what anyone, intellectual or not, can see almost with their eyes closed. Kolakowski expostulates:

> The long history of terrible errors that so many intellectuals in our century have committed in their political choices and of their noisy identification with the most cruel tyrannies is well known and has been described repeatedly; it probably has contributed to the significant decline of their authority as leaders in political matters.[14]

Judt focuses on Jean-Paul Sartre:

> Sartre never spoke out against Soviet anti-Semitism or in defense of the victims of the show trials, nor was he ever held to account by his followers and heirs for this, any more than for his more egregiously silly pronouncements from the early fifties. In other words, the years 1944-56 were not a golden era of intellectual responsibility but quite the reverse; never were French intellectuals so *irresponsible*, saying and writing whatever they desired, pronouncing angrily on a subject one month, neglecting it thereafter for years to come, at no cost either to their reputations or their skins.[15]

Judt selects as the epigraph for his study of French intellectuals Albert Camus's all too true dictum:

> Mistaken ideas always end in bloodshed, but in every case it is someone else's blood. That is why some of our thinkers feel free to say just about anything.[16]

Two of the most mistaken ideas held by intellectuals of the past two centuries are the identification of truth first with personal vision and, second, with ideology.

Nowhere is the first confusion more evident than in Ralph Waldo Emerson. In "The American Scholar," his Phi Beta Kappa address at

Harvard University in 1837, Emerson spoke in glowing terms of Man Thinking, the role to which thoughtful, intelligent "men" were to be called. Man Thinking links one human mind with the mind of the universe, with every other mind. For Man Thinking "learns that in going down into the secrets of his own mind he has descended into the secrets of all minds."[17] Emerson's vision here is predicated

---

If you who set yourselves to explain the theory of Christianity, had set yourselves instead to do the will of the Master, the one object for which the Gospel was preached to you, how different would now be the condition of that portion of the world with which you come into contact! Had you given yourselves to the understanding of his word that you might do it, and to be the quarrying of material wherewith to buttress your systems, in many a heart by this time would the name of the Lord be loved where now it remains unknown.

GEORGE MACDONALD
Creation in Christ

---

on his American pantheism, a secularized Eastern monism bereft of its gods and goddesses and peopled by men and women, each of whom participates in the "one soul that animates all men."[18]

The intellectual is not to be a mere thinker. The secrets, the knowledge, that emerge within Man Thinking are to be put in action:

> Without it [action], thought can never ripen into truth. . . . Inaction is cowardice, but there can be no scholar without the heroic mind. The preamble of thought, the transition through which it passes from the unconscious to the conscious, is action. Only so much do I know, as I have lived. Instantly we know whose words are loaded with life, and whose not.[19]

And again: "The mind now thinks, now acts, and each fit reproduces the other. . . . Thinking is the function. Living is the functionary."[20]

Ultimately the role of Man Thinking is "to cheer, to raise and to guide men by showing them facts amidst appearances."[21] So it is that intellectuals become the high priests of a brave new world of American transcendentalism.[22]

It is tempting to discount Emerson as an eccentric denizen of nineteenth-century New England. What twenty-first-century Americans are going to recant their materialism, their identity as producers and consumers of goods and services? Very few, I suspect. New Agers who accept the spirituality behind the material still think the

---

Why should intellectuals be specifically responsible, and differently responsible than other people, and for what? Their superiority, one may think, consists in a skill in using words; and if it is right to label them as seducers, they are able to seduce to either good or evil, of course. But as far as the distinction between good and evil is concerned—be it in moral or political matters—are they necessarily more reliable, are they less fallible guides than other people? Hardly.

LESZEK KOLAKOWSKI
Modernity on Endless Trial

---

material is quite real, quite worth buying and consuming. But there are good reasons for taking Emerson seriously, for one major element of his transcendentalism had already appeared in Enlightenment thought: a rejection of revelation and a confidence in human reason as such. Today that confidence is present in ideology. Man Thinking can refashion Man Not Thinking.

In short, the second confusion of modern intellectuals is to think that truth is identical with ideology. Take Karl Mannheim's comment:

> In every society there are social groups whose special task it is to provide an interpretation of the world for that society. We call these the "intelligentsia." The more static a society is, the more likely is it that this stratum will acquire a well-defined status or the position of a caste in that society. Thus the magicians, the Brahmins, the medieval clergy are to be regarded as intellectual strata, each of which in its society enjoyed a monopolistic control over the moulding of that society's world-view, and over either the reconstruction or the reconciliation of the differences in the naively formed world-views of other

strata. The sermon, the confession, the lesson, are in this sense means by which reconciliation of the different conceptions of the world takes place at less sophisticated levels of social development.[23]

Mannheim, working largely from a Marxist perspective, limits all explanations of social reality to material causes. Here he is supposedly describing reality, not prescribing what it should be. But with many intellectuals from such an *is* quickly comes an *ought*.

Václav Havel describes the position, one aptly labeled "holistic social engineering," by Karl Popper:

> He [Popper] used the term [holistic social engineering] to describe attempts to change the world for the better, completely and globally, on the basis of some preconceived ideology that purported to understand all the laws of historical development and to describe inclusively, comprehensively, and holistically a state of affairs that would be the ultimate realization of these laws.[24]

The application of such ideology has led to much violence and terror. It is this that prompted Camus to write: "Mistaken ideas always end in bloodshed, but in every case it is someone else's blood."[25]

Intellectuals make at least as many political, moral, and personal mistakes as anybody else. Ordinary folk, however, may not have the same capacity for self-deception as more high-powered minds.

PAUL ROAZEN
"Soft-Hearted Hannah," *The American Scholar*

Contrary to Nietzsche and his myriad followers, truth is not a "mobile army of metaphors" imagined by intellectuals and propagated by "strong poets" who by their rhetorical skill get us to speak their language.[26] Truth cannot be constructed. To live in ideology is, as Havel so eloquently reminds us, inevitably to *live in a lie*. Truth can only be revealed. We cannot be creators, only receptors.

And so as Christians we do well to be wise "readers" of this past century and wise responders to what we read. If our public intellectuals are mostly models for how *not* to think and act, they still provide a service.

Learning the Truth

The first half of living the truth is *learning the truth*. We have been discussing this from the very beginning of the book. There is little to add here, just more to emphasize.

First, learning the truth is primarily a matter of *receiving* something given to us. Truth is not wrested from reality as if we were on a mission of attack. This image smacks of Francis Bacon and René Descartes, not of the Bible or even of philosophy prior to the seven-

---

There are many who seek knowledge for the sake of knowledge: that is curiosity. There are others who desire to know in order that they may be known: that is vanity. Others seek knowledge in order to sell it: that is dishonorable. But there are some who seek knowledge in order to edify others: that is love [*caritas*].

ST. BERNARD OF CLAIRVAUX

---

teenth century. Rather, philosophy, the search for the truth about everything, begins in wonder. We are struck by the beingness of being. We receive knowledge as a gift from God via the natural, or created, world or the world of books, especially the Bible. Pieper puts it well:

> Not only the Greeks in general—Aristotle no less than Plato—but the great medieval thinkers as well, all held that there was an element of purely receptive "looking," not only in sense perception but also in intellectual knowing or, as Heraclitus said, *"Listening-in to the being of things."*
>
> The medievals distinguished between the intellect as *ratio* and the intellect as *intellectus. Ratio* is the power of discursive thought, of searching and re-searching, abstracting, refining, and concluding [*cf.* Latin *discurrere*, "to run to and fro"], whereas *intellectus* refers to the ability of "simply looking" (*simplex intuitus*), to which the truth presents itself as a landscape presents itself to the eye. The spiritual

knowing power of the human mind, as the ancients understood it, is really two things in one: *ratio* and *intellectus:* all knowing involves both. The path of discursive reasoning is accompanied and penetrated by the *intellectus'* untiring vision, which is not active but passive, or better *receptive*—a receptively operating power of the intellect.[27]

The active pursuit of truth involves, then, the passive reception of what is given us and the active work of our minds, what John Henry Newman called "the elastic force of reason."[28] In earlier chapters, especially six and seven, we have already seen how various deliberate disciplines can lead us into these twin modes of *ratio* and *intellectus*. So we need not pursue this further here.

Telling the Truth

The second half of *living the truth* involves telling the truth.

Havel's greengrocer took a simple method of living the truth. He just refused to continue living a lie. He stopped displaying the ideological slogans. Any Christian—intellectual or not—may do the same sort of thing. Publication is not necessary to living the truth. When a Christian family decides not to have a TV in the house or to severely limit its use, it has begun to live in truth. It will not be long

---

Jesus would be perfectly at home in any professional context where good is being done today. He would, of course, be a constant rebuke to all the proud self-advancement and the contemptuous treatment of others that goes on in professional circles. In this and other respects, our professions are aching for his presence.

DALLAS WILLARD
"Jesus the Logician"

---

before the neighborhood children will learn that there's no TV in the house (or none allowed to be used for programs with destructive texts or subtexts); they will ask why, and *telling* the truth will begin. One could multiply examples.

So much for any Christian. What does it mean for a Christian intellectual to tell the truth? At minimum it means to conduct one's ordinary communication with utter integrity, holding back nothing of who one is that is relevant to the situation. That is stated very generally. What it means in practice varies widely with the role one plays in society. What does one ordinarily write? Business letters, legal briefs, scientific reports, financial analyses? With whom does one ordinarily converse? Clients, students, employers, employees, neighbors, fellow air travelers?[29] That is the context for telling the truth.

Let's take an example from an area in which I have spent most of my life, university research and teaching. Secular intellectuals in universities have certainly never tired of telling us what they have either taken to be the truth or what they are currently constructing to masquerade as the truth. Christian intellectuals have also been active. But many both inside and outside the Christian world do not know this, or at least pretend not to.

Academic conferences are held, for example, but beyond the fields of philosophy, religion and biblical studies, the presence of Christians reading papers with distinctive Christian content is minimal. I suspect that there are many more Christian academics than those whose academic papers reflect a Christian worldview. This may not be so troublesome in mathematics and the natural sciences

---

In the case of intellectuals, the only specific matter they are professionally responsible for is the good use—that is, the upright and least misleading use—of the word. It is less a matter of truth, since nobody can promise that he will never be mistaken; but it is possible to preserve the spirit of truth, which means never to abandon a vigilant mistrust of one's own words and identifications, to know how to retract one's own errors, and to be capable of self-correction. That *is* humanly possible, and one should expect it from intellectuals since, for obvious reasons, the common human qualities of vanity and greed for power among intellectuals may have particularly harmful and dangerous results.

LESZEK KOLAKOWSKI
Modernity on Endless Trial

of chemistry, physics and much of biology. But in the study of biological origins, and certainly in psychology, sociology and anthropology, as well as in history, literature and the arts, some revealed truths of the Christian worldview are so relevant that not to bring them into the picture constitutes *living a lie*.

Is not the most important fact about us that we are made *in the image of God?* Yet what textbook, scholarly paper or research program in psychology, sociology, anthropology, history, literary theory even mentions the idea? It is considered, if not simply false, utterly irrelevant to the field. What papers published in reputable academic journals or books published by scholarly presses can we point to as examples of Christian scholarship in those fields? There are a few. I can point to two: *The Political Meaning of Christianity* by Glenn Tinder, a professor of political science at the University of Massachusetts at Boston; and *The American Hour: A Time of Reckoning and the Once and Future Role of Faith* by Os Guinness, a sociologist and Senior Fellow at the Trinity Forum.[30] Guinness is perhaps best described as both a Christian and an independent, public intellectual.

Or in the natural sciences, is not the most important fact about the so-called natural order that, in a most important sense, it is not "natural" at all? John Henry Newman's challenge is apt:

> Admit a God, and you introduce among the subjects of your knowledge, a fact encompassing, closing in upon, absorbing, every other fact conceivable. How can we investigate any part of any order of knowledge, and stop short of that which enters into every order? All true principles run over with it, all phenomena converge to it.[31]

Where in the scientific literature, a considerable portion of which is written by Christians in the sciences, is there any acknowledgment of the fact of creation and the immanence of God?[32]

Christian scholars at secular universities, and tragically many at distinctively Christian colleges as well, have been entrapped by the ideology of naturalism.[33] Like Havel's greengrocer, many teachers have, wittingly or not, displayed the various naturalist placards appropriate to their academic discipline, changing them as the specific ideology of their discipline changes:

☐ "All history is written by the winners."

☐ "History is best told from the bottom up."

☐ "Polarized views—this is right, that's wrong—don't take history's questions seriously."[34]

☐ "In science only material factors enter into our explanations; we cannot talk of design."[35]

☐ "Literature is an ideology."[36]

☐ "No text has an author."

☐ "Observe the functioning of Christ-images in this story; don't ask about Christ himself."

☐ "Systematic theology is the study of what systematic theologians have written or believed; it is not about the object of belief."[37]

☐ "The effects of truth are produced within discourses which in themselves are neither true nor false."[38]

☐ "Human beings construct their own nature."[39]

Beneath all of these may rest the most decadent principle of all (this was actually overheard at an academic conference on religion): "None of us believes any of what we are discussing, but this is how we get paid."[40] In such an academic arena it has not been easy to display any obvious placard of Christian faith.

Political scientist John C. Green writes:

> If a professor talks about studying something from a Marxist point of view, others might disagree but not dismiss the notion. But if a professor proposed to study something from a Catholic or Protestant point of view, it would be treated like proposing something from a Martian point of view.[41]

It must have come as something of a shock to hear Charles Habib Malik deliver the Pascal Lectures on Christianity and the University at the University of Waterloo, Ontario, Canada. Malik's academic credits include professorships at Harvard, Dartmouth and the Catholic University of America; his political credits include president of the General Assembly of the United Nations and of its Security Council. Now picture him addressing an academic audience at a secular university. Who is the final critic of the university? he asked:

> The critic in the final analysis is Jesus Christ himself. We are not offering our opinion; we are seeking his judgment of the university. . . . Jesus Christ exists in himself and he holds the entire world, including the university, in the palm of his hands. . . . We are asking, seeking, knocking to find out exactly what Jesus Christ thinks of the university.[42]

Malik's lectures were a stunning tour de force as the rhetoric lent power to his shrewd analysis of the sciences and humanities. His was at the time almost a lone voice.

Of course there have always been a few Christians who have dared to admit to their Christian faith in the secular academic arena. One thinks here first and foremost of C. S. Lewis. Then one struggles

---

[Harvard students in the 1880s:] It was an idyllic, haphazard, humouristic existence, without fine imagination, without any familiar infusion of scholarship, without articulate religion: a flutter of intelligence in a void, flying into trivial play, in order to drop back, as soon as college days were over, into the drudgery of affairs.

GEORGE SANTAYANA
Character and Opinion in the United States

---

to think of anyone else. In fact, it is only in the past few years that Christian scholars have thought seriously about their public role, the open relevance of their Christian faith to their academic disciplines.[43] Among the most visible of these have been a trio of academics with roots in Calvin College: Nicholas Wolterstorff, Alvin Plantinga and George Marsden, all of whom have taken posts at major Ph.D.-granting institutions. The first two are philosophers and have been at the forefront of creating a visible scholarly presence of Christians in philosophy. The latter is a historian, two of whose books, *The Soul of the American University* and *The Outrageous Idea of Christian Scholarship*, are published by Oxford University Press.[44] Marsden in fact was fêted with a front-page photo in *The Chronicle of Higher Education*, with a backdrop of a giant mural of Jesus seen on TV by many on Saturday afternoons in the fall, just over the top of the Notre Dame football stadium.[45] It would be marvelous if all Christian academics were to think and act as if Jesus really were looking over their shoulders. (He is, you know.)

In general, however, Christian intellectuals have been conspicuous by their absence from the corridors of education and political power. They have often known the truth but either have had no public platforms from which to proclaim it or have squandered their opportunities by fear of being marginalized even further.[46]

"But wait," I hear some of my friends say. "Aren't you forgetting about the hundreds of books that Christians have written that do precisely what you are calling for? Didn't you as editor of InterVarsity Press encourage and publish many such books? And didn't Eerdmans do this both before and after you did so? Haven't Zondervan

---

The point of Christian scholarship is not recognition by standards established in the wider culture. The point is to praise God with the mind. Such efforts will lead to the kind of intellectual integrity that sometimes receives recognition. But for the Christian that recognition is only a fairly inconsequential by-product. The real point is valuing what God has made, believing that the creation is as "good" as he said it was, and exploring the fullest dimensions of what is meant for the Son of God to "become flesh and dwell among us." Ultimately, intellectual work of this sort is its own reward, because it is focussed on the only One whose recognition is important, the One before whom all hearts are open.

MARK NOLL
The Scandal of the Evangelical Mind

---

and some others followed suit? Just look at the long list of books in the bibliography at the end of your own *Discipleship of the Mind*."[47]

The point is well taken. Yes, all that is true.[48] But actually it proves my point. These books—excellent as they are—are published by evangelical Christian publishers. Eerdmans and IVP after it have only just emerged as acceptable publishers of books worthy to be read by scholarly readers outside the narrow confines of the evangelical Christian world. Moreover, most of their publications are on specifically religious topics. There still remain only a handful of quality books based on specifically Christian premises in the disciplines of psychology, sociology, anthropology and economics or the humanities and fine arts.[49]

It is clearly time to obey the slogan of the campaign in which my politician brother-in-law backed a candidate running against his colleague, the governor of the state: "Tell the truth, Terry!" I must sadly report that the campaign was unsuccessful. Terry was reelected. But success in telling the truth, as I have said before, is not measured by results. The graduate student who tells the truth may jeopardize his chances of achieving the Ph.D. The assistant professor may lessen the chance of receiving tenure. The Christian scholar may not get his or her paper in the top journals of the field.

But Noll is correct: "Ultimately, intellectual work of this sort is its own reward, because it is focussed on the only One whose recognition is important, the One before whom all hearts are open."[50]

Take my intellect, and use
Every power as thou shalt choose.

FRANCES R. HAVERGAL
"Take My Life and Let It Be"

Unfortunately, Camus too is right—figuratively as well as literally: "Mistaken ideas always end in bloodshed, but in every case it is someone else's blood."[51] The blood that is shed by the mistaken ideas of others—those preventing the dissemination of Christian scholarship, for example—may be that of Christian scholars. Telling the truth may indeed be hazardous to one's professional health. Remember, though, what we discussed in chapter six: courage is one of the intellectual virtues. It is absolutely necessary for Christians in the academic world today.

Responsible to God

While we are responsible *for* living in truth—learning the truth and telling the truth—it is *to God* that we are responsible. Beyond our responsibility to our families, our communities of faith, our neighbors, our country, the world around us, we are primarily responsible to our Creator, our Lord, our Savior—Father, Son and Holy Spirit.

The general responsibility to glorify God takes precedence over any of the specific responsibilities we have as intellectuals or intellectual wannabes, for glorifying God is a full-time task engaging all we are. This prayer might well be offered at the beginning and end of each day:

> Let me use all things for one sole reason: to find my joy in giving You great glory.[52]

Notes

Preface

[1]Os Guinness, *The Call: Finding and Fulfilling the Central Purpose of Your Life* (Nashville: Word, 1998), p. 73.

[2]Miguel de Unamuno, *The Tragic Sense of Life*, trans. J. E. Crawford Flitch (New York: Dover, 1954), p. 16.

[3]Ibid., p. 1.

[4]Attributed to an old Jew of Galicia by Czeslaw Milosz, *The Captive Mind*, trans. Jane Zielomko (New York: Vintage, 1955), p. 2.

[5]Petrarch's letter to Giovanni Colonna di San Vito, dated September 25, 1342, as quoted by David Lyle Jeffrey, *People of the Book: Christian Identity and Literary Culture* (Grand Rapids, Mich.: Eerdmans, 1996), p. 170.

[6]George Santayana, *Character and Opinion in the United States* (Garden City, N.Y.: Doubleday/Anchor, 1920), p. 52.

[7]Okay. These Latin words are a bit much. Centuries ago they were sung by a child and overheard by Augustine, encouraging him over and over to "pick it up and read, pick it up and read" (*Confessions* 8.12). He did and read Romans 13:13-14. His highly emotional and spiritual conversion quickly followed. A bit too much to quote here? Who knows?

Chapter I: Confessions of an Intellectual Wannabe

[1]Denis Diderot, *Rameau's Nephew* and *D'Alembert's Dream*, trans. Leonard Tanock (Harmondsworth, U.K.: Penguin, 1966), p. 33. Of course it takes an act of considerable imagination to picture a story by this eighteenth-century French *philosophe* in *The Saturday Evening Post*. Still, the *Post* carried stories that intrigued me as a child with an insatiable hunger to read.

[2]This definition is close to that given in jest by President Eisenhower: "a man who takes more words than are necessary to tell more than he knows" (quoted by Richard Hofstadter, *Anti-intellectualism in American Life* [New York: Alfred A. Knopf, 1969], p. 10; Hofstadter also lists other uncomplimentary descriptions of intellectuals [pp. 9-10]).

[3]Paul Roazen comments, "Intellectuals make at least as many political, moral, and personal mistakes as anybody else. Ordinary folk, however, may not have the same capacity for self-deception as more high-powered minds" ("Soft-Hearted Hannah," review of *Hannah Arendt/Martin Heidegger/Elzbieta Ettinger*

by Elzbieta Ettinger [New Haven, Conn.: Yale University Press, 1995], *The American Scholar*, summer 1996, p. 459).

[4]Bertrand Russell, quoted by Russell Kirk, "The American Intellectual: A Conservative View," in *The Intellectuals: A Controversial Portrait*, ed. George B. de Huszar (Glencoe, Ill.: Free Press, 1960), p. 309.

[5]J. I. Packer summarizes Johnson's notion of an intellectual as "one who pontificates about how others should live while being unable or unwilling to live that way himself" (J. I. Packer, "The Substance of Truth in the Present Age," *Crux*, March 1998, p. 5).

[6]Paul Johnson, *Intellectuals* (New York: Harper & Row, 1988). Johnson's full description is as follows: "The secular intellectual might be deist, sceptic or atheist. But he was just as ready as any pontiff or presbyter to tell mankind how to conduct its affairs. He proclaimed, from the start, a special devotion to the interests of humanity and an evangelical duty to advance them by his teaching. He brought to this self-appointed task a far more radical approach than his clerical predecessors. He felt himself bound by no corpus of revealed religion. The collective wisdom of the past, the legacy of tradition, the prescriptive codes of ancestral experience existed to be selectively followed or wholly rejected entirely as his own good sense might decide. For the first time in human history, and with growing confidence and audacity, men arose to assert that they could diagnose the ills of society and cure them with their own unaided intellects: more, that they could devise formulae whereby not merely the structure of society but the fundamental habits of human beings could be transformed for the better. Unlike their sacerdotal predecessors, they were not servants and interpreters of the gods but substitutes. Their hero was Prometheus, who stole celestial fire and brought it to earth" (pp. 1-2).

[7]Johnson is only one of many critics to define and criticize "intellectuals" as a class. Thomas Molnar, for example, takes a more nuanced view in *The Decline of the Intellectuals* (New York: World, 1961). He argues that the term *intellectual* used in a historical context should be limited to a "class" of thinkers living between 1350 and 1950. All of them were ideologues, but not by any means of one mind: they included liberal humanists, Marxists, progressives, reactionaries; most were secularists, but some continued to maintain belief in Christianity. All were interested in bringing about their utopian visions, but in every case their plans shipwrecked on the rocky shores of human nature: People could not be refashioned by visions and ideologies. If one is to see the transformation of human beings, it will be through the power of Christ and the coming of the kingdom of God. As Joseph de Maistre (1753-1821) wrote, "One can only smile somewhat scornfully at a man who promises us a *new man*. Let us leave that expression for the Gospel. The human spirit is what it has always been" (quoted by Crane Brinton, *The Shaping of Modern Thought* [Englewood Cliffs,

N.J.: Prentice-Hall, 1963], p. 175). Lydia Alex Fillingham's capsule definition of an intellectual begins by identifying Jean-Paul Sartre as one who "really defined the type: a thinker, with thoughts on a wide variety of subjects, popularly recognized as an important national resource, expected to say brilliant, unexpected things, to get involved in politics from time to time, and to symbolize knowledge and thought for the nation and the world" (*Foucault for Beginners* [New York: Writers and Readers, 1993], p. 3). Among the more balanced treatments are Leszek Kolakowski, "The Intellectuals," in *Modernity on Endless Trial* (Chicago: University of Chicago Press, 1990), pp. 32-43; and Lewis A. Coser, *Men of Ideas: A Sociologist's View* (New York: Free Press, 1965), pp. vii-ix.

[8]Hofstadter, *Anti-intellectualism*, p. 280, comments that in the late nineteenth century and the early years of the twentieth "not many farmers sent their sons [to college]; and when they did, the sons took advantage of their educational opportunities to get out of farming—usually to go into engineering."

[9]See Ranald Macauley and Jerram Barrs, *Being Human: The Nature of Spiritual Experience* (Downers Grove, Ill.: InterVarsity Press, 1978), pp. 147-53; and J. P. Moreland, *Love God with All Your Mind* (Colorado Springs, Colo.: NavPress, 1997), pp. 57-59. John Stott's *Your Mind Matters* (Downers Grove, Ill.: InterVarsity Press, 1972), an excellent brief book encouraging Christians to use their minds, also counters such anti-intellectual readings of Paul.

[10]Perhaps it would be better to say that anti-intellectualism is a major characteristic of Americans in general. After I had contemplated this possibility for some time, it was somewhat of a relief to find that it may be a major characteristic of the English as well; at least that's what one promoter of rational thought tries to demonstrate (see L. Susan Stebbing, *Thinking to Some Purpose* (Harmondsworth, U.K.: Penguin, 1939), in a chapter subtitled "Are the English Illogical?" pp. 11-22.

[11]Mark Noll, *The Scandal of the Evangelical Mind* (Grand Rapids, Mich.: Eerdmans, 1994), p. 3. See also Os Guinness, *Fit Bodies, Fat Minds* (Grand Rapids, Mich.: Baker, 1994). Both books are sustained pleas for evangelical Christians to live up to their responsibilities—to love God with all the mind.

[12]The number of definitions of *intellectual* (noun) and *anti-intellectual* (noun) could be multiplied. Thomas Molnar, for example, briefly identifies four definitions of *intellectual*: "André Malraux defines the intellectual as a man whose life is guided by devotion to an idea; Peter Viereck holds that he is a full-time servant of the Word, or of the word,' that is, a kind of priest either of a lofty ideal, or of literary, artistic, philosophical, pursuits" (Thomas Molnar, *The Decline of the Intellectual* [Cleveland, Ohio: World, 1961], p. 7). He notes as well that Maurice Barrés calls intellectuals "pen pushers and leftists" (ibid.). After identifying three of his own distinct "anti-intellectualisms," Crane Brinton

concludes, "If Graham Wallas, William James, Freud, Nietzsche, Bergson, Tristan Tzara, Kafka, Alfred Rosenberg, Hitler, Stalin, and the late Senator McCarthy all belong in the same boat, it must be a pretty big boat, with several water-tight, or better, air-tight compartments" ("On the Discrimination of Anti-intellectualisms," *The Fate of Man*, ed. Crane Brinton [New York: George Braziller, 1961], p. 313).

[13]Jacques Barzun lists three main reasons for the rampant anti-intellectualism in current American society: modern art (which has taken a distinctly antirational turn in both form and justification), science (with its emphasis on the "numerical, objective, [and] certain") and philanthropy (which promotes education among the less capable to the detriment of the more capable) (see Jacques Barzun, *The House of Intellect* [New York: Harper & Brothers, 1959], pp. 1-30). The first two reasons seem reasonable; the latter provides some rational justification for the anti-intellectualism it is said to cause!

[14]Hofstadter, *Anti-intellectualism*, p. 27.

[15]Another image than ax in the forest is digging one's own grave, suggested by Peter Berger and used imaginatively by Os Guinness in *The Gravedigger File* (Downers Grove, Ill.: InterVarsity Press, 1983), pp. 13-27. See Peter Berger, *The Sacred Canopy* (Garden City, N.Y.: Doubleday/Anchor, 1969).

[16]See as well Barzun, *House of Intellect*, pp. 4-5.

[17]Hofstadter, *Anti-intellectualism*, p. 27. Jacques Barzun takes exception to this distinction: "Every mind capable of ideas must live for them as well as by them. Living exclusively for ideas does not define an intellectual but an emotional type" (Barzun, *House of Intellect*, p. 26).

[18]The ideological mindset is always a temptation to one who thinks: "The ideological mind-set, formed as it is at bottom by a desire to dominate rather than illuminate, is an intruder in philosophy and the arts. It is closed in upon itself and resentful of competition. Instead of cultivating the openness to new influences that marks real philosophy and art and letting itself be exposed to the possible intellectual turmoil of fresh insight, ideology shunts inconvenient thought and imagination aside. Ideologues produce propaganda, although sometimes propaganda of a sophisticated kind. When such individuals set the tone, the intellectual and artistic life suffers" (Claes G. Ryn, "How Conservatives Have Failed 'the Culture,' " *Modern Age* 32, no. 2 [winter 1996]: 118). Hofstadter here comes close to Paul Johnson: "[The intellectual] lives for ideas—which means that he has a sense of dedication to the life of the mind which is very like a religious commitment. . . . The noblest thing, and the closest possible to divinity, is the act of knowing" (Hofstadter, *Anti-intellectualism*, pp. 27-28).

[19]Jacques Barzun, writing about "the educated mind," comments, "Indeed one test of a true education is that it sits lightly on the possessor. He knows better

than anybody else how thin in spots is the mantle which others would pluck from him" ("The Educated Mind," in *Begin Here: The Forgotten Conditions of Teaching and Learning* [Chicago: University of Chicago Press, 1991], p. 211).

Chapter II: John Henry Newman as an Intellectual

[1] John Henry Newman, *The Idea of a University*, ed. Frank M. Turner (New Haven, Conn.: Yale University Press, 1966), p. 101.

[2] John Henry Newman, *Apologia Pro Vita Sua*, ed. David DeLaura (New York: W. W. Norton, 1968), p. 18.

[3] Ker comments, "On 1 May 1808 Newman was sent to a private boarding-school at Ealing, run by a Dr Nicholas. Although it was not a private school, it enjoyed a considerable reputation" (Ian Ker, *John Henry Newman* [New York: Oxford University Press, 1988], p. 1). Much of the biographical information in this chapter comes from Ker's masterful biography as well as *Apologia Pro Vita Sua*, Newman's own autobiography.

[4] Ker, *John Henry Newman*, p. 15.

[5] Regarding his constant involvement in controversy, in 1861 Newman reflected, "I have been in constant hot water, of one sort or degree or another, for thirty years—and it has at last boiled me"; Ker adds, "The worry was 'sucking life' out of him" (ibid., p. 503, quoting *Letters and Diaries*, 10:35-36).

[6] Charles Frederick Harrold and William D. Templeman, "John Henry Newman," in *English Prose of the Victorian Era* (New York: Oxford University Press, 1938), p. 1616.

[7] Newman, *Apologia*, p. 22; David DeLaura describes Whately as one of Oriel College's " 'Noetics' (intellectuals) who freely criticized traditional religious orthodoxy" (ibid., p. 22 n.). Newman himself wrote, "As to Dr. Whately, his mind was too different from mine for us to remain long on one line" (ibid., p. 22).

[8] Ker, *John Henry Newman*, p. 328.

[9] Newman, *Apologia*, p. 2.

[10] Ker, *John Henry Newman*, p. 745.

[11] Owen Chadwick, *Newman* (Oxford: Oxford University Press, 1983), p. 2.

[12] Ker calls *Letters on Justification* "a pioneering classic of 'ecumenical' theology" (Ker, *John Henry Newman*, p. 157).

[13] Chadwick, *Newman*, p. 11.

[14] Quoted by Ker, *John Henry Newman*, p. 32.

[15] Ker, *John Henry Newman*, p. 738.

[16] Quoted in ibid., p. 150, from *The Letters and Diaries of John Henry Newman*, ed. Charles Stephen Dessain et al. (Oxford, 1978-1984), 6:193.

[17] Newman, *Apologia*, p. 17.

[18] Ker, *John Henry Newman*, p. 724 notes, quoting from *Letters and Diaries*, 10:343,

368, 168: "What had made him [Newman] write was 'the sight of a truth and the desire to show it to others.' "

[19]Quoted by Ker, *John Henry Newman*, p. 312, from *An Essay on the Development of Christian Doctrine*; see also Ker, *John Henry Newman*, p. 704.

[20]Ibid.

[21]Ker, *John Henry Newman*, p. 35, quoting Newman, *Letters and Diaries*, 2:129-31.

[22]Quoted by Ker, *John Henry Newman*, p. 72.

[23]Newman, "The Tamworth Reading Room," quoted by Ker, *John Henry Newman*, p. 209.

[24]From a letter to Mrs. W. Froude, quoted by Ker, *John Henry Newman*, p. 298.

[25]Newman, "Intellect, the Instrument of Religious Training," in *Sermons Preached on Various Occasions*, quoted by Ker, *John Henry Newman*, p. 434.

[26]Stanley L. Jaki, introduction to *Newman Today*, Proceedings of the Wethersfield Institute (San Francisco: Ignatius, 1989), p. 11.

[27]*John Henry Newman: Autobiographical Writings*, ed. Henry Tristram (London, 1950), p. 200, quoted by Ker, *John Henry Newman*, p. 21.

[28]John Henry Newman, *Parochial and Plain Sermons* (San Francisco: Ignatius, 1997), p. 220.

[29]Ibid., pp. 1477-78.

[30]Ibid., p. 11.

[31]In an entry in his private journal marked March 28, 1839, Newman described a regimen of severe fast and abstinence that he was to engage in for the next ten years. But he eventually abandoned this for an "ordinary path to holiness" which he describes in "A Short Road to Perfection": "Do not lie in bed beyond the due time of rising; give your first thoughts to God; make a good visit to the Blessed Sacrament; say the Angelus devoutly; eat and drink to God's glory; say the Rosary well; be recollected; keep out bad thoughts; make your evening meditation well; examine yourself daily; go to bed in good time, and you are already perfect" (Newman, *Prayers, Verses and Devotions* [San Francisco: Ignatius, 1989], p. 329, quoted by Michael Sharkey, "Newman's Quest for Holiness in His Search for Truth," in Jaki, *Newman Today*, p. 177).

[32]Newman, *Historical Sketches*, quoted by Ker, *John Henry Newman*, p. 484.

[33]See Michael Sharkey, "Newman's Quest for Holiness in his Search for Truth," in Jaki, *Newman Today*, pp. 175-87; and Ian Ker, "The Christian Life," in *Newman on Being a Christian* (Notre Dame, Ind.: University of Notre Dame Press, 1990), pp. 119-52.

[34]See Ian Ker, "Revelation," in *Newman on Being a Christian*, pp. 17-38, for a more detailed description of Newman's notion.

[35]Newman, *Tract 73*, quoted by Ker, *John Henry Newman*, p. 121.

[36]Newman, *Tract 73*, quoted by Ker, *John Henry Newman*, pp. 121-22.

[37]Newman, *The Arians of the Fourth Century* (London: Longmans, Green, 1908), p.

50, quoted by Ker, "Newman and the Postconciliar Church," in *Newman Today*, p. 131.

[38]Ibid.

[39]Newman, sermon "Implicit and Explicit Reason," quoted by Ian Ker, *The Achievement of John Henry Newman* (Notre Dame, Ind.: University of Notre Dame Press, 1990), p. 43.

[40]Jaki notes that the term "illative sense" is not original with Newman, but it is one he "certainly made popular" (Jaki, "Newman's Assent to Reality, Natural and Supernatural," in *Newman Today*, p. 196).

[41]Newman in a letter to Miss M. Holmes, March 8, 1943, quoted by Ker, *John Henry Newman*, p. 273.

[42]Newman, *An Essay in Aid of a Grammar of Assent* (hereafter cited as *Grammar*; Notre Dame, Ind.: University of Notre Dame Press, 1979), p. 240.

[43]Ker, *John Henry Newman*, p. 631.

[44]Newman, *Grammar*, p. 304. Given the pluralistic world in which most people in the West grow up, it is not clear to me that Newman would maintain such a universality in the specific content of conscience.

[45]Ibid., pp. 106-7.

[46]See quotation above (p. 40) from Ker, *John Henry Newman*, p. 121.

[47]Ker, *John Henry Newman*, p. 558.

[48]Newman, *Letters and Diaries*, pp. 425-26, quoted by Ker, *John Henry Newman*, p. 523.

[49]Ronald Begley examines this tension in "Metaphor in the *Apologia* and Newman's Conversion," in *Newman and Conversion*, ed. Ian Ker (Notre Dame, Ind.: University of Notre Dame Press, 1997), pp. 59-74.

[50]Ker, *John Henry Newman*, p. 523.

[51]Ibid., p. 558.

[52]Newman, *A Letter to the Duke of York*, in *Certain Difficulties Felt by Anglicans in Catholic Teaching* (London: Longmans, Green, 1898), 2:247-50, quoted in Ker, *John Henry Newman*, p. 688.

[53]Ibid., p. 688.

[54]Ibid., p. 689.

[55]Ibid., p. 690.

[56]Newman, *Grammar*, p. 106. In *Certain Difficulties Felt by Anglicans* Newman writes: "Conscience is not a long-sighted selfishness, nor a desire to be consistent with oneself; but it is a messenger from Him, who, both in nature and grace, speaks to us behind a veil, and teaches and rules us by His representatives. Conscience is the aboriginal Vicar of Christ, a prophet in its informations, a monarch in its peremptoriness, a priest in its blessings and anathemas, and, even though the eternal priesthood throughout the Church should cease to be, in it the sacerdotal principle would remain and would have a sway" (2:248-49;

quoted by Halbert Weidner, *Praying with Cardinal Newman* [Winona, Minn.: St. Mary's, 1977], p. 71).

[57]For a detailed analysis of Newman's conception of certitude, see Terrence Merrigan, *Clear Heads and Holy Hearts: The Religious and Theological Ideal of John Henry Newman* (Louvain, Belgium: Peeters, 1991), esp. pp. 193-228; and M. Jamie Ferreira, *Doubt and Religious Commitment: The Role of the Will in Newman's Thought* (Oxford: Clarendon, 1980).

[58]Newman credits Edward Hawkins, then vicar of St. Mary's, Oxford, with teaching him "to weigh my words, and to be cautious in my statements" (quoted by Ker, *John Henry Newman*, p. 22).

[59]Quoted by Ker, *John Henry Newman*, p. 253.

[60]Newman, *Parochial Sermons*, quoted by Ker, *John Henry Newman*, p. 97.

[61]See Newman, *Grammar*, pp. 25-92.

[62]It takes Ker thirteen pages to summarize Newman's argument (Ker, *John Henry Newman*, pp. 637-50).

[63]Newman, *Grammar*, p. 163.

[64]Ibid., p. 181.

[65]Ibid., p. 276. See William J. Wainwright's sympathetic explication of Newman's epistemology, especially his comments on the illative sense (*Reason and the Heart: A Prolegomenon to a Critique of Passional Reason* [Ithaca, N.Y.: Cornell University Press, 1995], pp. 55-83).

[66]I have discussed Nietzsche's critique of Descartes's search for certitude in "On Being a Fool for Christ and an Idiot for Nobody: Logocentricity and Postmodernity," in *Christian Apologetics in the Postmodern World*, ed, Timothy R. Phillips and Dennis L. Okholm (Downers Grove, Ill.: InterVarsity Press, 1995), pp. 116-20.

[67]Avery Dulles, "Newman: The Anatomy of a Conversion," in *Newman and Conversion*, p. 28.

[68]Newman, *Apologia*, p. 81.

[69]Harrold and Templeman, "John Henry Newman," p. 1617.

[70]Newman, *Apologia*, p. 98.

[71]Translated from *Contra epistolain Parmenian* (3.4.24) in ibid., p. 98 n.

[72]Ibid., p. 98.

[73]Ibid., p. 99.

[74]Newman, letter to Frederic Rogers, October 3, 1839, quoted by Ker, *John Henry Newman*, p. 183.

[75]Newman, *Apologia*, p. 99.

[76]Ibid., p. 100.

[77]Letter to H. Wilberforce, October 30, 1884, quoted by Ker, *John Henry Newman*, p. 292.

[78]Ibid.

[79]Letter to John Keble, November 21, 1844, quoted by Ker, *John Henry Newman*, p. 294.

[80]Letter to Mrs. J. Mozley, November 24, 30 and December 2, quoted by Ker, *John Henry Newman*, p. 294.

[81]Ker, *John Henry Newman*, p. 293.

[82]Chadwick, *Newman*, p. 5.

Chapter III: The Perfection of the Intellect

[1]Frank M. Turner, "Newman's University and Ours," in John Henry Newman, *The Idea of a University*, ed. Frank M. Turner (New Haven, Conn.: Yale University Press, 1996), p. 283.

[2]Jaroslav Pelikan attempts to interpret the implications of *The Idea of a University* for secular education, but in trying to secularize Newman's ideas Pelikan so distorts them as to make the book useless for Christians and for secular education as well (see Jaroslav Pelikan, *The Idea of a University: A Reexamination* [New Haven, Conn.: Yale University Press, 1992]). A far more helpful book alluding to Newman's *Idea of a University* is George Marsden's *The Outrageous Idea of Christian Scholarship* (New York: Oxford University Press, 1997); see also Mark R. Schwehn, *Exiles from Eden: Religion and the Academic Vocation in America* (New York: Oxford University Press, 1993); and Arthur F. Holmes, *The Idea of a Christian College*, rev. ed. (Grand Rapids, Mich.: Eerdmans, 1987).

[3]Newman, *Idea*, p. 100.

[4]Ibid, pp. 97-98.

[5]Ibid., pp. 100-102.

[6]Newman, "Christianity and Scientific Investigation," in *Idea*, p. 221.

[7]Newman, sermon "Implicit and Explicit Reason," quoted by Ian Ker, *The Achievement of John Henry Newman* (Notre Dame, Ind.: University of Notre Dame Press, 1990), p. 43.

[8]Newman, *Idea*, p. 60.

[9]Newman, *An Essay in Aid of a Grammar of Assent* (hereafter cited as *Grammar*; Notre Dame, Ind.: University of Notre Dame Press, 1979), p. 228.

[10]Ker, *John Henry Newman*, p. 3.

[11]See the discussion of *real* and *unreal* in chapter two (p. 46).

[12]Newman, *Idea*, p. 60.

[13]Ibid., p. 53.

[14]Ibid., p. 45. Note also: "I have said that all branches of knowledge are connected together, because the subject-matter of knowledge is intimately united in itself, as being the acts, and the work of the Creator. Hence it is that the Sciences, into which our knowledge may be said to be cast, have multiplied bearings one on another, and an internal sympathy, and admit, or rather demand, comparison and adjustment. They complete, correct, balance

each other" (ibid., p. 76).

[15]Ibid., p. 54.

[16]Ibid., p. 53.

[17]Newman, *Grammar*, p. 275.

[18]Granted some theologians, Karl Barth for example, question the sort of natural theology implied by Newman's notion of discerning something of God in creation. Moreover, we are not required at this point to follow Newman in believing in the infallibility of the Roman Catholic Church or of the pope. If Newman is right about that—and he thinks he is—then we must follow. But that is a position subsequent to the common theological presuppositions that undergird the "perfection of the intellect."

[19]Ker, *John Henry Newman*, p. 35, quoting *Letters and Diaries*, 2:129-31.

[20]Newman, *Grammar*, pp. 106-7 and 304.

[21]See, for example, Newman, *Idea*, p. 66.

[22]Ibid., p. 63.

[23]George Marsden, *The Soul of the American University* (New York: Oxford University Press, 1994); and James Tunstead Burtchaell, *The Dying of the Light: The Disengagement of Colleges and Universities from Their Christian Churches* (Grand Rapids, Mich.: Eerdmans, 1998). A short version of this may be found in Burtchaell, "The Decline and Fall of the Christian College" (in two parts), *First Things*, April 1991, pp. 16-29; May 1991, pp. 30-38.

[24]Ker, *John Henry Newman*, p. 649.

[25]See, for example, Stanley L. Jaki, "Newman's Assent to Reality, Natural and Supernatural," in *Newman Today*, Proceedings of the Wethersfield Institute (San Francisco: Ignatius, 1989), pp. 189-220; John Macquarrie, "Newman and Kierkegaard on the Act of Faith," in *Newman and Conversion* (Notre Dame, Ind.: University of Notre Dame Press, 1997), pp. 75-88; Cyril Barrett, "Newman and Wittgenstein on the Rationality of Belief," in *Newman and Conversion*, pp. 89-99; and William J. Wainwright, *Reason and the Heart: A Prolegomenon to a Critique of Passional Reason* (Ithaca, N.Y.: Cornell University Press, 1995).

[26]The major mystery of the mind is not how reasoning is conducted by the conscious mind; it is rather how the brain has a mind, how consciousness arises. For a fascinating reflection on this see John Searle's comments from the standpoint of a materialist (*The Mystery of Consciousness* [New York: New York Review of Books, 1997]).

[27]Newman, *Idea*, p. 89.

[28]Ibid., p. 151.

[29]Ibid.

[30]John Henry Newman, *Apologia Pro Vita Sua*, ed. David DeLaura (New York: W. W. Norton, 1968), p. 191.

Chapter IV: How Thinking Feels

[1]John Henry Newman, sermon "Implicit and Explicit Reason," quoted by Ian Ker, *The Achievement of John Henry Newman* (Notre Dame, Ind.: University of Notre Dame Press, 1990), p. 43.

[2]A. G. Sertillanges, *The Intellectual Life: Its Spirit, Conditions, Methods,* trans. Mary Ryan (Washington, D.C.: Catholic University of America Press, 1987), p. viii.

[3]Tim Stafford, quoting from an interview with Ellen Charry, "New Theologians," *Christianity Today*, February 8, 1999, p. 47.

[4]Sertillanges, *Intellectual Life*, p. 71.

[5]And babies, especially grandchildren, but that should go without saying, so I didn't say it in the text. Aren't you glad you found this in an endnote that didn't disturb your flow of thought?

[6]Drusilla Scott, *Everyman Revived: The Common Sense of Michael Polanyi* (Grand Rapids, Mich.: Eerdmans, 1985), p. 40; then she quotes Polanyi, *Personal Knowledge: Toward a Post-critical Philosophy* (New York: Harper & Row, 1964), p. 134: "The excitement of the scientist making a discovery is an *intellectual* passion, telling that something is *intellectually* precious, and more particularly that it is *precious to science*."

[7]Enrique Krauze, "In Memory of Octavio Paz (1914-1998)," *The New York Review of Books*, May 28, 1998, p. 24.

[8]Everett Knight, *The Objective Society* (New York: George Braziller, 1960), p. 8.

[9]Jacques Barzun, *The House of Intellect* (New York: Harper & Brothers, 1959), p. 95.

[10]See chapter two, p. 34. The passage there is quoted from *The Letters and Diaries of John Henry Newman*, ed. Charles Stephen Dessain et al. (Oxford, 1984), 6:212-13, by Ker, *Achievement of John Henry Newman*, p. 150. The book Newman was referring to is his *Lectures on Justification* (1838).

[11]See chapter 7, pp. 135-36.

[12]David Hansen, *A Little Handbook on Having a Soul* (Downers Grove, Ill.: InterVarsity Press, 1997), p. 79.

[13]Gilbert Highet, *Man's Unconquerable Mind* (New York: Columbia University Press, 1954), p. 36.

[14]Josef Pieper, *In Defense of Philosophy: Classical Wisdom Stands Up to Modern Challenges*, trans. Lothar Krauth (San Francisco: Ignatius, 1992), p. 47; Plato, Martin Heidegger and Hannah Arendt agree (see Hannah Arendt, "For Martin Heidegger's Eightieth Birthday," in *Martin Heidegger and National Socialism: Questions and Answers*, ed. Günther Neske and Emil Kettering, trans. Lisa Harries [New York: Paragon House, 1990], p. 213, citing Plato *Theaetetus* 155d).

[15]Pieper, *In Defense of Philosophy*, p. 47.

[16]Josef Pieper discusses this distinction in *Leisure, the Basis of Culture* (South Bend, Ind.: St. Augustine's, 1998), pp. 11-12, apparently translating Heracli-

tus's Greek (in Fragment 112) *theoreto* as "listening-in"; Kathleen Freeman in *Ancilla to the Pre-Socratic Philosophers* (Cambridge, Mass.: Harvard University Press, 1957), p. 32, translates *theoreto* less dramatically as "paying heed."

[17]Josef Pieper in fact points to the necessity of leisure to the formation of culture (*Leisure: The Basis of Culture*).

[18]Lewis A. Coser, *Men of Ideas: A Sociologist's View* (New York: Free Press, 1965), p. ix.

[19]Michael Ignatieff, "On Isaiah Berlin (1909-1997)," *The New York Review of Books,* December 18, 1997, p. 10.

[20]Jacques Barzun, "The Educated Mind," in *Begin Here: The Forgotten Conditions of Teaching and Learning* (Chicago: University of Chicago Press, 1992), p. 211 (first published in *Life* magazine, October 15, 1950).

[21]Wendell Berry, "Notes: Unspecializing Poetry," in *Standing by Words* (San Francisco: North Point, 1983), p. 85.

[22]Mary Jo Weaver, "Rooted Hearts/Playful Minds: Catholic Intellectual Life at Its Best," *Cross Currents,* Spring 1988, p. 74.

[23]George Steiner, "The Cleric of Treason," in *George Steiner: A Reader* (New York: Oxford University Press, 1984), pp. 197-98.

[24]I do not wish to put all sociologists of knowledge into the "mere" category. Many, like Max Weber, Peter Berger and Robert Bellah, are intellectuals in their own right.

[25]Stuart Hampshire, "On Isaiah Berlin (1909-1997)," *The New York Review of Books,* December 18, 1997, p. 11.

[26]Leon Wieseltier, "The Trouble with Multiculturalism," review of *Dictatorship of Virtue: Multiculturalism and the Battle for America's Future* by Richard Bernstein, *New York Times Book Review,* October 23, 1994, p. 11.

[27]I have outlined the panorama of contemporary worldviews—theism, deism, naturalism, nihilism, existentialism, Eastern pantheistic monism and postmodernism—in *The Universe Next Door,* 3rd ed. (Downers Grove, Ill.: InterVarsity Press, 1997).

Chapter V: The Moral Dimension of the Mind

[1]A. G. Sertillanges, *The Intellectual Life: Its Spirit, Conditions, Methods.* trans. Mary Ryan (Washington, D.C.: Catholic University of America Press, 1987), p. 172.

[2]From James Allen, *As a Man Thinketh,* quoted by Rueben P. Job and Norman Shawchuck, *A Guide to Prayer for Ministers and Other Servants* (Nashville: Upper Room, 1983), pp. 337-38.

[3]Sertillanges, *Intellectual Life,* pp 67-68.

[4]I recommend most highly Dallas Willard, *The Spirit of the Disciplines* (San Francisco: Harper & Row, 1987); Richard Foster, *Celebration of Discipline* (San Francisco: Harper & Row, 1982); and Job and Shawchuck, *Guide to Prayer for*

Ministers and Other Servants.

[5]The first sentence in Aristotle's *Metaphysics.*

[6]The phrasing is Josef Pieper's, but the concept is Aristotle's (*Metaphysics* 2.1.993b.20) (see Josef Pieper, *Defense of Philosophy* [San Francisco: Ignatius, 1992], pp. 45-46).

[7]The best book I know that takes on the task of showing how knowing and doing fit together and how this unity can be realized in both personal practice and educational pedagogy is Steven Garber's *The Fabric of Faithfulness* (Downers Grove, Ill.: InterVarsity Press, 1996). See also Harvard professor Robert Coles's poignant essay "The Disparity Between Intellect and Character," *The Chronicle of Higher Education,* September 22, 1995, back page.

[8]Sertillanges, *Intellectual Life,* p. 19.

[9]Ibid., pp. 17-18.

[10]E. Michael Jones, *Degenerate Moderns: Modernity as Rationalized Sexual Misbehavior* (San Francisco: Ignatius, 1993), p. 258.

[11]If it is true that desire masks truth, what a gloomy prospect we face if Habermas is correct: "Habermas, probably the ablest defender of modernity, sees only the triumph of desire over reason in the postmodern vision of the world" (Philip Sampson, "The Rise of Postmodernity," in *Faith and Modernity,* ed. Philip Sampson, Vinay Samuel and Chris Sugden [Oxford: Regnum Books International, 1994], p. 40, reflecting on J. Habermas, *The Philosophical Discourse of Modernity* [Polity, 1987]).

[12]Jones, *Degenerate Moderns,* p. 259.

[13]Ibid.

[14]See Stephen K. Moroney, "How Sin Affects Scholarship: A New Model," *Christian Scholar's Review,* spring 1999, pp. 432-51, for a philosophic/theological assessment of the noetic effect of sin.

[15]Eugene (Fr. Seraphim) Rose, *Nihilism: The Root of the Revolution of the Modern Age* (Forestville, Calif.: Fr. Seraphim Rose Foundation, 1994), p. 65.

[16]Jones, *Degenerate Moderns,* pp. 19-41; Jones also has major chapters on Alfred Charles Kinsey (of the infamous Kinsey Report), Anthony Blunt (art critic and spy), Stanley Fish and Jane Tompkins (literary critics), Pablo Picasso, Sigmund Freud, Carl G. Jung and Martin Luther (!). In *Dyonysos Rising: The Birth of Cultural Revolution out of the Spirit of Music* (San Francisco: Ignatius, 1994) Jones continues his analysis of rationalized sexual misbehavior in relation to Richard Wagner, Friedrich Nietzsche, Arnold Schönberg, Theodor Adorno, Aleister Crowley and Mick Jagger. Jones's critique of Kinsey is more than supported by James H. Jones, "Annals of Sexology: Dr. Yes," *The New Yorker,* August 5 and September 1, 1997, pp. 99-113, who writes that rather than being an objective scientist letting carefully collected scientific data guide his conclusions, Kinsey was "a covert crusader who was determined to use science to free American

society from what he saw as the crippling legacy of Victorian repression" (p. 100). His methodology was flawed from start to finish, and his life given over to sexual obsessions: "He was both a homosexual and, from childhood on, a masochist who, as he grew older, pursued an interest in extreme sexuality with increasing compulsiveness" (p. 101). George Steiner reflects on the impact of Anthony Blunt's homosexuality on his treason in "The Cleric of Treason" in *George Steiner: A Reader* (New York: Oxford University Press, 1992), pp. 194-97, but refuses to decide whether Blunt's sexual orientation or even his treason had a deleterious effect on his scholarship: "Blunt's performance as an art historian stands luminous. Are 'monuments of unageing intellect'—Yeats's proud phrase—susceptible to moral or political denial? I just don't know" (p. 202).

[17]The phrase is Derek Freeman's in the book that broke the story of Mead's bad scholarship (see his *Margaret Mead and Samoa: The Making and Unmasking of an Anthropological Myth* [Cambridge, Mass.: Harvard University Press, 1983], p. 284, as quoted by Jones, *Degenerate Moderns*, p. 32).

[18]Jones, *Degenerate Moderns*, p. 32.

[19]Ibid., p. 33.

[20]Ibid., p. 37.

[21]Ibid., p. 40. For Freeman reference see note 17 above.

[22]This is the translation used by Jones.

[23]Sertillanges, *Intellectual Life*, p. 22.

[24]Quoted by Nicholas Lasch in his introduction to John Henry Cardinal Newman, *An Essay in Aid of a Grammar of Assent* (Notre Dame, Ind.: University of Notre Dame Press, 1979), p. 9.

[25]Newman, *Grammar*, pp. 106-7. Newman continues, "Then they are brought into his presence as that of a Living Person, and are able to hold converse with Him, and that with a directness and simplicity, with a confidence and intimacy, *mutatis mutandis*, which we use towards an earthly superior; so that it is doubtful whether we realize the company of our fellow-men with greater keenness than these favoured minds are able to contemplate and adore the Unseen, Incomprehensible Creator" (p. 107).

[26]Okay. Here's the second part of your assignment. Turn over your paper and write the number of hours (minutes?) you spend praying each week. Get it?

[27]Ian Ker, *John Henry Newman* (New York: Oxford University Press, 1988), p. 138.

[28]Quoted by Tim Stafford, "New Theologians," *Christianity Today*, February 8, 1999, p. 36.

[29]Ibid., p. 45.

[30]I have written already in *Discipleship of the Mind* about the integral relationship between knowing and doing, another way of putting the dichotomy (see chapters five and six).

[31]Lesslie Newbigin, *Proper Confidence: Faith, Doubt and Certainty in Christian Disci-

pleship (Grand Rapids, Mich.: Eerdmans, 1995), p. 14.

[32]The text Newbigin quotes is a slightly different translation from the one I quote here from Dietrich Bonhoeffer, *The Cost of Discipleship* (New York: Macmillan, 1959), p. 54.

[33]Again, see chapters five and six of my *Discipleship of the Mind.*

[34]A second equation is similar though not quite so stark: ethically, anger is murder: "You have heard that it was said to the people long ago, 'Do not murder, and anyone who murders will be subject to judgment.' But I tell you that anyone who is angry with his brother will be subject to judgment" (Mt 5:21-22).

[35]For an explanation of the various problems posed by this passage and the solutions given by scholars, see John Stott, *Romans: God's Good News for the World* (Downers Grove, Ill.: InterVarsity Press, 1994), pp. 205-14. In an earlier treatment of Romans 5—7 (*Men Made New* [Downers Grove, Ill.: InterVarsity Press, 1966], pp. 71-75), Stott argues that in Romans 7:14—8:4 Paul was referring to himself and by extension to all Christians; in *Romans*, pp. 205-11, he rejects both this view and the view that these verses refer to the unregenerate person. Instead he takes the rather subtler position that these verses describe a person still living under the sway of the Old Testament, not recognizing the presence or power of the indwelling Holy Spirit, who enables believers to do what they most desire to do: live in conformity with the law.

[36]Stott, *Romans*, p. 221.

[37]Ibid., pp. 217-36; I am, however, quoting here from Stott's earlier, shorter study of Romans 5—8: *Men Made New*, pp. 85-94; on the issue addressed here Stott seems not to have changed his mind.

[38]Ibid., pp. 86-87.

[39]Ibid., p. 91.

[40]Ibid., p. 92.

[41]Michael Casey, *Sacred Reading: The Ancient Art of Lectio Divina* (Ligouri, Mo.: Triumph, 1996), p. 75. Casey goes on to quote Bernard of Clairvaux: "Therefore, my advice to you, friends, is to turn aside from troubled and anxious reflection on your own progress, and escape to the easier paths of remembering the good things God has done. In this way, instead of becoming upset by thinking about yourself, you will find relief by turning your attention to God. . . . Sorrow for sin is, indeed, a necessary thing, but it should not prevail all the time. On the contrary, it is necessary that happier recollections of God's generosity should counterbalance it, lest the heart should become hardened through too much sadness and so perish through despair" (SC 11.12, *Santi Bernardi Opera* [Rome: Editions Cistercienses, 1957], 1.55.12-19).

Chapter VI: The Intellectual Virtues

[1]John Henry Newman, *The Idea of a University*, ed. Frank M. Turner (New

Haven, Conn.: Yale University Press, 1996), pp. 100-102.

[2]Robert Browning, "Andrea del Sarto," lines 97-99.

[3]A. G. Sertillanges, *The Intellectual Life: Its Spirit, Conditions, Methods,* trans. Mary Ryan (Washington, D.C.: Catholic University of America Press, 1987), p. 13.

[4]W. Jay Wood, *Epistemology: Becoming Intellectually Virtuous* (Downers Grove, Ill.: InterVarsity Press, 1998), p. 45.

[5]Ibid., pp. 34-40. My list is not an exact duplicate (I have added some and omitted others he includes).

[6]Quoted by Patrick Henry Reardon, "Truth Is Not Known Unless It Is Loved," *Books & Culture,* September-October 1998, p. 44.

[7]Bernard of Clairvaux, *Sup. Cant.* 8.5-6, quoted by Jean LeClercq, *The Love of Learning and the Desire for God: A Study of Monastic Culture,* 3rd ed., trans. Catherine Misrahi (New York: Fordham University Press, 1982), p. 228.

[8]Blaise Pascal, *Pensées,* trans. A. J. Krailsheimer (Harmondsworth, U.K.: Penguin, 1966), no. 739, p. 256.

[9]Pavel Florensky, *The Pillar and the Ground of Truth,* trans. Boris Jakim (Princeton, N.J.: Princeton University Press, 1997), quoted by Reardon, "Truth Is Not Known Unless It Is Loved," p. 45.

[10]Sertillanges, *Intellectual Life,* p. 19.

[11]Wendell Berry, *The Hidden Wound* (San Francisco: North Point, 1989), pp. 65-66.

[12]David Lyle Jeffrey, "Knowing the Truth in the Present Age," *Crux,* June 1998, p. 20.

[13]Friedrich Nietzsche, *The Anti-Christ* (55), in *Twilight of the Idols/The Anti-Christ,* trans. R. J. Hollingdale (London: Penguin, 1968), p. 183.

[14]Kai Nielsen, *Ethics Without God* (London: Pemberton, 1973), p. 40.

[15]Quoted in Simone de Beauvoir, *Adieux: A Farewell to Sartre,* trans. Patrick O'Brian (London: Penguin, 1984), p. 434.

[16]There are, of course, strong—even compelling—arguments for the existence of God, though it is always possible to doubt the premises or fail to grasp the arguments themselves. See, for example, Peter Kreeft and Ronald K. Tacelli, *Handbook of Christian Apologetics* (Downers Grove, Ill.: InterVarsity Press, 1994), pp. 47-88; J. P. Moreland, *Scaling the Secular City: A Defense of Christianity* (Grand Rapids, Mich.: Baker, 1987), pp. 15-132; and J. P. Moreland and Kai Nielsen, *The Great Debate: Does God Exist?* (Nashville: Thomas Nelson, 1990).

[17]Friedrich Nietzsche, "Thus Spoke Zarathustra," in *The Portable Nietzsche,* trans. Walter Kaufmann (New York: Viking, 1954), pp. 378-79.

[18]Sertillanges, *Intellectual Life,* p. 215.

[19]Mary Jo Weaver, "Rooted Hearts/Playful Minds: Catholic Intellectual Life at Its Best," *Cross Currents,* Spring 1988, pp. 69-70.

[20]Sertillanges, *Intellectual Life,* p. 220.

[21]Eviatar Zerubavel, *Social Mindscapes: An Invitation to Cognitive Sociology* (Cam-

bridge, Mass.: Harvard University Press, 1997), p. 32.

[22]E. Harris Harbison, *The Christian Scholar in the Age of the Reformation* (New York: Charles Scribner's Sons, 1956), p. 80.

[23]Sertillanges, *Intellectual Life*, p. 253.

[24]Weaver, "Rooted Hearts/Playful Minds," p. 68. David Lyle Jeffrey notes, "Humility was regarded by medieval philosophers of education as a *sine qua non* for the serious pursuit of truth in reading (e.g., Hugh of St. Victor, *Didascalicon* 3.13)" (*People of the Book: Christian Identity and Literary Culture* [Grand Rapids, Mich.: Eerdmans, 1996], p. 219n).

[25]J. Richard Middleton, "Curiosity Killed the Cat: Or, The Outrageous Hope of Reformational Scholarship and Practice," *Perspectives* (Institute of Christian Studies), December 1998, p. iii.

[26]Richard John Neuhaus, "Encountered by the Truth," *First Things*, October 1998, p. 83.

[27]Leszek Kolakowski, *Modernity on Endless Trial* (Chicago: University of Chicago Press, 1990), pp. 39-40.

[28]Ibid., p. 40.

[29]Thomas Aquinas *Summa Theologiae* 1-2.q31.al5, quoted by Josef Pieper, *Leisure: The Basis of Culture*, trans. Gerald Malsby (South Bend, Ind.: St. Augustine, 1998), p. 110. Pieper himself puts it this way: "No man is wise and knowing, only God. And so the most that man can do is call someone a loving searcher of the truth, *philo-sophos*" (*Leisure*, p. 111).

[30]Lewis Thomas, "On the Uncertainty of Science," *Harvard Magazine*, September-October 1980, p. 20.

[31]Robert Coles describes Simone Weil's struggle with pride and humility: "Nowhere is her essentially Christian nature more evident than in her kind of anti-intellectualism—not a cheap, vulgar excess, calculated to curry the favor of ignorant, mean-spirited people, but a sincere acknowledgement on her part that the sin of pride is especially inconsistent—one moment on the Left, the next a stern, moralistic conservative—because she would not trust the intentions of her pride. The torment one senses in her is the awareness of an intellectual's *hauteur* coming up against a penitent Christian's recognition that humility is hard to achieve, even in small amounts" ("Simone Weil's Mind," in *Simone Weil: Interpretation of a Life*, ed. George Abbot White [Amherst: University of Massachusetts Press, 1981], p. 32).

[32]Albert Edward Day, *Discipline and Discovery* (The Disciplined Order of Christ, 1961), quoted by Rueben P. Job and Norman Shawchuck. *A Guide to Prayer for Ministers and Other Servants* (Nashville: Upper Room, 1983), p. 92.

Chapter VII: The Intellectual Disciplines

[1]William J. Wainwright, *Reason and the Heart: A Prolegomenon to a Critique of Pas-*

sional Reason (Ithaca, N.Y.: Cornell University Press, 1995), p. 15.

[2]As Josef Pieper says, "As much as a living philosophy 'happens' in the dialogue among different minds, even *as* dialogue: there can nonetheless be no teamwork in philosophy" (Josef Pieper, *In Defense of Philosophy: Classical Wisdom Stands Up to Modern Challenges*, trans. Lothar Krauth [San Francisco: Ignatius, 1992], p. 80).

[3]Dora Thornton quotes several contemporary descriptions of such rooms designed for scholars during the Renaissance (see her *The Scholar in His Study: Ownership and Experience in Renaissance Italy* [New Haven, Conn.: Yale University Press, 1997], as quoted by James Fenton, "A Room of One's Own," *The New York Review of Books*, August 18, 1998, pp. 52-53).

[4]Jacques Barzun, *The House of Intellect* (New York: Harper & Brothers, 1959), p. 204.

[5]There is some indication that certain kinds of music stimulate intellectual activity. Gordon L. Shaw has, perhaps, discovered a "Mozart effect"—that "some kinds of music [notably the carefully ordered music of Mozart] can actually enhance learning" (Ronald Kotulak, "Q & A [with Gordon L. Shaw]," *Chicago Tribune*, May 24, 1998, Perspective sec., pp. 1, 3).

[6]Quoted by Kathleen Norris, *Amazing Grace: A Vocabulary of Faith* (New York: Riverhead, 1998), p. 17.

[7]Ibid.

[8]Wendell Berry, *A Timbered Choir: Sabbath Poems 1979-1997* (Washington, D.C.: Counterpoint, 1998), poem I (1997), p. 207. Berry comments on the best circumstance in which this collection of poetry can be read: "These poems were written in silence, in solitude, mainly out of doors. A reader will like them best, I think, who reads them in similar circumstances—at least in a quiet room" (p. xvii).

[9]A. G. Sertillanges, *The Intellectual Life: Its Spirit, Conditions, Methods*, trans. Mary Ryan (Washington, D.C.: Catholic University of America Press, 1987), p. viii.

[10]Pieper, *In Defense of Philosophy*, p. 47.

[11]Ernest Dimnet, *The Art of Thinking* (New York: Pocket, 1942), p. 25.

[12]Ibid., p. 77.

[13]Ibid., p. 76.

[14]Ibid., p. 86.

[15]Simone Weil, *Waiting for God*, trans Emma Crauford (New York: Harper & Row, 1951), p. 110.

[16]Eviatar Zerubavel, *Social Mindscapes: An Invitation to Cognitive Sociology* (Cambridge, Mass.: Harvard University Press, 1997), p. 35.

[17]Quoted from Igumen Chariton of Valamo, *The Art of Prayer: An Orthodox Anthology* (Faber & Faber, n.d.) by Rueben P. Job, *A Guide to Retreat for All God's Shepherds* (Nashville: Abingdon, 1994), pp. 220-21.

[18]Weil, *Waiting for God*, p. 110-11.

[19]Ibid., p. 111.

[20]Ibid., pp. 111-12.

[21]See chapter 2, p. 45; and John Henry Newman, *Parochial Sermons*, quoted by Ian Ker, *John Henry Newman* (New York: Oxford University Press, 1988), p. 97; John Henry Newman, *An Essay in Aid of a Grammar of Assent* (Notre Dame, Ind.: University of Notre Dame Press, 1979), pp. 25-92.

[22]Contrasting the philosopher with the sophist, Josef Pieper writes, "The true philosopher, thoroughly oblivious of his own importance, and 'totally discarding all pretentiousness,' approaches his unfathomable object unselfishly and with an open mind. The contemplation of this object, in turn, transports the subject beyond mere self-satisfaction and indeed releases him from the fixation on selfish needs, no matter how 'intellectual' or sublime" (*In Defense of Philosophy,* p. 38).

[23]Anthony Bloom, *Living Prayer* (Templegate, n.d.), quoted by Job, *Guide to Retreat for All God's Shepherds,* pp. 308-9.

[24]Karl Barth, *The Faith of the Church: A Commentary on the Apostles' Creed According to Calvin's Catechism,* ed. Jean-Louis Leuba, trans. Gabriel Vahanian (New York: Living Age, 1958), p. 45.

[25]Ibid., p. 44.

[26]Earl F. Palmer, "Theological Themes in the Chronicles of Narnia," *Radix* 26, no. 2 (fall 1998): 7-8.

[27]Josef Pieper grounds this notion in Christian metaphysics: "The structural framework of Christian metaphysics as a whole stands revealed, perhaps more plainly than in any other single ethical dictum, in the proposition that prudence is the foremost of the virtues. That structure is built thus: that Being precedes Truth, and that Truth precedes the Good. Indeed, the living fire at the heart of the dictum is the central mystery of Christian theology: that the Father begets the Eternal Word, and that the Holy Spirit proceeds out of the Father and the Word" (Josef Pieper, *The Four Cardinal Virtues,* trans. Richard and Clara Winston [New York: Harcourt Brace Jovanovich, 1965], pp. 3-4, as quoted in Josef Pieper, *An Anthology* [San Francisco: Ignatius, 1989], p. 54).

[28]After I wrote this paragraph, Tim McGrew, philosophy professor at Western Michigan University, drew my attention to the support this receives from Matthew 25:31-46, in which those honored by Jesus are not aware of their service to him via service to others.

[29]Evelyn Underhill, *The Spiritual* Life (Harrisburg, Penn.: Morehouse, 1937), p. 20.

[30]Henry C. Simmons, *In the Footsteps of the Mystics* (New York: Paulist, 1992), anthologized in Job, *Guide to Retreat for All God's Shepherds,* p. 106.

[31]Sertillanges, *Intellectual Life,* pp. 72-73. Sertillanges goes on: "Every fact may

give rise to a great thought. In all contemplation, even that of a fly or of a passing cloud, there is a fit occasion for endless reflection. Every light striking on
an object may lead up to the sun; every road opened is a corridor to God" (p.
73).

[32]Also see chapter four, pp. 77-78.

[33]Edward De Bono, *New Think* (New York: Avon, 1971), p. 15. Robert Pirsig gives
a more interesting account in novel form in *Zen and the Art of Motorcycle Maintenance* (New York: Bantam, 1975), pp. 114-15, 272-82, 293-320.

[34]De Bono, *New Think*, p. 197.

[35]Yes, De Bono did say "even a library" (ibid., p. 155).

[36]John H. Westerhoff III and John D. Eusden, *The Spiritual Life* (New York:
Seabury, 1982), quoted by Rueben P. Job and Norman Shawchuck, *A Guide to
Prayer for Ministers and Other Servants* (Nashville: Upper Room, 1983), p. 221.

[37]Sertillanges, *Intellectual Life*, p. ix.

[38]Ibid., p. 31.

[39]Ibid., p. 133.

[40]Ibid., p. 52.

[41]Martin Heidegger, *Discourse on Thinking*, trans. John M. Anderson and E. Hans
Freund (New York: Harper & Row, 1966), p. 46.

[42]John Anderson, introduction to Heidegger, *Discourse on Thinking*, p. 24.

[43]Heidegger, *Discourse on Thinking*, p. 56.

[44]Anderson, introduction, p. 26.

[45]Heidegger, *Discourse on Thinking*, p. 68.

[46]Ibid., p. 85; also see Os Guinness, *The Call: Finding and Fulfilling the Central Purpose of Your Life* (Nashville: Word, 1998), p. 212.

[47]Many have rightfully criticized Heidegger for the implications, in his own life,
of replacing God with Being. Heidegger held with Nietzsche that the cultural
God of Western Christendom was dead; he seems never to have faced the possibility of a fully biblical God; and so he struggled to replace this loss with the
notion of Being. His more than flirting with Nazism and his failure to develop
any viable approach to ethics are more than lapses in his thought: they indicate
a serious weakness in his whole philosophic agenda. These problems need not
be examined at length here; there is much literature already devoted to them.
See, for example, Günther Neske and Emil Kettering, *Martin Heidegger and
National Socialism: Questions and Answers*, trans. Lisa Harries (New York: Paragon, 1990); Hans Sluga, *Heidegger's Crisis: Philosophy and Politics in Nazi Ger-
many* (Cambridge, Mass.: Harvard University Press, 1993; Rüdiger Safranski,
Martin Heidegger: Between Good and Evil, trans. Ewald Osers (Cambridge, Mass.:
Harvard University Press, 1998); and Robert Sokolowski's review of the latter
book, "Being, My Way," *First Things*, January 1999, pp. 54-57.

[48]Anderson, introduction, p. 29. As Heidegger develops these notions in the last

half of "Conversations on a Country Path," the language becomes more and
more complex; the more the ideas are unpacked in order to be explained, the
more baffling the text becomes. One is led into locutions such as "But if hereto-
fore the reigning essence of thinking has been that transcendental-horizonal
representing from which releasement, because of its belonging to that-which-
regions, releases itself; then thinking changes in releasement from such a representing to wait upon that-which-regions." Granted, these puzzling terms
have been defined in what precedes, but the task of understanding what is
being said is formidable.

[49]Sertillanges, *Intellectual Life*, p. 247.

[50]Doris Lessing, "An Evening with Doris Lessing," *Partisan Review* 65, no. 1
(1998): 12.

[51]Sertillanges, *Intellectual Life*, p. 42.

[52]Ibid., p. xiii.

[53]Ibid., p. 82.

[54]Blaise Pascal, fragment 370 of the *Pensées* as quoted by Emile Cailliet, *The Clue
to Pascal* (Philadelphia: Westminster Press, 1943), p. 83.

[55]Sertillanges, *Intellectual Life*, pp. 82-83.

[56]Ibid, p. 260.

Chapter VIII: Thinking by Reading

[1]Augustine *Confessions* 8.12.

[2]Ibid.

[3]The phrases "reading directs thinking" and "thinking directs reading" are
mine. After making this distinction I discovered that Heidegger's distinction
between "meditative thinking" and "calculative thinking" (discussed above in
chapter seven, pp. 138-40) parallels this, as do George Steiner's distinction
between "critic" and "reader" ("Critic/Reader," in *George Steiner: A Reader*
[New York: Oxford University Press, 1984], pp. 67-98) and David Lyle Jeffrey's
distinction between the "hard-hearted and the broken-hearted reader" (*People
of the Book: Christian Identity and Literary Culture* [Grand Rapids, Mich.: Eerdmans, 1996], p. 370).

[4]Lynne Sharon Schwartz writes, "Indeed what reading teaches, first and foremost, is how to sit still for long periods and confront time head-on. The dynamism is all inside, an exalted, spiritual exercise so utterly engaging that we
forget time and mortality along with all of life's lesser woes, and simply bask
in the everlasting present" (*Ruined by Reading: A Life in Books* [Boston: Beacon,
1996], p. 116).

[5]Alberto Manguel, *A History of Reading* (New York: Viking, 1996), p. 267.

[6]Jeffrey, *People of the Book*, pp. 84-85, reflecting on Augustine *On Christian Doctrine* 2.8.12-14.

[7]Manguel writes, "For centuries, Afro-American slaves learned to read against extraordinary odds, risking their lives in a process that, because of the difficulties set in their way, sometimes took several years" (*History of Reading*, p. 280).

[8]Ibid., p. 287.

[9]Virginia Woolf, *A Room of One's Own* (New York: Harcourt Brace Jovanovich, 1929), p. 76.

[10]A. G. Sertillanges, *The Intellectual Life: Its Spirit, Conditions, Methods*, trans. Mary Ryan (Washington, D.C.: Catholic University of America Press, 1987), p. 149.

[11]Sven Birkerts, *The Gutenberg Elegies: The Fate of Reading in an Electronic Age* (New York: Fawcett Columbine, 1994), p. 101.

[12]A more advanced form of Bible study (dubbed manuscript study) developed by Paul Byer for InterVarsity Christian Fellowship adapts the semitechnical methodology of New Criticism to analyze biblical texts from which modern paragraphing and verse numbers have been removed.

[13]Michael Casey, *Sacred Reading: The Ancient Art of Lectio Divina* (Liguori, Mo.: Triumph, 1996), pp. 9-10.

[14]Eugene Peterson, "Caveat Lector," *Crux*, March 1996, p. 2.

[15]Rueben P. Job and Norman Shawchuck, *A Guide to Prayer for Ministers and Other Servants* (Nashville: Upper Room, 1983).

[16]Ibid., p. 154.

[17]Casey, *Sacred Reading*, p. 8.

[18]Jean LeClercq, *The Love of Learning and the Desire for God: A Study of Monastic Culture*, 3rd ed., trans. Catharine Misrahi (New York: Fordham University Press, 1982), p. 73.

[19]It appears that perhaps everyone read aloud before St. Ambrose (340?-397). "Augustine's description of Ambrose's silent reading (including the remark that he never read aloud) is the first instance recorded in Western literature" (Manguel, *History of Reading*, p. 43).

[20]LeClercq, *Love of Learning*, p. 73.

[21]Ibid., p. 15.

[22]Peterson, "Caveat Lector," p. 6.

[23]Casey is not so demanding: "The formation of mind and heart that is due to *lectio divina* is realized only after a solid investment of time. I am thinking, for example, of a near-daily slot of about thirty minutes continuing over several years" (Casey, *Sacred Reading*, p. 21).

[24]Gordon Fee, "Exegesis and Spirituality: Reflections on Completing the Exegetical Circle," *Crux*, December 1995, p. 30.

[25]Peterson, "Caveat Lector," p. 6.

[26]Ibid., p. 7.

[27]Dylan Thomas, the first line of a poem by the same title.

[28]Casey, *Sacred Reading*, p. vi.

[29]Peterson, "Caveat Lector," p. 9.

[30]Ibid.

[31]Jacques Le Goff (*Intellectuals in the Middle Ages*, trans. Teresa Lavender Fagan [Cambridge: Blackwell, 1993]) overemphasizes the anti-intellectual cast of medieval monasticism and probably sees in medieval scholastic thought more modernity than was present—exemplifying G. K. Chesterton's comment that secular scholars either abuse the scholastics for being dogmatic or present them as scholars "in advance of their age," meaning "in agreement with our age" (G. K. Chesterton, *St. Thomas Aquinas* [Garden City, N.Y.: Doubleday Image, 1956 (orig. ed. 1933)], pp. 33-34). Still, Le Goff cites St. Bernard, a stellar example of a thoughtful monk, encouraging students to flee the universities in Paris: "You will find much more in forests than in books. The woods and the rocks will teach you much more than any master" (Le Goff, *Intellectuals in the Middle Ages*, p. 21). In contrast, Jean LeClercq finds St. Bernard the prime example of a fully integrated man: "From his arrival at Clairvaux to his entry into Heaven, the real, the only Bernard was indissolubly and simultaneously a learned man and a man of God, a thinker and a saint, a humanist and a mystic" (LeClercq, *Love of Learning*, p. 161).

[32]These pairs of terms derive from LeClercq, *Love of Learning*, pp. 2-3, 5, 199-203, 213-14, 216, 223, 226, 257. Alberto Manguel finds a parallel division in Jewish scholars in the sixteenth century: "One, centered around the Sephardic schools of Spain and North Africa, preferred to summarize the contents of a passage with little discussion of the details that composed it, concentrating on the literal and grammatical sense. The other, in the Ashkenazi schools based largely in France, Poland and the Germanic countries, analyzed every line and every word, searching for every possible sense" (Manguel, *History of Reading*, p. 89).

[33]G. K. Chesterton notes the world-affirming character of both St. Francis and St. Thomas. St. Francis affirmed the value and glory of the natural world; St. Thomas affirmed the value of the mental world trained on the physical world. "It was the paradox of St. Francis that while he was passionately fond of poems, he was rather distrustful of books. It was the outstanding fact about St. Thomas that he loved books and lived on books" (Chesterton, *St. Thomas Aquinas*, p. 21).

[34]Le Goff, *Intellectuals in the Middle Ages*, p. 89.

[35]Ibid., pp. 89-90.

[36]Ibid., p. 90.

[37]Ibid., p. 92.

[38]Ibid., p. 117.

[39]Sertillanges,. *Intellectual Life*, p. 173; Sertillanges is reflecting on the views of Abbé de Tourville.

[40]Josef Pieper, *The Silence of St. Thomas: Three Essays*, trans. John Murray and

Daniel O'Connor (South Bend, Ind.: St. Augustine's, 1999), p. 35.

[41]Ibid., p. 35, quoting Thomas Aquinas *Commentaria in Aristotelis De Caelo et mundo* 1.22.

[42]George Ledin Jr., liner notes to *Scriabin Études*, Alexander Paley, piano, Naxos, CD 8.553070 (1997). The verbal overload is relentless, extending throughout the four pages of notes.

[43]Schwartz, *Ruined by Reading*, p. 1.

[44]James W. Sire, *The Universe Next Door*, 3rd ed. (Downers Grove, Ill.: InterVarsity Press, 1997); *How to Read Slowly* (Downers Grove, Ill.: InterVarsity Press, 1978); reprinted as *The Joy of Reading* (Portland, Ore.: Multnomah Press, 1984); rev. ed. published as *How to Read Slowly* (Wheaton, Ill.: Harold Shaw, 1988).

[45]See Sire, *Universe Next Door*, pp. 17-18, for an elaboration on the definition of *worldview* and Sire, *How to Read Slowly*, pp. 23-53, for an extended example of reading an essay worldviewishly.

[46]Saul Bellow, *Mr. Sammler's Planet* (Greenwich, Conn.: Fawcett, p. 1970), p. 7.

[47]Ibid., pp. 21-22.

[48]"Mr. Sammler could not say that he literally believed what he was reading. He could, however, say that he cared to read nothing but this" (ibid., p. 231).

[49]Ibid., p. 284.

[50]Sertillanges, *Intellectual Life*, p. 150.

[51]Ibid., pp. 158-59; Sertillanges is quoting Victor Hugo.

[52]Ibid., pp. 169-70.

[53]Richard M. Weaver, *Ideas Have Consequences* (Chicago: University of Chicago Press, 1984), p. 1.

[54]Schwartz, *Ruined by Reading*, p. 101.

[55]Ibid., p. 1.

[56]Ibid., p. 106.

[57]John Baillie, *A Diary of Private Prayer* (New York: Simon & Schuster/Fireside, 1996), p. 89.

Chapter IX: Jesus the Reasoner

[1]In March 1997 Dallas Willard was addressing a meeting of InterVarsity Christian Fellowship staff members serving graduate students in the United States and Canada. Much of what follows has been stimulated by Willard in this address; a lecture he gave at the Following Christ, Shaping Our World conference in Chicago, sponsored by InterVarsity Christian Fellowship, December 31, 1998; two lectures entitled "Jesus: The Smartest Man Who Ever Lived," given at BIOLA University (June 1, 1999); Willard's scholarly article "Jesus the Logician" *The Christian Scholar's Review,* summer 1999, pp. 605-14; and his *The Divine Conspiracy: Rediscovering Our Hidden Life in God* (San Francisco: HarperSanFrancisco, 1998), pp. 93-95.

[2]E. Harris Harbison says much the same thing in somewhat more muted form: "The most obvious thing about Jesus of the Synoptic Gospels is that he is a teacher who is aware of his relation, and conscious of a call to shape it. To this extent, he is a 'scholar' " (*The Christian Scholar in the Age of the Reformation* [New York: Charles Scribner's Sons, 1956], p. 3).

[3]This includes Diogenes Allen: "Jesus does not have the greatness of the order of the body, as does Alexander the Great, nor the greatness of the order of the intellect, as does Einstein" (*Christian Belief in a Postmodern World* [Louisville, Ky.: Westminster John Knox, 1989], pp. 109-10). In support of this Allen quotes Blaise Pascal, who distinguishes between greatness of wealth, power, intellect, holiness and wisdom, noting that one could have any one of these without the other: "Jesus without wealth or any outward show of knowledge has his own order of holiness. He made no discoveries; he did not reign, but he was humble, patient, thrice holy to God, terrible to devils, and without sin" (*Pensée* 308); see Blaise Pascal, *Pensées*, trans. A. J. Krailsheimer (Harmondsworth, U.K.: Penguin, 1966), p. 124. Notice that Pascal does not say Jesus did not have greatness of intellect, only that he did not make "any outward show of knowledge," quite another matter. Humility does not preclude intelligence; rather, as I have argued in chapter six, pp. 122-24, genuine intelligence demands humility.

[4]C. S. Lewis, *Letters to Malcolm: Chiefly on Prayer* (London: Geoffrey Bles, 1964), pp. 62-63.

[5]Willard, "Jesus: the Smartest Man Who Ever Lived?" and *Divine Conspiracy*, p. 94.

[6]Direct quote from Willard's lecture at the Following Christ, Shaping Our World conference.

[7]Willard, "Jesus the Logician," pp. 613-14.

[8]For a basic presentation of the reliability of the sources, see Paul Barnett, *Is the New Testament Reliable?* (Downers Grove, Ill.: InterVarsity Press, 1986); more substantial treatments include R. T. France, *The Evidence for Jesus* (Downers Grove, Ill.: InterVarsity Press, 1986); James D. G. Dunn, *The Evidence for Jesus* (London: SCM Press, 1985); and Craig Blomberg, *The Historical Reliability of the Gospels* (Downers Grove, Ill.: InterVarsity Press, 1987).

[9]Question-answer period, Willard, "Jesus: The Smartest Man Who Ever Lived?"

[10]W. H. Werkmeister, *An Introduction to Critical Thinking* (Lincoln, Neb.: Johnson, 1948), p. 366.

[11]For example, Luke 11:11-12; 12:4-5; 6-7; 24; 27-28; 54-56; 13:14-16; 14:1-5; 18:1-8.

[12]Scholars agree that John 7:53—8:11 is not original to this Gospel but has been inserted here.

[13]William L. Lane, *The Gospel According to Mark* (Grand Rapids, Mich.: Eerdmans, 1974).

[14]Willard, "Jesus the Logician," pp. 607-10.

[15]Eta Linnemann, *Parables of Jesus*, trans. John Sturdy (London: SPCK, 1966), p. 74, as quoted by Robert H. Stein, *Introduction to the Parables of Jesus* (Philadelphia: Westminster Press, 1981), p. 77.

[16]Other parables that are open-ended: (1) The parable with Simon (Lk 7:36-50), in which Jesus leaves Simon dangling with the irony that he is more sinful than the woman of the streets and then goes on to forgive the woman and not Simon. (2) The prodigal son (Lk 15:11-32), in which the elder son is left in the field with a choice to make, just as Jesus leaves the Pharisees with a choice to make—will they accept the graciousness of the Father toward sinners? (3) The parable of binding the strong man (Mk 3:20-30), in which Jesus lays bare the illogic of the Pharisees who think Jesus has a demon; his charge to them is that what they are accusing him of is the unforgivable sin. He is possessed by the Holy Spirit, not the demons. Even the demons know more about who he is (v. 21) than the Pharisees do.

Chapter X: The Responsibility of a Christian Intellectual

[1]Eric Hoffer, a longshoreman with scant education, became well-known for his brilliantly insightful, if troubling, book *The True Believer*, a study of the mindless fanaticism that often accompanies those who claim to be absolutely certain they are right (New York: New American Library, 1958; orig. ed. 1951).

[2]I do not wish to address the issue of predestination or free will. It is enough to note what is common to any Christian treatment of human responsibility.

[3]Evelyn Underhill, *The Spiritual Life* (Harrisburg, Penn.: Morehouse, 1937), pp. 29-30.

[4]Karl Barth, *The Faith of the Church: A Commentary on the Apostles' Creed According to Calvin's Catechism*, trans. Gabriel Vahanian (New York: Meridian, 1958), p. 27.

[5]Ibid., p. 28.

[6]Havel credits the phrase to his own mentor, the Czech philosopher Jan Patočka.

[7]Havel reflects on why he feels responsible for paying the tram fare when there is no official to observe him: "Who, then, is in fact conversing with me? Obviously someone I hold in higher regard than the transport commission, than my best friends (this would come out when the voice would take issue with their opinions), and higher, in some regards, than myself, that is, myself as subject of my existence-in-the-world and the carrier of my 'existential' interests (one of which is the rather natural effort to save a crown). Someone who 'knows everything' (and is therefore omniscient), is everywhere (and therefore omnipresent) and remembers everything; someone who, though infinitely understanding, is entirely incorruptible; who is for me, the highest and utterly unequivocal authority in all moral questions and who is thus Law itself; some-

one eternal, who through himself makes me eternal as well, so that I cannot imagine the arrival of a moment when everything will come to an end, thus terminating my dependence on him as well; someone to whom I relate entirely and for whom, ultimately, I would do everything. At the same time, this 'someone' addresses me directly and personally (not merely as an anonymous public passenger, as the transport commission does)." Nonetheless, for various reasons Havel refuses to identify this "someone," this "Being" or "absolute horizon" with a fully personal God, let alone the God of the Bible (see Václav Havel, *Letters to Olga: June 1979-September 1982*, trans. Paul Wilson [New York: Henry Holt, 1989], pp. 345-46). I have analyzed Havel's concept of responsibility and its foundation in Being in "An Open Letter to Václav Havel," *Crux*, June 1991, pp. 9-14.

[8]Havel tells this story in "The Power of the Powerless," in *Living in Truth* (London: Faber and Faber, 1986), pp. 41-57.

[9]Ibid., p. 42.

[10]Ibid., p. 55.

[11]This is the title of a famous book by Julian Benda, himself an intellectual by most definitions; Benda charges that the intellectuals of his day—the early twentieth century—have abandoned their role as spokespersons for the transcendent and indulged instead in party politics (see Julien Benda, *The Treason of the Intellectuals* [*La trahison des clercs* (1928)], trans. Richard Aldington [New York: W. W. Norton, 1969]). According to Benda, the true intellectuals are "all those whose activity essentially is *not* the pursuit of practical aims, all those who seek their joy in the practice of an art or a science or metaphysical speculation, in short in the possession of non-material advantages, and hence in a certain manner say: 'My kingdom is not of this world' " (p. 43).

[12]The reference is to a "portrait" of Cyril Connolly appearing in a diary belonging to Barbara Skelton (whom Johnson calls "a beautiful intellectual's moll"), one of Connolly's wives (Paul Johnson, *Intellectuals* [New York: Harper & Row, 1988], p. 318.

[13]Ernest Gellner, "La trahison de la trahison des clercs," reprinted in Ian Maclean, Alan Montefiore and Peter Winch, *The Political Responsibility of the Intellectuals* (Cambridge: Cambridge University Press, 1990), pp. 17-27; Tony Judt, *Past Imperfect: French Intellectuals, 1944-1956* (Berkeley: University of California Press, 1992); Leszek Kolakowski, "The Intellectuals," in *Modernity on Endless Trial* (Chicago: University of Chicago Press, 1990), pp. 32-43; Archibald MacLeish, "The Irresponsibles," *The Nation*, May 18, 1940, pp. 618-19, 620-23, reprinted in *The Intellectuals: A Controversial Portrait*, ed. George B. de Huszar (Glencoe, Ill.: Free Press of Glencoe, 1960), pp. 239-46; Thomas Molnar, *The Decline of the Intellectual* (New York: World, 1961).

[14]Kolakowski, *Modernity on Endless Trial*, p. 39.

[15]Judt, *Past Imperfect*, pp. 306-7.

[16]Albert Camus quoted in ibid., p. v.

[17]Ralph Waldo Emerson, "The American Scholar," in *Selections from Ralph Waldo Emerson*, ed. Stephen E. Whicher (Boston: Houghton Mifflin, 1957), p. 74.

[18]Ibid., p. 78.

[19]Ibid., p. 70.

[20]Ibid., p. 72.

[21]Ibid., p. 73.

[22]American transcendentalism really should be called immanentism, for divine reality is finally equated with the spiritual essence that is the reality behind the material appearance.

[23]Karl Mannheim, *Ideology and Utopia*, trans. Louis Wirth and Edward Shils (New York: Harcourt, Brace & World, n.d.), p. 10.

[24]Václav Havel, "The Responsibility of Intellectuals," *The New York Review of Books*, June 22, 1995, p. 36.

[25]Camus quoted by Judt, *Past Imperfect*, p. v.

[26]Friedrich Nietzsche, "On Truth and Lie in an Extra-moral Sense," in *The Portable Nietzsche*, trans. Walter Kaufmann (New York: Viking, 1954), pp. 95-96; and Richard Rorty, *Contingency, Irony and Solidarity* (Cambridge: Cambridge University Press, 1989), especially chapters 2 and 3.

[27]Josef Pieper, *Leisure: The Basis of Culture* (South Bend, Ind.: St. Augustine's, 1998), pp. 11-12.

[28]John Henry Newman, *The Idea of a University*, ed. Frank M. Turner (New Haven, Conn.: Yale University Press, 1966), p. 100.

[29]Alan Wolfe discusses the role of Christian intellectuals—Elshtain, among others—in the Clinton-Lewinsky affair, commenting on their responsibility (see Alan Wolfe, "Judging the President: The Perplexing Role of Religion in Public Life," *Brookings Review*, spring 1999, pp. 28-31).

[30]Glenn Tinder, *The Political Meaning of Christianity: An Interpretation* (Baton Rouge: Louisiana State Press, 1989); the brief preface is a model of how a scholar can wisely announce a Christian stance without automatically giving offense or turning the study into an evangelistic tract. English literature professor Harold K. Bush Jr. believes that Christian scholarship is "changing [for the better] right before our eyes" (personal letter). He cites his own review of some such work in " 'Invisible Domains' and the Theological Turn in Recent Literary Studies," *Christianity and Literature*, fall 1999, pp. 91-109. He might also have cited his own *American Declarations: Rebellion and Repentance in American Cultural History* (Urbana: University of Illinois Press, 1999).

[31]Newman, *Idea of a University*, p. 29.

[32]Terrence Merrigan writes, "For Newman, the only truly adequate point of departure for the contemplation of the physical universe is the experience of

God's moral government which is, of course, primarily made manifest in the experience of the conscience" (*Clear Heads and Holy Hearts: The Religious and Theological Ideal of John Henry Newman* [Louvain, Belgium: Peeters, 1991], p. 135).

[33]Alvin Plantinga more precisely distinguishes between two university ideologies: *perennial naturalism* (the dominant strain, representing the continuing influence of the Enlightenment) and *creative antirealism* (a postmodern version of naturalism that includes such specific examples as deconstruction, perspectivalism and, implicitly, nihilism). I have not been concerned with precision in the list of placard clichés. See Alvin Plantinga, "On Christian Scholarship," *RTSF Bulletin*, no. 6 (November-December 1994): 9-17 (part of which was excerpted from *The Challenge and Promise of a Catholic University*, ed. Theodore M. Hesburgh [Notre Dame, Ind.: University of Notre Dame Press, 1994]).

[34]Lewis Perry, professor of history, Vanderbilt University, quoted by Jeff Sharlet, "In a New Book, Historians Conduct a Moral Inquiry," *The Chronicle of Higher Education*, May 21, 1999, p. A18.

[35]While methodological naturalism (which this statement summarizes) is still the reigning presupposition among most scientists—both secular and Christian—it has been seriously challenged by a number of scientists, philosophers and cultural critics. W. Christopher Stewart explains the conflict between Christians in "Religion and Science," in *Reason for the Hope Within*, ed. Michael J. Murray (Grand Rapids, Mich.: Eerdmans, 1999), pp. 318-44. For those opposed to methodological naturalism and arguing instead for "design" or "theistic" science, see especially the work of Michael J. Behe (*Darwin's Black Box: The Biochemical Challenge to Evolution* [New York: Free Press, 1996]); mathematician and philosopher William A. Dembski (*The Design Inference* [New York: Cambridge University Press, 1998], and *Intelligent Design: The Bridge Between Science and Theology* [Downers Grove, Ill.: InterVarsity Press, 1999]); law professor and culture critic Phillip E. Johnson (*Darwin on Trial* [Downers Grove, Ill.: InterVarsity Press, 1993], and *Reason in the Balance: The Case Against Naturalism in Science, Law and Education* [Downers Grove, Ill.: InterVarsity Press, 1995]); and chemist and historian of science Charles B. Thaxton and writer Nancy R. Pearcey (*The Soul of Science: Christian Faith and Natural Philosophy* [Wheaton, Ill.: Crossway, 1994]). Two collections of essays by a wide variety of scholars also focus on this topic: William A. Dembski, ed., *Mere Creation: Science, Faith & Intelligent Design* (Downers Grove, Ill.: InterVarsity Press, 1998); and J. P. Moreland, ed., *The Creation Hypothesis: Scientific Evidence for an Intelligent Designer* (Downers Grove, Ill.: InterVarsity Press, 1994). Some of the most lively, distinctive Christian scholarship will be found in the works of these scholars, and their work is beginning to receive recognition in secular university circles as a worthy challenge to the reigning secular paradigm.

[36]Terry Eagleton, *Literary Theory: An Introduction* (Minneapolis: University of Minnesota Press, 1983), p. 22.

[37]I am told by one of his colleagues that a systematic theologian at a major university in Denmark is an atheist; this is like an astronomer who does not believe in stars, but believes others believe in stars and so studies their belief.

[38]Adapted from Michael Foucault, "Truth and Power," in *Power/Knowledge* in *Foucault: A Reader* (New York: Pantheon, 1984), p. 60.

[39]Peter L. Berger and Thomas Luckmann, *The Social Construction of Reality: A Treatise in the Sociology of Knowledge* (New York: Doubleday/Anchor, 1966), p.49; the sentence actually reads, "While it is possible to say that man has a nature, it is more significant to say that man constructs his own nature, or more simply, that man produces himself," but slogans must be ideologically correct.

[40]Told to me a few years ago by a fellow attendant at a meeting of the Academy of Religion and the Society of Biblical Literature.

[41]John C. Green made this remark as reported by Peter Steinfels, "Universities Biased Against Religion, Scholar Says," *New York Times*, November 26, 1993, p. A22, further quoted by George Marsden, *The Outrageous Idea of Christian Scholarship* (New York: Oxford University Press, 1997), p. 7.

[42]Charles Habib Malik, *A Christian Critique of the University* (Downers Grove, Ill.: InterVarsity Press, 1982), pp. 15-16.

[43]Mark Noll tells the long, often sad story of evangelical anti-intellectualism—where it got its start, how it grew and now how perhaps an evangelical intellectual renaissance may be emerging (see Noll, *Scandal of the Evangelical Mind*, esp. pp. 211-53; a brief analysis is also to be found in James C. Turner, "Something to Be Reckoned With: The Evangelical Mind Awakens," *Commonweal*, January 1999, pp. 11-13). For an even more compact historical sketch of Catholic intellectual life from the church fathers to the present, see Mary Jo Weaver, "Rooted Hearts/Playful Minds: Catholic Intellectual Life at its Best," *Cross Currents*, spring 1998, pp. 61-74; other studies of Christian intellectual life include Jean LeClercq, *The Love of Learning and the Desire for God: A Study of Monastic Culture*, 3rd ed., trans. Catharine Misrahi (New York: Fordham University Press, 1982); Jacques Le Goff, *Intellectuals in the Middle Ages*, trans. Teresa Lavender Fagan (Cambridge: Blackwell, 1993); E. Harris Harbison, *The Christian Scholar in the Age of the Reformation* (New York: Charles Scribner's Sons, 1956); David Lyle Jeffrey, *People of the Book: Christian Identity and Literary Culture* (Grand Rapids, Mich.: Eerdmans, 1996); and James Tunstead Burtchaell, *The Dying of the Light: The Disengagement of Colleges and Universities from Their Christian Churches* (Grand Rapids, Mich.: Eerdmans, 1998). A short version of this last may be found in James Tunstead Burtchaell, "The Decline and Fall of the Christian College" (in two parts), *First Things*, April 1991, pp. 16-29, and May 1991, pp. 30-38. In these articles Burtchaell's prescription for a

change in Catholic institutions of higher learning is so radical that most Christian academics would cringe at the reformation necessary in their own performance. But given Burchaell's passion for a fully Christian and Catholic university (he is a Holy Cross priest), it is hard to fault it. An evangelical Protestant version of these recommendations would be equally challenging.

[44]George Marsden, *The Soul of the American University: From Protestant Establishment to Established Nonbelief* (New York: Oxford University Press, 1994), and *The Outrageous Idea of Christian Scholarship* (New York: Oxford University Press, 1997). See also Mark Schwehn, *Exiles from Eden: Religion and the Academic Vocation in America* (New York: Oxford University Press, 1993); Nicholas Wolterstorff, "The Professorship as a Legitimate Calling," *The Crucible,* spring 1992, pp. 19-22; and Walter R. Hearn, *Being a Christian in Science* (Downers Grove, Ill.: InterVarsity Press, 1997). On a personal level, see Paul M. Anderson, ed., *Professors Who Believe* (Downers Grove, Ill.: InterVarsity Press, 1998); Kelly James Clark, *Philosophers Who Believe* (Downers Grove, Ill.: InterVarsity Press, 1993); and Thomas V. Morris, *God and the Philosophers: The Reconciliation of Faith and Reason* (New York: Oxford University Press, 1994). Perhaps the best short statement of the situation and the responses most appropriate is Plantinga, "On Christian Scholarship."

[45]See *The Chronicle of Higher Education,* May 4, 1994, pp. A1, A18.

[46]At a conference on Christian higher education, I suggested to some thirty new faculty at a Christian university that they reflect on the presuppositions undergirding their academic disciplines, identify those that square with their Christian faith and those that don't, and seek to ground their own teaching and scholarship in presuppositions that are commensurate with a Christian worldview. The almost universal response was suspicion that I was suggesting a "fundamentalist" approach to scholarship, and an anger that if they did what I suggested their work would not be published in reputable journals. At the minimum, what I was trying to say was misunderstood; at most, what I was recommending was rejected wholesale.

[47]The bibliography, "A Bibliography We Can't Live Without," in James W. Sire, *Discipleship of the Mind* (Downers Grove, Ill.: InterVarsity Press, 1980), pp. 219-43, came from Brian J. Walsh and J. Richard Middleton.

[48]When I was a graduate student at Washington State College (now University), I constructed a bibliography of articles and books on the relationship between Christianity and literature. I found only ten entries. Granted, the library there did not exhaust the sources; today there would be thousands of entries. Still, most of them could have been written by atheists, Hindus or Buddhists, there being little or no hint in most of the entries that the truth of any given religious notion is at stake.

[49]Most of the books footnoted by Noll to illustrate the growth in evangelical

scholarship are published by two publishers: Eerdmans and InterVarsity Press (see Noll, *Scandal of the Evangelical Mind*, pp. 211-53).

[50]Ibid., pp. 248-49.

[51]Camus quoted by Judt, *Past Imperfect*, p. v.

[52]Thomas Merton, *Seeds of Contemplation* (New York: Dell, 1949), p. 29.

Index